Internet Programming with OmniMark

Internet Programming with OmniMark

Edited by

Mark Baker

KLUWER ACADEMIC PUBLISHERS
BOSTON / DORDRECHT / LONDON

A C.I.P. Catalogue record for this book is available from the Library of Congress.

ISBN 0-7923-7237-9

Published by Kluwer Academic Publishers,
P.O. Box 17, 3300 AA Dordrecht, The Netherlands.

Sold and distributed in North, Central and South America
by Kluwer Academic Publishers,
101 Philip Drive, Norwell, MA 02061, U.S.A.

In all other countries, sold and distributed
by Kluwer Academic Publishers,
P.O. Box 322, 3300 AH Dordrecht, The Netherlands.

Printed on acid-free paper

Printed in the Netherlands.

Table of contents

Introduction: Why OmniMark?

Why choose OmniMark for Internet programming? There are already many programming languages to choose from for developing Internet applications. There is Java, Perl, C/C++ and XSLT. What does OmniMark have to offer that these languages do not? The answer is the streaming programming model.

The streaming programming model

What is the streaming programming model? The streaming programming model is based on a very simple idea. Conventional approaches to programming concentrate on building data structures, manipulating those data structures, and finally writing the data out from the data structures. The streaming approach concentrates on processing the data as it flows, or streams, from one place to another, without building unnecessary intermediate data structures.

What is a stream? Very simply, a stream is data on the move. Streams are what carry data into a program and out of a program to some destination or another. Streams are the central players in I/O – input and output. I/O has been one of the most neglected aspects of programming practice and programming language design for many years. While the creation and management of data structures, and the code that manipulates them, has become increasingly sophisticated with the development of object oriented programming practices and languages, I/O is hardly more sophisticated than it was in the days of punch cards.

Most programming languages offer little high level support for I/O. You can read data in fixed width records, in lines, or byte by byte. As you read data the only thing you can do to it is to put it into some kind of data structure: a variable, a buffer, or an object. There is no ability to process the data as it is input. And there is no abstraction of data sources and destinations. You must write different code to read from or write to a file, a TCP/IP connection, or a database field. I/O is treated as an odious low level chore that must be endured in order to get the data into data structures where the real work can begin. During I/O a typical program touches every byte of its input data, and yet does not do a thing to process it. This is an enormous opportunity lost. Streaming programming sees the data movement involved in I/O as a golden opportunity to do much if not all of the processing that the program has to do.

Impact of the Internet revolution

Before the Internet revolution began, desktop applications were a primary focus of software development. The first priority of a desktop application is to ensure rapid and smooth interactivity with the user at the keyboard. This requires that the application provide high speed random access to the data the user is working on. To do this, it is essential to create data structures that will support that rapid random access. File I/O is an infrequent event, occurring only when the user opens or saves a file. The development of increasingly sophisticated object oriented programming languages has supported these requirements very well.

But the Internet is a very different environment from the desktop. The crucial applications that deliver value on the Internet run on the server, not the client. The user makes a request to a service running somewhere on the Internet and expects a response as quickly as possible. Internet applications run as batch processes, taking all their input at the beginning and providing all their output at the end. They do not interact with the user in the middle of processing a request. An interactive application on the Internet consists not of a monolithic application maintaining a massive data structure, but of many distributed batch processes (server, or CGI programs) receiving requests and generating responses. For such applications, building complex data structures is a luxury they cannot afford – a luxury that is too expensive in execution time, in resource usage, and in programmer time. For such applications, the opportunity to process data during I/O is not to be missed.

There are already many classes of Internet applications that take a streaming approach. From the progressive display of graphics to streaming audio and video, more and more applications are processing data and outputting results as the input is received, rather than waiting for the end of the data and building data structures to represent it. The time for streaming programming, and for programming languages that support it, is now.

The Internet is really nothing more than a vehicle for directing streams of data. I/O and data streaming has never been more important. And I/O has never been more complex. There are many different types of data sources, each with their own protocols. And the data streams they produce are more and more complex. HTTP packets contain complex HTML and XML documents, which may call upon schemas and style sheets, or SOAP protocol packets. The XML data encodes a huge variety of business and entertainment data based on hundreds of different schemas. Middleware applications call on complex databases and other data sources in response to complex form data and requests from other applications. Programmers trying to contain this massive flux and flow of complex data without any more sophisticated stream processing than is provided by traditional programming languages are facing an uphill battle. It is time to look for languages designed to handle streaming data in more sophisticated ways.

What is a stream?

A stream is a complex object with important characteristics. A stream has a source and a destination, it has movement, and it has structure. A stream is of unknown length. These are features that a streaming language must support, expose, and exploit. Let's look at each in turn.

A stream has a source and a destination

A stream is a flow of data between a source and a destination. The source could be anything on the Internet from a web server, or an LDAP server, to a file on your own hard drive. The destination also can be anywhere and anything, from a mail server to a database to an ftp server. Each of these sources and destinations has its own particular way of sending or receiving data. The method by which a stream is connected to its source and its destination is therefore particular to the type of source or destination involved. But between source and destination, all streams are alike: they are a succession of bytes.

When dealing with a stream, therefore, the programmer has the opportunity to separate the issue of how streams are connected to their sources and destinations from the issue of processing the sequence of bytes as it flows. This allows the programmer to write code that works identically on any stream, no matter what its source or destination. In conventional practice, this abstraction is achieved by copying input data into data structures and operating on the data structures. In streaming programming, it is achieved at the level of the stream itself.

A stream has movement

A stream is a flow of data. Therefore, a stream has movement. When analyzing the content of a variable, a programmer must either write code to move the data byte-by-byte from one location to another, or write code to move a pointer through the data. When dealing with a stream, however, the programmer can exploit the movement that is already taking place. In the streaming model you do not write data movement code in order to process data, you take advantage of the movement that is natural to the stream.

A stream has structure

All useful data has structure, and all programs that process data work on that structure. But you don't need data structures to have structured data. The order of bytes in a data stream is never random. It always has meaning. If there were no structure in the stream of input data, it would not be possible to build a data structure from it.

Most of the data flowing over networks is encoded in a hierarchical structure of some kind. Hierarchy is simply the best and easiest way to describing structure in a linear stream. XML has garnered huge interest as a vehicle for general data exchange precisely because its hierarchical nature is suitable for encoding much of the data transmission on the Internet.

Since virtually every data stream has a hierarchical structure, a streaming language can be designed specifically to support the processing of hierarchically structured data. This does not mean that streaming languages cannot process streams with non-hierarchical structures. It does mean that a streaming language can bring a high level of sophistication to the decoding and management of hierarchical data streams which can largely remove the need to create data structures as a processing step.

The virtues of XML as the lingua franca of the Internet arise fundamentally from its linear nature. The Internet is an environment of streams. Streams are linear data in motion. Data structures live statically in computer memory. Streams of structured linear data move across networks. Whether the structure of those streams is encoded in XML or in some other format, the streaming approach to programming lets you process that streaming data directly and efficiently.

Streams are of unknown length

One of the most important characteristics of a stream is that you don't know its length until you get to the end of it. One of the things that makes XML so flexible as a data description format is that it has no length constraints. An XML document can grow from two kilobytes to two gigabytes while remaining perfectly valid.

Data structure oriented programming is very difficult if you don't know the length of the data you are dealing with. This is one of the principle reasons that data structure oriented programs buffer their entire input without processing it during I/O. It also why so many data structure oriented programs fail unexpectedly when the size of the data increases. Streaming programming, by contrast, handles data of unknown length easily and straightforwardly. The data stream is processed as it flows through the program. The input is not buffered, so its length is not important. Streaming programs scale up easily from handling two kilobytes of data to handling two gigabytes.

A streaming programming language

There is a difference between an approach to programming and a programming language that supports that approach. You can program in an object-oriented fashion in any language, but an object-oriented language makes it much easier to do so. The same is true of streaming programming. You can take a streaming approach to programming in any language, but it is much easier if you use a streaming language.

These are the key features of a streaming programming language:

- source and destination abstraction
- high level data scanning features
- high level context management
- placeholder capability
- data structures where required
- broad based connectivity
- co-routine support
- robust high level server programming support

Source and destination abstraction

Every stream has a source and a destination. There are many different source and destination types, each with its own interface and protocols. However, the particular mechanism by which a stream is connected to its source and its destination do not affect any of its other properties as a stream and should not affect the way the data in the stream is processed. Therefore, a streaming language should provide an abstract stream object which can be attached to any source or destination but which in itself has a single uniform set of properties against which the user can program.

High level data scanning features

A streaming language must provide powerful high-level features for finding and interpreting structures in streaming data. This requires sophisticated means for finding patterns in the streaming data. Such features must be implemented in a way that allows them to be applied directly to the data stream without halting its flow or capturing it into data structures. They must make it simple and transparent to insert data into the stream as it flows to its destination.

High level context management

When complex structures are encoded in linear data, the encoding is usually based on nested structures. (That is to say, it is hierarchical.) Each change in nesting level or hierarchy represents a change in context. Data within a given context has meaning in that context. It is not enough to recognize a pattern in the input data, you must recognize that pattern in context. Patterns have meaning only in context.

This means that a streaming language must have sophisticated high level support for managing context in the interpretation of a data stream. Furthermore, it means that managing that context should not require building data structures to represent the hierarchy of the data. Rather, context management should be a feature of the language itself.

Placeholder capability

The biggest challenge to a pure streaming approach to programming is that presented by differences in order between the input data and the output data. Streaming audio is easy because the order of output is exactly the same as the order of input. But in many other cases data does not go out in the same order as the source data comes in.

At this point, I will point out that there is a distinction to be made between three different places in a program where you might want to build a data structure. You may build a data structure to represent your input. You may build one to provide process control within your program, and you may build a data structure to represent the output of your program. Streaming programming attempts to minimize all three, but to different extents. A streaming program never builds a data structure to represent its input. Streaming programs commonly build data structures for process control (though the context management features of a streaming language lessen the need for such structures). Streaming programs sometimes build a data structure to represent the output. This usually occurs in analytical type programs in which it is not possible to generate any of the output until all the data has been processed. A program to count words in a document is a simple example of such a program.

Between streaming audio players and word counting programs, however, lie a vast range of applications in which most of the output can be generated in immediate response to the streaming input, but in which it is sometimes necessary to generate some of the output before the data required to generate it occurs in the input stream. In this case it is inevitable that the output will have to be buffered until the required data is available. But it is not necessary for the programmer to be forced to do that buffering, essentially dropping back into a data-structure-centered approach. Instead, a streaming language should provide a mechanism by which the programmer can output a placeholder to the output stream and supply a value for that placeholder later. The language then provides all the required buffering, in a highly optimized fashion, and allows the programmer to continue programming in a streaming fashion.

Data structures where required

Because data structures are often needed, even in a streaming language, a streaming language must provide an adequate set of data structures. Of course, the most fundamental data structure that a streaming language must provide is a stream. Even data that is buffered within the program, either for process control or output modeling, should be treated as streams so that all the facilities of the language for processing data in streams can be used to process the data structures.

(It is worth noting that, for this reason, streaming programming languages do not need pointers. You never move a pointer through the data, you stream the data and process it as it streams.)

Broad-based connectivity

Since streaming programming is appropriate for environments like the Internet where data is streamed from many different sources to many different destinations, a streaming programming language needs broad-based connectivity support. That support must be implemented in a way that complements source and destination abstraction. That is to say, each connectivity option must support the connection of a generic stream for sending or receiving data.

Co-routine support

Sometimes it is necessary to make more than one pass over a data source in order to produce a final input. That is, the data must pass through more than one process in order to create the desired output. The naive way to accomplish this is to run the data through the first process, capture the result, and then run it through the second process and so on for all subsequent processes. This involves buffering the complete output of each process. It is inefficient and resource intensive. The streaming approach to a problem of this type is to run each process as a co-routine without buffering the outputs between processes. In a co-routine environment, the final process drives a chain of co-routines. The lead process asks the preceding process for just enough data to get going. That process makes the same request down the line to the trailing process. The trailing process runs just long enough to supply the needs of the process it is feeding and then relinquishes control. The processes thus cooperate with one another to accomplish all the processing steps on a single data stream.

A streaming language should provide high level support for the creation of co-routines.

Robust high level server programming support

Because streaming programs commonly run in a network environment and act as servers, a streaming programming language should provide high level support for robust server programming.

This means more than simply providing a high-level interface to TCP/IP sockets. It means providing, at a high level, the ability to catch and survive program errors and to return a server application to a consistent and known-good state after every request is serviced, even when errors occur in servicing the request.

The benefits of streaming programming

The advantages of streaming programming in a streaming programming language can be summed up in three words: performance, robustness and productivity.

Performance

Streaming programming provides high performance because it avoids data copying and limits the number of times the program looks at the data. For instance, compare the streaming approach to transforming an XML document with the data-structure-oriented approach.

Data structure oriented:

1. Use a DOM based parser to build a DOM tree (first complete pass over the data, first copy of the data).

2. Traverse the DOM tree, selecting the required information and populate a second DOM tree representing the output (second complete pass over the data, second copy of the data).

3. Serialize the second DOM tree to create the output document (third pass over the data).

Streaming:

1. Parse the XML document with a parser that reports elements as they occur and allows you to create an immediate response. Output the new tagging directly into the data stream. Use the inherent context management features of the language to make sure all the opening and closing tags drop into the right places (one pass over the data, no copying).

Robustness

Streaming programs provide a high level of robustness because they greatly reduce or eliminate the use of variables and more complex data structures.

Data structures are a huge source of program errors. Uninitialized variables and variables with incorrect values are a major source of program bugs. As long as a piece of data is held in memory it is subject to accidental change and erasure. One of the principal arguments for the adoption of object oriented programming was to reduce errors due to data corruption by limiting access to data structures. It does this by hiding data structures in objects where it can only be manipulated by code belonging to the object itself.

The streaming model takes this safety measure one step further by greatly reducing the need to create data structures at all. This reduces the opportunity to introduce errors into the program. Eliminating the variables eliminates the places where bugs can hide and breed. Similarly, by eliminating unnecessary copying of data, the streaming approach eliminates errors due to mistakes in copying. You are dealing with originals, not copies.

Productivity

Streaming programming provides a high degree of programmer productivity because it eliminates so much of the overhead associated with conventional programming approaches. There are fewer data structures to design, build, and test. There are fewer bugs to detect and fix. There is no low level data access or data movement code to write and no need to code your own context management support.

Streaming programming tend to produce programs that are very process-oriented. That is, the working part of the program tends to describe the actions actually being performed on the input to produce the output, rather than describing abstract manipulations of data structures and objects. This makes it easier to read and understand the programs, which makes them both easier to write and easier to maintain.

Finally, because the streaming approach is naturally efficient and naturally minimizes the use of resources, there is usually no need for performance tuning of a streaming program after it is complete. Streaming programs are naturally fast and frugal.

What are streaming programming languages good for?

Streaming languages are good for writing software that runs in batch mode. That is, software that takes all its input up front in the form of input data and runs to completion without user interaction to create an output. This includes server programs, most of which are essentially remotely invoked batch programs. A server services each request in batch mode, and then waits for another request.

Data-structure languages are more appropriate for developing interactive applications such as word processors and spreadsheets. In a batch-oriented program the input data is dealt with sequentially. In an interactive application, users access the data randomly, and a sequential approach to processing the data is not appropriate. The application relies on building a complex data structure that provides speedy random access to the data.

Note, however, that distributed interactive applications – the Web is the most prominent example – often consist of interactive clients accessing back-end services that run in batch mode. All CGI scripts, for instance, run in batch mode, as does the web server itself. The browser needs to build a data structure representing the document model of the page it is displaying in order to provide equally rapid response no matter which link the user clicks or which field they choose to enter data. But the CGI script that processes a form submission processes the data it receives serially and creates a response page serially, without user interaction. The user's requirements from a CGI script are not random access but rapid response, and the overhead associated with building elaborate data structures does not help meet that need.

Is streaming programming a low-level approach?

Because streaming programming deals directly with streamed data, rather than with data structures, some people regard it as a low level approach. But surely it is not a hallmark of low level programming that it requires less code and less time to write that code than high level programming. The truth is that building data structures may encapsulate data, and it may hide data, but it does not provide a higher level abstraction of data. No such abstraction is possible. The data is ultimately what every programmer must deal with. The question is, will you deal with it directly using high level tools, or will you build it up into complex data structures and then manipulate those data structures with relatively crude low level operations? Unless you need data structures to provide random access to data for an interactive application, your choice should be the streaming programming model.

Are there any other streaming programming languages?

XSL and XSLT have some features of a streaming programming languages, though I know of no implementations that are streaming in practice. CSS is a streaming language, of a kind. But the only fully general streaming programming language available today is OmniMark. As such, OmniMark is the only streaming programming language capable of being used for a wide variety of Internet programming tasks.

Streaming languages vs. object-oriented languages

Do you have to choose between a streaming language and an object-oriented language? Today, yes, because OmniMark is the only full streaming language available and it is not yet fully object oriented, though it has several object-oriented features. But the ideas of streaming programming and object oriented programming are not opposed to each other. Indeed, streaming programming's concept of a stream as a high level object abstracted from any specific source or destination of data is a clear application of object-oriented programming principles. The streaming and object-oriented paradigms are perfectly compatible with each other. Streaming programming stands in contrast to data-structure-oriented programming, not object-oriented programming.

While it is at heart a streaming language, OmniMark, like all successful programming languages, borrows features and ideas from many different programming paradigms. It has a full set of conventional structured programming tools; loops, branches, blocks, arrays, and functions. Its OMX architecture uses component-based software model for language extensions and access to external data sources. OmniMark's fundamental building blocks are its sources and streams, which are high level objects. Many of the keywords of the OmniMark language can be thought of as either method calls or property assignments on source and stream objects.

Future versions of OmniMark will add full object-orientation to the language. OmniMark will then be both a fully streaming language and a fully object-oriented language. In the meantime, OmniMark is the best language to choose for streaming programming and streaming programming is the best approach to use for most Internet programming tasks.

About this book

This book will teach you about streaming programming in OmniMark. It is designed for working Internet programmers who are looking for a way to work faster and smarter. OmniMark is the first and only language designed from the ground up for streaming programming. It will make every Internet programming chore you do, from writing CGI scripts to transforming data into HTML, to creating and processing XML, faster and easier. The book is designed to get you using OmniMark productively as soon as possible. Though I will be explaining the principles of streaming programming along the way, this is a practical book, not a theoretical one. I assume you have a working knowledge of computer programming in general and of Internet programming in particular.

I asked a bunch of programmers how they like to learn a programming language. Most said, "I start with the examples, and once I get them to run I play with them". That's how this book is organized. Each chapter will present one or more OmniMark programs that solve common Internet programming problems. The programs presented are designed for learning, and to give you opportunities to play and explore. They are not necessarily designed to be production ready programs.

In each chapter, I'll explain the programs and the problem solving approach they use. Then I'll explain the main OmniMark language features used in the program. (I will only deal with the OmniMark syntax actually presented in the program. For the full details on all language features, you should consult the OmniMark documentation.) Finally, I'll suggest some ways you can play with the program to make sure you understand what it does and how it does it.

Throughout this book, I'll assume you are using the OmniMark IDE. If you are using OmniMark C/VM instead, you will have to adapt some of the instructions slightly, but all the examples will work just the same.

All the sample programs and code are listed in full in the text or in Appendix 3. You can also download them from www.omnimark.com/ipwithom/.

Have fun. You're going to enjoy programming in OmniMark.

1: Hello world

I'll start with the obvious, the classic "Hello World" program. In the Internet age, however, it is not enough to print "Hello World" to the screen. This chapter will show you how to build hello world programs that write to many different destinations and that run as CGI and server programs as well as desktop applications. At the same time, you'll see how OmniMark abstracts data destinations, allowing you to use the same method to output data to any destination.

Here is the classic "Hello World" program in OmniMark:

```
;hello.xom
process
    output "Hello World%n"
```

Here's what you need to know about this program:

- The ; introduces a comment.
- The keyword **process** begins the working part of an OmniMark program (it may be preceded by declarations, as we shall see later).
- The keyword **output** is an instruction to send what follows to output.
- The text "Hello World%n" is a literal string.
- The "%n" is the escape sequence for a line feed.

To run this program:

1. Fire up the OmniMark IDE. (If you don't have access to the IDE, see below for instructions on using the command-line compiler/virtual machine, OmniMark C/VM, instead.)
2. Click the "New File" button.
3. Type in the program.
4. Click the "Run" button.
5. Click the "Continue" button.

The output of the program will appear in the log window of the IDE. The stuff that appears in the log window before "Hello World" is the command required to run your program on the command line. OmniMark is intended for server-side applications, so it doesn't include GUI building options. The normal place to run an OmniMark program is on the command line. The IDE is a development environment only.

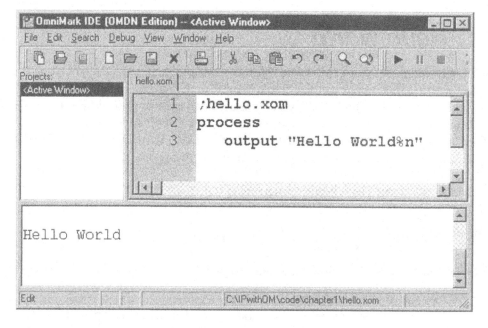

The Hello World program in the OmniMark IDE.

So, now that the "Hello World" program is developed and running properly, it is time to move it to the command line. First, save the program to disk. Use any location and file name you like. Now run it again in the IDE. This gives you the proper command line for running the saved version of the program.

Now, to run the program on the command line:

1. Open a command prompt (a "DOS box" under Windows).
2. Type in the command line as it appears in the log window of the IDE.
3. Hit "Enter".

OmniMark will print out "Hello World". The stuff before "Hello World" is OmniMark's copyright and version information. To suppress it, change the "-s" on the command line to "-sb".

If you don't have access to the IDE, the command-line syntax is:

```
omnimark -s <path to program file>
```

Hello World CGI

Now let's change the program to run as a CGI script:

```
#!omnimark/omnimark -sb
;hellocgi.xom
include "omcgi.xin"
process
   output "Content-type: text/html"
       || crlf
       || crlf
       || "<h1>Hello World</h1>%n"
```

Here's what you need to know about this program:

*   The #! (hash-bang) tells a UNIX shell which executable to use to run the program. OmniMark itself treats this line as a comment, so it is ignored if your program is run under Windows (unless you use Apache for Windows, which will use the hash-bang line itself).
*   Like the previous program, this program outputs to standard output, but in this case, standard output is the web server. This is because of the way the web server launches a CGI program, and has nothing to do with how the program is coded.
*   The line include "omcgi.xin" includes the file "omcgi.xin" (OmniMark's CGI support library) in our program. (".xin" is the standard extension for OmniMark include files. Program files have the extension ".xom".)
*   I have added HTML tagging to the "Hello World" text and added a minimal HTTP header ("Content-type: text/html").
*   The double bar (||) is OmniMark's concatenation operator. It joins string

expressions together. It is good programming style to line up the concatenation operators under the output keyword as shown, creating a clear and legible text block on the right.

- crlf is a macro defined in omcgi.xin. As you might expect, crlf represents a carriage return/line feed combination.

To run this program as a CGI, you must first set up your web server to run OmniMark CGI programs. You will find the necessary instructions in Appendix 2.

Hello World server

I'll explain all the details later, but just for fun, here is a Hello World server program:

```
;hellosrv.xom
include "omtcp.xin"

process
   local TCPService service
   set service to TCPServiceOpen at 5432
   repeat
      local TCPConnection connection
      local stream  response
      set connection to TCPServiceAcceptConnection service
      open response as TCPConnectionGetOutput connection
      using output as response
       output "Hello "
           || TCPConnectionGetPeerName connection
           || "%n"
   catch #program-error
   again
```

To run this program, type it into the IDE (or load it from the samples) and run it as before. It won't produce any immediate output, because it is waiting for a client program to connect to it. To see what the program does (assuming your computer has a TCP/IP stack running):

1. Fire up telnet (under Windows, choose Run from the Start menu and type in "telnet").
2. Connect to host "localhost" or "127.0.0.1" (either of which is your own machine) using port "5432".

Telnet will display the words "Hello localhost".

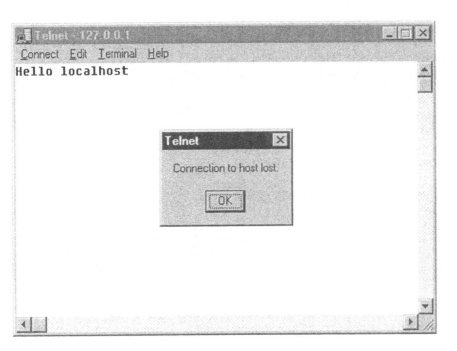

Telnet after connecting to the Hello World server. The server drops the connection as soon as it sends the greeting.

You can do this as often as you like, since the server keeps running. The program personalizes the greeting so that it greets the individual user rather then the whole planet. It greets the user using the network names of the machine the client is running on (or "localhost" if it is running on the same machine).

To see this dynamic greeting in action:

1.   Leave the server running in the IDE on your machine.
2.   Go to another machine on your network.
3.   Use telnet to connect to port 5432 on the machine the server is running on (you will need to know that machine's real network address or name).

The program will greet you appropriately.

When you are tired of this game, shut down the server by pressing the stop button in the IDE.

Writing "Hello World" to a file

Now that you can write "Hello World" to the screen, a web page, and a network client, how about writing it to something simple like a file. Here is the program:

```
;hellofile.xom
process
   local stream output-file
   open output-file as file "hello.txt"
   using output as output-file
   do
      output "Hello World%n"
   done
```

Run this program in the IDE. It will create a file called "hello.txt" and write "Hello World" to it.

Technique

These simple programs illustrate some very important techniques that underlie all OmniMark programs, especially those that run in a web environment.

The universal output mechanism

In all the versions of the Hello World program, you may have noticed that one thing is constant. No matter what other stuff goes into the program to make it work in a particular environment, the line that outputs the "Hello World" message stays the same. It is simply the keyword output followed by the message to be output.

There are similar keywords in other languages. C has printf. Perl and Basic both use Print. Each of these sends data to standard output. So, in C, Perl, and Basic in turn, you can write:

```
printf("Hello World\n")
Print "Hello World\n"
Print "Hello World"
```

And in OmniMark:

```
output "Hello World%n"
```

These all work identically as long as you are outputting to standard output (usually the screen). When it comes to writing to a file, however, in the other languages you have to specify where the output goes in each output statement. In C, you need a different keyword to write to a file:

```
fprintf( outfile, "Hello World/n")
```

In Basic and Perl you can use the same command, but you must supply a file handle as a parameter to the "Print" command. In Basic it looks like this:

```
Print #outfile, "Hello World"
```

In Perl it looks like this:

```
Print outfile "Hello World/n"
```

In OmniMark, however, output never takes any kind of destination parameter. It is always simply output. Where the output goes is established by the using output as statement.

In OmniMark, the question of where the output goes and the question of what the output is are two separate issues. First you must establish the destination for your output. Then you can generate the output to that destination.

Managing output destinations with output scopes

The program "hellofile.xom", uses using output as to establish the file "hello.txt" as the destination for output and then does the output.

We say that using output as establishes an *output scope*. Any output created in an output scope goes to the destination established for that scope. For instance, if a function is called in the middle of an output scope, any output generated by that function goes to the destination of that output scope. This means that the function will output to different destinations depending on the output scope in which it is called. Once an output scope ends, the previous output scope is restored. There is always a current output scope in an OmniMark program, and all output goes to the current output scope.

using output as is a prefix and establishes a new output scope for the duration of the statement it prefixes. In "hellofile.xom", it prefixes a code block delimited by the keywords do and done. Every output statement between the do and the done will send its output to the destination specified by the using output as statement.

Because using output as is a prefix, and there is only one output statement, you can reduce the program a little by eliminating the do...done block and prefixing the output statement itself with using output as:

```
;hellofile2.com
process
   local stream output-file
   open output-file as file "hello.txt"
   using output as output-file
    output "Hello World%n"
```

I indent the output statement under the using output as to remind myself that using output as is a prefix to that statement, and that statement only. To make sure you understand this, run the following program and observe the effects:

```
;hellofile3.xom
process
   local stream output-file
   open output-file as file "hello.txt"
   using output as output-file
   output "Hello file%n"
   output "Hello screen%n"
```

The words "Hello file" will be written to the file "hello.txt". The words "Hello screen" will be written to the log window because the second output statement is not affected by the using output as statement. You can restore the do...done block to give you control over the scope of the using output as statement:

```
;hellofile4.xom
process
   local stream output-file
   open output-file as file "hello.txt"
   using output as output-file
   do
      output "Hello file%n"
      output "More for the file%n"
   done
   output "Hello screen%n"
```

Run this program and see what happens. Why do the words "Hello screen" go to the screen? Because standard output (the screen) is the default destination of the default output scope of an OmniMark program. That scope was established at the beginning of the program and restored after the done.

Output scopes can be nested, so you can write a program like this:

```
;hellofile5.xom
process
    local stream hello-file
    local stream goodbye-file
    open hello-file as file "hello.txt"
    using output as hello-file
    do
        output "Hello file%n"
        open goodbye-file as file "goodbye.txt"
        using output as goodbye-file
        do
            output "Goobye cruel world!%n"
        done
        output "More for the hello file%n"
    done
    output "Hello screen%n"
```

Play with this program until you are comfortable with how output scopes work.

Streams

Now that you're comfortable with output scopes, let's take a closer look at the parameter that using output as takes when establishing an output scope. In the line using output as goodbye-file, what kind of thing is goodbye-file?

As you have probably figured out from the code, goodbye-file is a variable of the type "stream". You may think it looks a lot like a file handle, but an OmniMark *stream* is not a file handle. To see the difference, compare the following OmniMark and Basic open statements.

Basic first:

```
dim goodbye-file as integer
goodbye-file = freefile
open "goodbye.txt" for input as #goodbye-file
```

Now OmniMark:

```
local stream goodbye-file
open goodbye-file as file "goodbye-txt"
```

Notice the difference? Both use an **open...as** syntax. But in Basic you open the file "as" the file handle, while in OmniMark you open the stream "as" the file. Why? Because while a Basic file handle is a low-level means of communicating with the operating system, an OmniMark stream is a high-level object in the language. You don't open files in OmniMark; you open streams and attach those streams to files or other data destinations.

The job of actually completing the attachment between a stream and a file belongs to the **VOS** (Virtual Operating System). Like Java, OmniMark runs on top of a virtual machine. But OmniMark's virtual machine has a virtual operating system as well, which provides a high-level interface between your program and your computer's real operating system. When you open an OmniMark stream "as" a file, you are asking the VOS to form that attachment for you. How it does this on each of the platforms that OmniMark runs on is up to the VOS. You never open a file in an OmniMark program. You open a stream and attach it to a file. The VOS opens the file. This makes OmniMark programs extremely portable.

What is a stream? Essentially, a stream is a pipe through which data can flow to a destination. When you use an OmniMark stream, you don't have to worry about what destination it is attached to, or even the kind of destination it is attached to. An OmniMark stream behaves exactly the same no matter what destination it is attached to. Here's a snippet from the Hello World server showing a stream being opened with an attachment to a TCP/IP connection. Once the connection is established, the stream is used just like any other stream:

```
local TCPConnection connection
local stream   response
set connection to TCPServiceAcceptConnection service
open response as TCPConnectionGetOutput connection
using output as response
 output "Hello "
```

Directing output to multiple destinations

Here's another difference between file handles and streams. You can establish more than one stream as the destination for an output scope:

```
;hellofile6.xom
process
   local stream hello-file
   local stream greeting-file
   open hello-file as file "hello.txt"
   open greeting-file as file "greeting.txt"
```

```
using output as hello-file and greeting-file
   output "Hello file%n"
        || "More for the file%h"
```

This program sends the same output to two different files simultaneously. (Run it and see for yourself.)

Can you send the output to the screen and a file simultaneously?

Yes:

```
;hellofile7.xom
process
   local stream hello-file
   open hello-file as file "hello.txt"
   using output as hello-file and #process-output
       output "Hello file%n"
            || "More for the file%n"
```

#process-output is a built-in OmniMark stream that is attached to standard output. This program outputs not only to two different destinations, but also to two different kinds of destinations. Can you output the same data simultaneously to the screen, a TCP/IP connection, two files, three FTP sites, and a buffer in memory? Yes you can. You just need to know how to make the proper attachments. Your output code won't change at all. OmniMark streams are the great equalizers.

Here's another cool trick. This program keeps adding new streams to the set of output destinations:

```
;hellofile8.xom
process
   local stream file-one
   local stream file-two
   local stream file-three
   output "zero%n"
   open file-one as file "one.txt"
   using output as file-one and #current-output
   do
       output "one%n"
       open file-two as file "two.txt"
       using output as file-two and #current-output
```

```
do
    output "two%n"
    open file-three as file "three.txt"
    using output as file-three and #current-output
     output "three%n"
    output "two%n"
  done
  output "one%n"
done
output "zero%n"
```

#current-output is an OmniMark keyword that acts as an alias for all the streams already in the current output scope. You can use it to establish an output scope that has all the current output destinations plus a new one. Examine the output of this program carefully, both the output written to the screen and the output written to the three files. Make sure you understand exactly why each piece of output ended up where it did. Play around with the program until you're sure you know what it does. Understanding how streams work with attachments, how using output as establishes an output scope with one or more streams, and how output always outputs to the current output scope are fundamental to successful programming in OmniMark.

Line end and network protocols

You may have noticed something odd about the output of the Hello World CGI program. It uses two different methods to create a line end, "%n" and crlf:

```
output "Content-type: text/html"
        || crlf
        || crlf
        || "<h1>Hello World</h1>%n"
```

What's the difference between "%n" and crlf and why do they both occur in the output of the program?

"%n" is LF (ASCII 10). The crlf macro is defined as CR (ASCII 13) followed by LF.

Windows and DOS systems use CR followed by LF to indicate a line end. UNIX systems use LF alone. In a network environment, however, there is no guarantee that the system receiving data will be running the same OS as the one sending the data. Therefore there are protocols designed for network communication that specify data formats, including line end sequences, which network applications must obey regardless of the OS the application is running on.

The four lines of text output by the program involve the use of two network protocols, or, to be more precise, one protocol contained in another. In a CGI program, you use two protocols: HTTP and HTML. The HTTP protocol is used to transport web pages (and other web-accessible formats) across the Web. It consists of a header followed by the data. The end of the header is indicated by a blank line. For the HTTP header, the required line end format is CRLF, regardless of the conventions of the sending or receiving system. Thus you should use the `crlf` macro to insert the proper line end sequence in the HTTP header.

HTML follows the rules of SGML, which says that either CRLF, or LF, or even CR, is acceptable as a line end character. Since the protocol imposes no restrictions, you can use "%n" for the HTLM portion of your output. (Note, however, that if your CGI program runs on a UNIX platform and a Windows user attempts to view the HTML source of your page using an editor that expects a CRLF line end combination, they will see your entire file displayed without line breaks. If this concerns you, use `crlf` for all the line ends you output.)

Syntax

Let's look at the principal syntax elements introduced in this chapter. I'll just hit the highlights here. For the full nitty-gritty, see the OmniMark documentation. First a quick overview of the general syntax rules of an OmniMark program.

General OmniMark syntax rules

One question that many people ask on first seeing an OmniMark program is how the compiler can tell where things end. OmniMark does not use braces the way C and Java do. Nor is it a line-based language like Basic. Every token in an OmniMark program has a precise meaning based on the context in which it occurs. No further delineation of structures is required.

OmniMark is designed to be written as a free-form language. It is conventional to place one action per line and to indent the content of blocks and loops, but it is not required. You can write a whole OmniMark program on one line, or you can break complex actions over many lines to make them clear.

Only two OmniMark structures are sensitive to where lines end: comments and strings.

OmniMark comments begin with ";" and extend to the end of the current line:

```
;this is a comment
```

OmniMark strings are contained between double or single quotation marks and must begin and end on a single line. You can build long strings with the concatenation operator (||):

```
output "This is one line of text.%n"
    || 'This is another line of text.%n'
```

Keywords

Now let's look at the OmniMark keywords introduced in this chapter:

process

process introduces the working part of an OmniMark program. process is in fact a *rule header*, a concept I'll explore in the next chapter.

output

output sends data to the current output scope.

stream

A stream is a variable used to direct output to a destination. Unlike variables in a conventional language, a stream is not a container itself, but a conduit to a container. Before it can be used, a stream must be attached to a suitable container. The container to which it is attached may be of any type and may be located on a different machine.

using output as

You can use using output as to set the destination of output in an OmniMark program. using output as creates an output scope containing one or more streams attached to different destinations. The output destinations can be of any type, and you can freely mix and match destinations of different types.

In OmniMark, the question of where output goes is entirely separate from the act of creating output.

local

The keyword `local` declares a variable that is local in scope. I will get to global variables later in the book.

open

In OmniMark you must open a stream for that stream to receive data. When you open the stream, you must attach it to an output destination. The output destination may be of any type. All output in an OmniMark program is directed to streams in the current output scope. There are no special output commands for different types of output destinations. Streams allow the OmniMark programmer to treat all output destinations the same way.

You can apply a number of modifiers to a stream when you open it. See the OmniMark documentation for details.

#current-output

The keyword `#current-output` represents all the streams in the current output scope. You can use `#current-output` to add new output streams to the current set when creating a new output scope.

```
using output as #current-output and output-file
```

#process-output

`#process-output` is a built-in OmniMark stream that is attached to standard output.

"%n"

"%n" is a string escape for the newline character (ASCII 10). C programmers may expect there to be a corresponding "%r", but OmniMark does not have a "%r". Instead you can use "%13#". Any character code can be written this way, as "%" followed by a decimal number between 0 and 255, followed by "#". "%n" is equivalent to "%10#".

||

`||` is the OmniMark concatenation operator. You can use `||` to join strings and string expressions.

Review

The following are the main points covered in this chapter. If you don't understand any of the statements below, go back and review the material in this chapter before you go on.

- In OmniMark, the question of where output goes is separate from the task of generating output.
- The statement using output as creates an output scope. All output generated in the current output scope goes to the destination established by using output as.
- An OmniMark stream is used to direct output to an attached destination. All streams work the same way, regardless of the destination they are attached to.
- The keyword process starts the working part of an OmniMark program.
- The keyword output sends output to the current output scope.
- The keyword #current-output is an alias for all the streams in the current output scope.
- An OmniMark stream is a conduit through which data flows to a destination. A stream can be attached to any kind of data destination. Thanks to streams, the OmniMark programmer can output to all destinations in exactly the same way.
- In network programming, the conventions of a particular operating system are irrelevant; it is the conventions of the network protocol that matter.

Exercises

1. Play with the programs in this chapter and make sure you understand how they work.
2. Rewrite the programs in this chapter to serve up the current time and data. To get the current time and date, use the date keyword. Check the OmniMark documentation for the proper syntax.

2: Converting text to HTML

The previous chapter showed you how OmniMark streams its output, and how the language abstracts data destinations, allowing you to use the same basic techniques to write to any destination. In this chapter I will show you how OmniMark abstracts data sources and how you can establish an input data stream.

You will also learn how to process data directly as it streams from input to output, without the use of intermediate data structures. OmniMark processes streaming data by recognizing meaningful patterns in the data and executing the appropriate actions. You specify the patterns to be recognized and actions to take when those patterns occur. In this chapter, we will examine this concept using a simple text-to-HTML translation.

Suppose you have a set of text files containing nursery rhymes and you want to convert that data to make HTML pages for a nursery rhyme website. Here is a sample data file, "mary.txt":

```
Mary had a little lamb
by Mother Goose

Mary had a little lamb
Its fleece was white as snow;
And everywhere that Mary went
The lamb was sure to go
```

```
It followed her to school one day
Which was against the rule.
It made the children laugh and play
To see a lamb at school.
```

Here is an OmniMark program to convert it to a very basic HTML. It operates by detecting and acting on patterns in the data such as the use of the word "by" to introduce the author's name, and the use of blank lines to separate verses:

```
;nursery.xom
process
    output "<HTML><BODY>%n<H1>"
    using input as file #args[1]
     submit #current-input
    output "</BODY></HTML>"

find "%nby"
    output "</H1>%n<B>by</B>"

find "%n%n"
    output "<P>%n"

find "%n"
    output "<BR>%n"
```

Here is what the output looks like in a browser.

The output of the nursery rhyme program in a browser window.

Here's what you need to know about this program:

- **#args** gives you access to the items typed on the command line.
- **using input as** establishes an input scope, making input data available for processing.
- **submit #current-input** initiates processing of the current input data by find rules.
- **find** introduces a find rule. Find rules process the input data by matching patterns in the input and responding accordingly. Data not matched by a find rule streams straight to the current output scope.

Technique

This program illustrates the most fundamental ideas behind streaming programming: abstraction of data sources and the processing of streamed input data by scanning.

Establishing sources with "using input as"

Just as you can use using output as to establish an output scope, you can use using input as to establish an input scope. In this program, the input comes from a disk file and output goes to another disk file. The program reads the file names from the command line using the built-in variable #args. #args is a special type of multi-value object called a *shelf*, but for now you can just think of it as an array. You can access items in #args by specifying the item number in square brackets (shelf indexes start at 1, not 0):

```
using input as file #args[1]
```

To input command-line arguments for your program while it is running in the IDE, add them to the "Arguments" tab in the Project Options dialog box.

using input as is different from using output as in one important respect, however. As I said before, using output as takes one or more OmniMark streams as arguments. Streams are used in OmniMark to direct data to output destinations. They are not used to read data from sources. Instead, using input as takes a source as an argument. Sources are not high-level objects in OmniMark the way streams are. When the source is a file, you access it with the file keyword. You can also use a literal string as a source:

```
using input as "Mary had a little lamb."
```

We will look at ways of accessing other types of sources later.

For reasons that should be obvious, you cannot read from multiple simultaneous sources the way you can output to multiple simultaneous destinations.

Scanning the input stream

Once you have established an input scope, you are ready to act on the input. In most programming languages, the first thing you do with an input source is to read it into a variable or allocate a block of memory and copy it into the allocated block. Once the data has been read into memory, you write code using variable names or pointers to manipulate the data.

OmniMark works differently. You will notice that the data is never read into a variable. In fact, the only variable in the whole program is the local stream established to funnel the output. In OmniMark, you act directly on the input data as it flows. You do this by a process known as *scanning*. When you scan the data, you look for patterns in the data as it flows by and act on those patterns.

(Even if you wanted to capture the data into variables, you would do so by scanning the data, finding the pattern you wanted to capture, and assigning it to a variable. But while capturing data in this way will sometimes be necessary, it usually is not. In a good OmniMark program you will act directly on the data as it flows without ever building intermediate data structures.)

You will also notice that there is no data movement code in this program. You don't explicitly read the data a byte at a time and do comparisons on each byte as you might in other languages. Data movement is automatic in OmniMark. All you have to do is initiate the scanning of the current input source.

In this program I initiate the scanning of the current input with the submit keyword. As you might expect, the syntax is:

```
submit #current-input
```

There are others ways to initiate scanning, which I will come to later. submit is used to initiate scanning by *find rules*. submit activates the find rules and starts the current input source data flowing.

OmniMark processes data in motion. You never write code to move over data. Start the data moving and use rules to process it.

Setting traps for data using find rules

A find rule is a trap for data flowing from the current input source. Once scanning begins, as a result of a submit, data flows from the current input to the current output. As the data flows, the *patterns* specified by the find rules are matched against the data. If a pattern matches the data, the find rule is fired and any actions associated with the rule are executed. An output statement in the body of a find rule sends output to the current output scope and thus inserts data into the stream flowing from current input to current output. nursery.xom, uses output in find rules to insert HTML markup into the steam of text data at the appropriate places.

OmniMark tries find rules in the order they appear in a program. When a pattern matches, the data matched is consumed and does not pass to the output stream.

You can see this at work in the two find rules that deal with line ends. The data uses one line end between lines of a verse and two line ends between verses. The code translates one line end into an HTML "<BR>" tag and two into an HTML "<P>" tag.

```
find "%n%n"
    output "<P>%n"

find "%n"
    output "<BR>%n"
```

The important thing to note is that the find rule for two line ends comes before the find rule for one. This is essential if the rule for two line ends is ever to fire. If the single-line-end rule came first, it would fire twice for two line ends in a row, consuming them both and never letting the two-line-end rule get a chance at the data.

You must always arrange your find rules from the most specific to the most general. A specific rule will never fire if preceded by a more general rule that can match the same data.

A rule that is unique in the data it matches (that is, no other rule can match what it matches) can come anywhere in the program. An example is the first rule in the program:

```
find "%nby"
    output "</H1>%n<B>by</B>"
```

This rule looks for the word "by" at the beginning of a line (that is, immediately following a line end) and outputs the word "by" (which has, of course, been consumed from the input) surrounded by bold tags. It also outputs the end "</H1>" tag to end the title.

In this program, I do not attempt to identify the title line per se. Instead, I rely on what I know about the data to output the H1 tagging in the right place. I know the title is the first line of the file, so I can simply output the "<H1>" at the start of the file. I do this immediately before the submit statement. I know that the second line of the file is the byline and it always starts with the word "by". I also know that the file contains a nursery rhyme, so all the other lines will start with capital letters. Therefore, a line end followed by the word "by" is the start of the byline and therefore the end of the title. So I output the end tagging for the title and the special markup for "by" and I'm done.

The first rule of text processing is "know thy data".

Of course, I could be in trouble if, unknown to me, someone slipped an e. e. cummings poem into the data. e. e. cummings wrote poems without capital letters, so a "by" at the beginning of any line in the poem would fire the first find rule.

The second rule of text processing is also "know thy data".

There are, of course, other ways to process this kind of data, such as keeping a count of lines or implementing a state machine to keep track of where you are in the data. These might be the first recourse when working in another language, but in OmniMark simple patterns can take you a long way, if you know your data. Programs based on pattern recognition alone are simple and easy to write and very appropriate for quick, simple problems. Later I will look at how to implement more sophisticated text processing techniques in OmniMark.

Notice that this program uses "%n" to match a line end. As I said before, "%n" is LF (ASCII 10). Since this program processes text files, OmniMark will normalize line ends to LF on input, so "%n" will match line ends correctly on all platforms.

Rules and the structure of OmniMark programs

As we have seen, OmniMark uses find rules to process data. OmniMark is a rule-based language. Different types of rules are used for different purposes. Find rules are used to scan a data source. We will look at other rules types as we go along.

To write a rule, you create a rule header that describes the event and a rule body that describes the actions to take when the event occurs. In the following lines the word find followed by the pattern "%nby" forms the rule header. The output statement forms the rule body.

```
find "%nby"
    output "</H1>%n<B>by</B>"
```

The keyword process, which starts the working part of an OmniMark program, is in fact a rule type, just like find. The keyword process begins a *process rule*. A process rule is simply a rule that is fired when the program starts. The body of a process rule contains the base code of your application, just as function "main()" contains the base code of your application in a function-based language like C or Visual Basic.

In these lines, the word process by itself is the rule header. The rest of the lines form the body of the process rule. The process rule body contains the submit action which activates the find rules in the program.

```
process
   output "<HTML><BODY>%n<H1>"
   using input as file #args[1]
      submit #current-input
   output "</BODY></HTML>"
```

Watch and learn

Run the program "nursery.xom" in the OmniMark IDE and step through it line
by line. Observe when the rules fire. Watch the data scopes to see how the data is
matched and consumed. Watch the log window to see how the output is produced.
Once you understand how the program works, play around with it. Try to make it
match different input data or output different tagging.

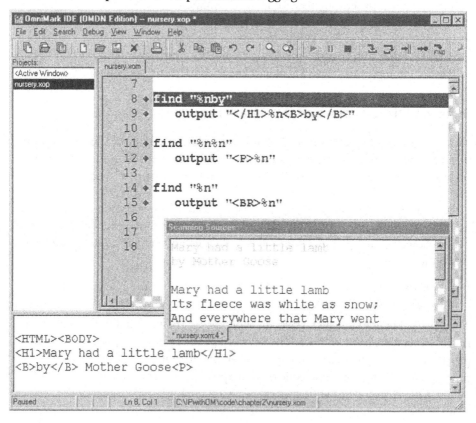

*nursery.xom running in the IDE. Note the throttle, which is used to control the speed of execution
and to step through the code. Also note the datascope (the window labeled "Scanning sources") that
shows the input data being matched and consumed.*

Establishing sources directly

As you have seen, you can establish a source with the expression using input as. However, OmniMark provides a shortcut for establishing current input and initiating scanning. You can skip the use of using input as and name a source directly in a submit statement. Thus this code:

```
using input as file #args[1]
using output as out-file
do
    output "<HTML><BODY>%n<H1>"
    submit #current-input
    output "</BODY></HTML>"
done
```

can be reduced to:

```
using output as out-file
do
    output "<HTML><BODY>%n<H1>"
    submit file #args[1]
    output "</BODY></HTML>"
done
```

Functionally this makes no difference at all. The longer version has the advantage of being slightly easier to read because the input and output are established right at the top of the program. This makes it a little easier to glance at a program and see what's going on. The shorter version has the advantage of being shorter and it is by far the more common approach in OmniMark programming.

Syntax

These are the new syntax items introduced in this chapter.

#args

#args is a built-in shelf containing the items typed on the command line. Items beginning with "-", such as "-sb", and the parameters used by those items, such as the name of your OmniMark program following "-sb", are not included. More on shelves later.

You access items on the #args shelf by specifying an index number in square brackets. Indexes start at 1.

#current-input

You can use #current-input to represent the current input source. If you use #current-input as the argument of submit, you initiate scanning of the current input source.

submit

The submit statement initiates the scanning of the current input source (that is, the source in the current input scope) by find rules. If used with a source as an argument, submit both establishes the current input scope, using that source, and initiates scanning. If used with #current-input as an argument, submit initiates scanning of the currently established input scope.

using input as

The using input as statement establishes the current input scope with the named source attached to it. By itself, using input as does not initiate processing of the data.

find

The find keyword introduces a find rule. find must be followed by a pattern. When the pattern occurs in the input data being scanned, the find rule fires and its associated actions are performed. Any output generated in the body of a find rule is directed to the current output scope.

Review

The following are the main points covered in this chapter. If you don't understand any of the statements below, go back and review the material in this chapter before you go on.

- All input in an OmniMark program comes from the source attached to the current input scope. An input scope can be created using the statement using input as or the keyword submit. (I will explore other methods in later chapters.)
- OmniMark allows you to scan input data for patterns.
- Find rules fire when the patterns they describe are found in the data.
- A more specific find rule must always occur before a more general find rule that can match the same data.

- The first rule of text processing is "know thy data".
- OmniMark is a rule-based language.

Exercises

1. Write an OmniMark program to translate a memo from text to HTML.
    An example of the memo format is as follows (memo.txt in the samples):

```
MEMO

From: Tom
To: Dick, Harry
Date: 2000-01-04
Subject: OmniMark

Hey guys, I just discovered this great programming language.
OmniMark is an Internet processing language with integrated XML
support and great connectivity, including high-level ODBC and
TCP/IP support.

You can write web applications quickly and easily. It will really
improve our productivity. The code is also very readable, which
will make maintenance a snap.

I think OmniMark is the solution to all our Internet programming
problems!
```

3: Converting an ASCII table to HTML

In a streaming programming language, you process data by recognizing and responding to patterns in the data. Mastery of a streaming language, therefore, requires a mastery of pattern matching technique. Pattern matching is a familiar technique to Perl programmers and to users of the UNIX utilities from which Perl borrowed its regular expression language. Perl's regular expressions are tuned for use in a data structure oriented language. OmniMark's pattern language is designed for use in a streaming language, and is designed to fit in with the overall scanning and context management features of the language. In this chapter, and in many chapters to come, we will talk about pattern matching techniques and how the OmniMark pattern matching language works. Perl programmers will find a summary of the key differences between pattern matching in OmniMark and Perl in Appendix 1.

In the last chapter, I showed you how to use find rules to match literal text in the input data and substitute different text in its place. In this chapter, I will show you how to match text that occurs a variable number of times.

As an Internet programmer, you get information coming to you in many different forms. Here is one example, a table drawn with ASCII characters ("ascii table.txt"):

```
Below are the results for each sales territory for the year 1999.

+------+----+----+----+----+----+----+----+----+----+----+----+
|      |Jan |Feb |Mar |Apr |May |Jun |Jul |Aug |Sep |Oct |Nov |Dec |
```

```
+------+----+----+----+----+----+----+----+----+----+----+----+
|North |123 |456 |789 |234 |567 |890 |345 |678 |901 |987 |654 |321 |
+------+----+----+----+----+----+----+----+----+----+----+----+
|South |345 |678 |901 |987 |654 |321 |123 |456 |789 |234 |567 |890 |
+------+----+----+----+----+----+----+----+----+----+----+----+
|East  |234 |567 |890 |345 |678 |901 |987 |654 |321 |123 |456 |789 |
+------+----+----+----+----+----+----+----+----+----+----+----+
|West  |123 |456 |789 |234 |901 |987 |654 |321 |567 |890 |345 |678 |
+------+----+----+----+----+----+----+----+----+----+----+----+
```

Note the poor results in the southern territory during the summer months.

The western sales team is to be congratulated on their excellent
numbers in the months of May and June.

For use on the Internet, you need to convert this memo to HTML. To do this, you
need to generate HTML table markup in place of the ASCII characters used to draw
the table in the text version. Here is an OmniMark program to do the conversion:

```
;asciitable.xom
process
    output "<HTML><BODY><P>%n"
    submit file #args[1]
    output "</BODY></HTML>%n"

;find the start of the table
find line-start "+"
    output "%n<TABLE BORDER=%"1%">"

;find a dividing line and start of the next row
find ("-"+ "+")+ "%n|"
    output "<TR><TD>"

;find the last dividing line
find ("-"+ "+")+
    output "%n</TABLE>"

;find the end of a row
find "|%n+"
    output "</TD></TR>%n"

;find a cell divider
find "|"
```

```
output "</TD>%n<TD>"

;find a paragraph break
find "%n%n"
    output "%n<P>"
```

Technique

The first pattern matching lesson here is about where to look for patterns. Many programmers are tempted to look for, and try to capture, the data they want to keep: the contents of the rows and columns of the table. If you were to approach this problem by building a data structure, this is exactly the approach you would have to take. But it is not the right approach with OmniMark. Instead, you should approach a problem like this by ignoring the data and looking for the markup.

There is markup in the original text file, just as there is HTML markup in the output that the program creates. The markup in the input file consists of the "+", "-", and "|" characters used to draw the borders of the table. The program replaces that input markup with the output markup. The data itself just streams through.

It is not for nothing that an OmniMark find rule consumes the data it matches and allows unmatched input to fall through to output. It works like this because this is the correct way to approach a transformation problem. For many projects, you will certainly need to capture data and output it in a different form. But your basic approach to transforming data should always be to look for the markup, transform it, and leave the content alone.

The problem with the markup in the input data, in this case, is that it does not seem, at first glance, to correspond very well to the HTML markup to be created. How will the program distinguish a "+" that begins the whole table from a "+" that is merely an intersection of two lines? How will it distinguish a "|" at the beginning of a row from a "|" between two cells?

The answer is to look for patterns. And the secret to looking for patterns, in this case, is to look for them across line ends. For instance, the pattern "|%n+", a "|" at the end of one line followed by the "+" at the beginning of another signifies the end of a row. No other occurrence of "|" matches this pattern.

Similarly, this pattern signals the beginning of a row: ("-"+ "+")+ "%n|". This is a more complex pattern, but fairly easy to understand. First we have something new, an **occurrence indicator**, in this case a plus sign (+), which stands for "one or more occurrences". Thus the pattern "-"+ means a hyphen occurring one or more times in a row. Within the larger pattern, this item is a **sub-pattern**. A pattern may consist of many sub-patterns. The next sub-pattern is the literal character "+". (Try not to get confused between the literal "+" signs and the + occurrence indicator.) Taken together, these two sub-patterns match one or more hyphens followed by a plus sign. So this pattern would match any of the following:

```
-+
-----+
---------------------------------------------------------+
```

In the ASCII table, the pattern of "one or more hyphens followed by a plus sign" occurs repeatedly as, for example, in the first line of the data:

This repeating pattern is represented by grouping the sub-patterns "-"+ and "+" with parentheses and applying the + occurrence indicator to the group:

```
("-"+ "+")+
```

Finally the last sub-pattern, "%n|", captures the line end and opening bar. This does two things. First, it prevents the last line of the input from matching this pattern. The last line does not start a new row. Secondly, it consumes the leading "|" on the next line. Combined with the pattern "|%n+", which consumes the last "|" of lines ending in "|", that leaves us with all the other "|" characters in the file representing cell boundaries. That makes it very simple to write a rule for cell boundaries:

```
find "|"
    output "</TD><TD>"
```

Note that it is essential that this rule appear after the rule with the pattern "|%n+", or it will match the "|" characters that that rule is interested in. The rule that deals with the last line is similarly position sensitive:

```
find ("-"+ "+")+
    output "</TABLE>"
```

The pattern used here is a subset of the pattern ("-"+ "+")+ "%n|". The only difference is that it does not look for the line end and the opening "|" of the next line. This allows it to match the last line of the table, which is where the end-of-table markup needs to go. For obvious reasons, this rule must come later than ("-"+ "+")+ "%n|".

(If it isn't obvious, don't go on until you figure it out.)

Finally, there is the rule that matches the start of the table:

```
find line-start "+"
    output "<TABLE BORDER=%"1%"">"
```

You might not think that `line-start "+"` is a sufficient pattern to uniquely match the start of the table, considering that half the line in the table start with "+". But the secret here is that no other rule ever leaves the data in a state where "+" is the first unmatched character. Therefore, this rule can only ever fire on the very first occurrence of "+". For this reason also, this rule is not position dependent. The program will work the same no matter where it is placed.

The `line-start` pattern is a positional pattern that matches a particular position in the data without matching any actual data. I use it here so that the program will only recognize "+" as the start of a table if it occurs at the beginning of a line.

Take some time to play with this program. Explore its weaknesses as well as its strengths. How much of a change in the data can it tolerate?

Syntax

A pattern can be composed of several sub-patterns. These sub-patterns can be of different types. So far, we have looked at patterns made up of literal strings and occurrence indicators. Let's take a more detailed look at these.

Literal strings

A literal string in OmniMark is contained between double or single quotation marks. It may not span more than one line of the program. It may contain escape sequences, which begin with a percent sign. You have already met one such escape, "%n", the line end character. In OmniMark these escape sequences are called *format items*. I will cover other format items later in the book. For a complete list, see the OmniMark documentation.

You can join strings together with the concatenation operator, | |. When composing a long string, it is considered good form to put each element on a new line and line up the concatenation operators under the last two letters of the preceding action, as shown in earlier examples.

line-start

`line-start` is a positional pattern. It matches a position in the data rather than a character in the data. We will see other positional patterns later.

Occurrence indicators

Occurrence indicators allow you to indicate that a pattern may occur a number of times in succession. You have already seen the one-or-more occurrence indicator, +.

Here is a complete list:

+	pattern occurs one or more times
?	pattern occurs zero or one times
*	pattern occurs zero or more times
**	pattern occurs zero or more times up to the following pattern
++	pattern occurs one or more times up to the following pattern
{6}	pattern occurs six times exactly
{3 to 9}	pattern occurs at least three times but no more than nine times
{7}+	pattern occurs seven times or more

Groups

You can use parentheses to group sub-patterns into a unit. You can then apply occurrence indicators to these groups just as if they were simple sub-patterns:

```
find ("-"+ "+")+
```

Review

The following are the main points covered in this chapter. If you don't understand any of the statements below, go back and review the material in this chapter before you go on.

- When converting data from one form of markup to another, the best method is to match the source markup and output the destination markup, letting the data itself simply stream through.
- Useful patterns are often found across line ends.
- Matched data is consumed. Sometimes you consume data just to get it out of the way so that it won't be matched by another pattern.
- A set of patterns works together to process the input. One pattern may work only because the other patterns leave the data in a predictable state.
- A pattern can consist of a number of sub-patterns.
- Sub-patterns can be combined into groups.
- An occurrence indicator allows you to specify how many times a pattern, sub-pattern, or group can occur.

Exercises

1. Step through the program in the IDE. Use the datascope and the output window to observe how the pattern matching works and how the HTML markup is generated in the right places. Make sure you understand this thoroughly before going on.
2. Adapt the program to output the HTML to a file. Pass the file name on the command line.
3. Write a program to strip email quoting from an email or newsgroup message. Make it support multiple levels of quoting. Try it on a selection of real email or newsgroup messages.

4: Finding links in a web page

Converting data from one form to another is an important Internet programming task. Another important task is analyzing data to pull out certain critical pieces of information. In this chapter, I will show you how to match variable data in an OmniMark program and how to create output that is not simply a translation of the input.

In the program in the last chapter, the streams were set up so that data flowed from the source to the destination. As it flowed, the program trapped certain patterns in the data. The matched data was consumed and did not flow to output. In its place, data generated by output statements flowed to the output stream.

The program in this chapter will be organized the same way, except that, in this case, all the data coming from the source will be matched and consumed, and the data flowing to output will be entirely generated by output statements in the find rules (or, in this case, a single find rule).

Though there is no data flowing completely through the program, this is still very much a streaming program. The input data is being streamed into the find rules, where it is consumed and discarded. But it is never copied into data structures. Similarly, the output is streamed out as we find the information we are looking for, without building any data structures to buffer output.

In this chapter, you will also learn a new pattern matching technique: matching variable data.

Suppose that you need to process an HTML page and make a list of the URLs it contains. What you need to do is scan the page for URLs. Here's a program that does this:

```
;findurl.xom
process
   output "URL listing%n"
        || "===========%n%n"
   submit file #args[1]

find
 (letter+
  "://" [\ white-space or "%"'>"]+
 ) => url
   output url || "%n"

find any
```

Load this program into the IDE, pick a web page of your choice, and run the program. You should see a nice list of all the URLs in the web page.

Technique

There's quite a bit of new material in these few lines of code, so let's take it one step at a time.

A sponge rule

The previous programs were matching the material to be discarded and let the material to be kept stream through to output, along with the markup that was added. This program does exactly the opposite. It outputs the data that it matches and throws the unmatched data away.

Throwing away the unmatched data is easy. The second find rule of the program handles it:

```
find any
```

The keyword any is a ***character class***. A character class is a collection of characters. If a character in the data matches any one of the characters in the character class, you have a match. The character class any, as you might expect, matches any character.

Find rules are tried in order, so if the first rule in findurl.xom does not match at the current point in the input data, the find any rule will match a single character and consume it. Then the first rule will try again at the new position in the input. Nothing will fall through to output. Every single character in the input will be matched by one rule or the other.

The find any rule doesn't do anything with the characters it matches. It isn't supposed to. It is simply there to prevent characters streaming through to output. find any is a "sponge rule". It soaks up all the data we're not interested in. We will see some more sophisticated sponge rules later that can soak up more than one character at a time.

Using character classes

The previous pattern matching examples were matching specific characters: "by", "%n", "+", "-", or "|". To match a URL, however, findurl.xom has to match a pattern that contains some specific characters and some variable data. To do this, it will again make use of character classes.

URLs are fairly easy to find because they contain the unusual literal string "://". It is unlikely that the string "://" will occur on a web page as part of anything other than a URL. (It is not impossible, of course. For example, any discussion of URLs, such as this one, may quote the string "://" outside of a URL.)

The program can identify URLs because they contain "://", but it still has to deal with the fact that they don't begin that way. They begin with "http" or "ftp" or "mailto" or another of the half dozen or so available method names. On the other hand, they don't begin with character strings that contain numbers, white space, or punctuation. All of the various method names in current use consist entirely of letters. To find them, the program matches a series of letters followed by the literal string "://".

To do this, it uses the OmniMark character class letter. This character class contains all the uppercase and lowercase letters of the alphabet. The expression letter+, therefore, means "one or more letters". (Which you had probably figured out for yourself.) So, the pattern to match one or more letters followed by "://" is:

```
letter+ "://"
```

Now there is a choice to make. How should the program grab the rest of the URL? Should it describe each part of the URL syntax in detail, or just match up to the first character that cannot possibly be part of the URL? The second approach is the easy way. In HTML markup, a URL ends at the first white space, quotation mark, or tag close character, ">". None of those characters can occur in a URL, so matching all the characters that are not part of that set will effectively match to the end of the URL.

This is a job for a character class, but there is no built-in OmniMark character class for this job, so I define my own. Here it is: [\ white-space or "%"'">"].

OmniMark uses square brackets to define a character class. You can define character classes by enumerating the allowed characters or by adding or subtracting characters from an existing character class. The character class [\ white-space or "%"'">"] means "any character so long as it is not white space (space, tab, carriage return, or line feed), a single or double quote, or a greater-than sign (>)". I'll go into the mechanics of user defined character classes later in this chapter, but the construction of this one is fairly simple. The backslash character is the "except" operator. It means that the character class matches all characters except those named. white-space is a built-in OmniMark character class that matches white space characters. The quoted string is a list of characters. To include the double quote character in a literal string, it must be escaped with %, so %" in a quoted string means the quote character. The or simply joins the quoted string and the white-space character class.

By itself, the character class says: "Match one character as long as it is not white space, ", ', or >."

The pattern as a whole therefore says: "Match one or more letters, followed by the string "://", followed by one or more characters that are not white space, ", ', or >."

This is not a complete description of a URL. There are other characters that are prohibited in a URL, besides the ones mentioned above, and URLs use periods, slashes, "?", and "#" in specific and well-defined ways. However, you don't need to go through all of that to tell where a URL ends in an HTML file.

A pattern does not have to be a complete representation or description of the thing you are looking for. Unless you are trying to validate the data, a pattern only has to be specific enough to distinguish the thing you are looking for from the surrounding data. Anything more is just extra work for you. That said, it is possible, if not likely, for this pattern to generate false hits, and you could reduce that possibility with a more exacting pattern. I'll leave that task to the exercises.

Capturing matched data: Pattern variables

Now that the program can match a URL, how does it capture it so that it can display it? It uses a *pattern variable*. A pattern variable is a variable used in a pattern to capture some or all of the data matched by a pattern.

Findurl.xom needs to capture the entire matched pattern. The code looks like this:

```
find (letter+
    "://" [\ white-space or "%"'>"]+
    ) => url
```

Here => is the *pattern variable assignment operator*. In fact, => both declares the pattern variable name and assigns the value to it. I have given the pattern variable the name "url", since that is the data it will contain. You can, of course, give a pattern variable any name you like. The value assigned to a pattern variable is the value of the immediately preceding sub-pattern. Since I want to capture the whole pattern in this rule, I wrap the whole pattern in parentheses to make it a group. The value matched by the group is then assigned to the pattern variable url.

Now that I have the matched pattern captured to the pattern variable url, I can output it:

```
output url || "%n"
```

Finding data in context

Sometimes you will find that the pattern that you are looking for is not sufficiently distinct from the surrounding data to identify on its own, no matter how precisely you describe it. You will need to identify it in the context of the surrounding data. In fact, using context is a better approach to the problem of finding URLs. Consider this version of the program:

```
;findurl2.xom
process
    output "URL listing%n"
        || "===========%n%n"
    submit file #args[1]

find
 ul "<a" white-space+
 ul "href" white-space*
 "=" white-space*
 "%"" white-space*
 [\ white-space | "%""]* =>url
```

```
white-space* "%""

    output url || "%n"


find
 ul "<a" white-space+
 ul "href" white-space*
 "=" white-space*
 "'" white-space*
 [\ white-space | "'"]* =>url
 white-space* "'"

    output url || "%n"


find
 ul "<a" white-space+
 ul "href" white-space*
 "=" white-space*
 [\ white-space | ">"]* =>url
 white-space* ">"

    output url || "%n"

find any
```

This program does not look for the pattern of a URL at all, but for the HTML anchor markup that surrounds a URL. Its strategy is to find the entire anchor tag and then pluck the URL out of the middle of it.

This program is an improvement on the previous one in several ways. Run this version and you will probably notice a difference in the output. This version lists relative URLs, which do not contain "://". It is not going to pick up stray occurrences of "://" in the text. It isn't going to pick up plain-text URLs from the body of a page. However, it is still not infallible. For one thing, it will miss any anchor that has another parameter before "href".

The reason there are three almost identical rules for URLs in this program is to account for different quoting styles. Parameter values in HTML may be quoted with double quotes, or single quotes, or may not be quoted at all. There are ways to combine all these alternatives into one rule, but the divide-and-conquer approach works well enough in this case.

Case insensitive pattern matching

"findurl2.xom" needs to match HTML anchor markup "a" and "href". However, HTML markup is case insensitive, so the program needs to match these strings case insensitively. To do this it uses the ul pattern modifier. The ul modifier (think "upper/lower") makes the pattern that follows match case insensitively. Thus, the sub-pattern ul "href" will match "href" or "HREF" (or even "Href" or "hReF").

You can apply ul to a pattern group, so instead of using it twice, as in this rule:

```
find ul "<a" white-space+
    ul "href" white-space*
    "=" white-space*
    [\ white-space or ">"]* =>url
    white-space* ">"
    output url || "%n"
```

You can group the whole pattern and make it all match case insensitively:

```
find ul ("<a" white-space+
    "href" white-space*
    "=" white-space*
    [\ white-space or ">"]* =>url
    white-space* ">")
    output url || "%n"
```

Capturing partial patterns

The first version of the program used the pattern variable url to capture the whole matched pattern. The second version, captures only part of the matched data. It does this by applying the => operator only to the part of the pattern that contains the URL:

```
find ul "<a" white-space+
    ul "href" white-space*
    "=" white-space*
    "%"" white-space*
    [\ white-space or "%""]* =>url
    white-space* "%""
    output url || "%n"
```

In this pattern, only the characters matched by the sub-pattern [\ white-space or "%"""]* are assigned to the pattern variable url.

As we shall see in later chapters, you can capture many different parts of a pattern to different pattern variables.

More on character classes

Character classes are one of the most important parts of the pattern matching language. A character class used in a pattern matches one character from the input if that character is a member of the character class. Thus the find rule:

find letter

will fire each time the input data contains a character from the Latin alphabet. The rule:

find digit

will fire each time the input data contains an Arabic numeral.

Character classes come in two flavors, built-in and user defined.

Built-in character classes

We have already covered a number of built-in character classes. Here is the complete list:

Class	Characters
any	any character
any-text	any character except a carriage return or line feed
blank	any space or a tab character
digit	any Arabic numeral: "0123456789"
lc	any lowercase letter of the Latin alphabet
letter	any uppercase or lowercase letter of the Latin alphabet
space	a space character
uc	any uppercase letter of the Latin alphabet
white-space	any carriage return, line feed, space, or tab

User defined character classes

You can build your own character classes. Here is a character class for vowels:

```
["AEIOUaeiou"]
```

A character class is defined between square brackets. The string it contains is the list of all the characters in the character class.

You can also define a character class by adding characters to a built-in character class. The following defines a character class for hex digits, by adding the letters used for expressing hex values to the existing digit character class (it assumes that the letter digits are written using upper case letters):

```
[digit or "ABCDEF"]
```

You can also define a character class by excluding characters from a built-in character class using the "except" operator. This is a character class for consonants:

```
[letter \ "AEIOUaeiou"]
```

A very common use of this technique is to define a character class consisting of any character except one or a chosen few. If you wanted to match any character except an exclamation mark, you could define a character class like this:

```
[\ "!"]
```

Notice that your character classes behave just like the predefined ones. Unless you add an occurrence indicator, they match only a single character. Thus to match one or more consonants, you would write a pattern like this:

```
[letter \ "AEIOUaeiou"]+
```

And to match one or more characters that are not exclamation marks, you would write:

```
[\ "!"]+
```

A common mistake with character classes is to confuse them with patterns. For example, there is a built-in character class digit that is equivalent to ["0123456789"]. You may want to find numbers in your data, but you soon realize that digit is not sufficient for this purpose because a number can contain a decimal point, or a minus sign, as well as digits. You may be tempted to extend the digit character class like this:

```
[digit or ".-"]
```

And then write a find rule for a number like this:

```
find [digit or ".-"]+
```

But this won't work. This rule will match all kinds of things that are not numbers. It will match periods at the end of sentences. It will match hyphens in hyphenated words. It will match expressions such as "12.3-4.57".

The problem is that a number is a complex pattern. It cannot be represented by a character class alone. A number may begin with a minus sign, but can't contain one in any character position but the first. A number can contain a decimal point, but only one, and not as the first or last character, and not as the second character if the first character is a minus sign. A more appropriate find rule for a number would be this one, which uses a carefully defined pattern:

```
find "-"? digit+ ("." digit+)?
```

Study this pattern and make sure you understand why it works and why the character class approach does not.

Of course, this is not the only possible pattern for a number. Numbers are represented in different ways. Try writing a rule to find numbers written using parentheses instead of minus signs to express negative amounts. Remember that you should only match the trailing ")" if there is an opening one.

A third common mistake with character classes is to try to use them to match up to a multi-character delimiter. Using a character class is the right way to look for all the characters up to a single-character delimiter. Take the following data for example:

```
skifngjtridm937v8d;=-#ajdifmel;018205
```

To find all the characters up to the "#", you can use a character class that excludes "#":

```
find [\ "#"]+
```

But to find anything up to a table end tag in an HTML document, the following will not work:

```
find [\ "</table>"]+
```

This rule says to match any character that is not any one of "<", "/", "t", "a", "b", "l", "e", and ">". It will cease matching as soon as it encounters any one of those characters. To match up to a multi-character delimiter, use the "one-or-more-upto" occurrence indicator:

```
find any++ lookahead "</table>"
```

This simply matches one or more of any character until it sees the string "</table>". The lookahead operator causes "</table>" to be matched but not consumed, meaning that it stays in the current input and can be matched by another rule.

You can also use this form to match up to single character delimiters. Thus you can write

```
find any++ lookahead "#"
```

rather than

```
find [\ "#"]+
```

Notice however, that wile the second form will match the characters "def" in the string "abc#def", the first form will not, since it will not match characters unless they are followed by "#". To fix this, you can reformulate the first form as:

```
find any++ lookahead ("#" | value-end)
```

This will accept either the "#" or the end of the source as a delimiter and thus works exactly the same as `find [\ "#"]+`.

There is no performance difference between these two approaches. You can use whichever you find more expressive in the program you are writing.

Using macros to encapsulate character classes

You can use macros to encapsulate common character classes so that you can use them by name in your program. For example, let's define our consonant character class using a macro:

```
macro consonant is [letter \ "AEIOUaeiou"] macro-end
```

You can then use this in a pattern:

```
find consonant+
```

Using macros to encapsulate common patterns

In the same way, you can use a macro to encapsulate and name a common pattern. Here is our pattern for "number", defined as a macro:

```
macro decimal-number is ("-"? digit+ ("." digit+)?) macro-end
```

I call this macro "decimal-number" to avoid confusion with other kinds of numbers. I use parentheses around the pattern to make sure that it is treated as a whole if I decide to assign it to a pattern variable:

```
find decimal-number => the-number
```

Try this with and without the parentheses in the macro and observe the results.

Syntax

These are the new syntax items introduced in this chapter.

pattern variable assignment operator (=>)

The pattern variable assignment operator, =>, causes the data matched by the pattern on the left to be assigned to the pattern variable on the right:

```
find letter+ => word
```

This find rule will match a sequence of letters and assign them to the pattern variable word.

You can have more than one pattern variable in a pattern. The following code matches a date in the form "1999-09-09 13:50:23" and separately captures the years, months, days, hours, minutes, and seconds in pattern variables:

```
find digit{4} => year
     "-"
     digit{2} => month
     "-"
     digit{2} => day
     space
     digit{2} => hours
     ":"
     digit{2} => minutes
     ":"
     digit{2} => seconds
```

You can even nest pattern variables so that one captures a larger part of the matched data than another. The following code does all that the previous code does, but also captures the whole date-time string into another pattern variable, date-and-time:

```
find (digit{4} => year
     "-"
     digit{2} => month
```

```
  "_"
  digit{2} => day
  space
  digit{2} => hours
  ":"
  digit{2} => minutes
  ":"
  digit{2} => seconds
) => date-and-time
```

=> both declares the pattern variable and performs the assignment. You cannot assign a pattern to an existing variable. You cannot declare the same pattern variable twice in the same pattern.

User defined character classes

You can use square brackets to create a user defined character class. The characters in a character class can be defined by listing them inside quotes:

```
["AEIOUaeiou"]
```

Or they can be defined by adding characters to, or subtracting characters from, a built-in character set. To subtract characters from a built-in character set, use the except operator:

```
[\ "AEIOUaeiou"]
```

To add characters to a built-in character set use or:

```
[digit or "ABCDEF"]
```

You can also add or subtract one built-in character set from another:

```
[white-space \ space]
[letter or digit]
```

ul

The pattern modifier ul is used to force the following pattern to match case insensitively. Thus the pattern:

```
find ul "http"
```

will match "http" or "HTTP" or any other combination of uppercase and lowercase letters.

lookahead

The keyword lookahead is used in a pattern to test if, at the current point in the data, the next string of characters matches a certain pattern. The data matched by lookahead is not consumed and is still available for subsequent matching.

The expression lookahead not is used in a pattern to test if, at the current point in the data, the next string of characters does not match a certain pattern.

Review

The following are the main points covered in this chapter. If you don't understand any of the statements below, go back and review the material in this chapter before you go on.

- When you are pulling individual pieces of data from an input, you need a "sponge rule" to prevent the rest of the input from falling through to output.
- A character class matches any one of a set of characters.
- You cannot use a character class to match a complex pattern such as a number.
- You can capture matched data using pattern variables.
- It is often easier to recognize the context of the data you are looking for than to recognize the data itself.
- You can use character classes to match data up to a single-character delimiter, but not a multi-character delimiter.
- You can use the one-or-more-upto occurrence indicator with lookahead to match data up to a multi-character delimiter.

Exercises

1. Write a pattern to match a number expressed in scientific notation. Write a program to test it.
2. Write a program to process a file to find telephone numbers with area codes. Print out a list of the numbers. (This may be an easier exercise for readers in North America, where telephone numbers conform to a strict and well-known pattern.)
3. Adapt your telephone number program to handle telephone numbers that use letters instead of numbers (for example, 1-800-COLLECT).

4. Rewrite the first URL-matching program to define the pattern of a URL more precisely. To prove you are successful, write an HTML page that will produce false hits with the original program, but which your program will handle properly. Make sure your program does not miss any legitimate URLs.

5. Rewrite findurl2.xom to handle anchor tags that contain other parameters besides "href". You are going to have to think about the various forms that a parameter can take, and remember all the places that white space is allowed in HTML.

5: Displaying the CGI environment variables

Data does not always come to you in a single stream. In CGI, the web server communicates with the CGI program by setting environment variables.
You have to be able to handle data presented as a set of key/value pairs.
To accommodate data of this type, OmniMark provides the shelf data structure.
The shelf is a powerful and flexible data structure. We will explore its properties in several chapters.

Even though you don't have a single data stream for your input, you can still stream output in a CGI program. And you can use streaming methods to process the data in the input data structure. In this chapter I will present a common tool in every webmaster's toolbox, the program that dumps CGI variables. Displaying the CGI environment variables isn't much use as a final product, but it makes a great test script. To make the display a little clearer, the program formats the result as an HTML table. This means we will need to scan each CGI variable to escape the HTML markup characters "<", ">", and "&".

Reading and using information from the CGI environment is the basis for many important techniques in CGI programming. This program shows how to read data from the CGI interface using the OmniMark CGI library.

```
;cgiinfo.xom
include "omcgi.xin"
```

```
process
   local stream cgi-data variable

   cgiGetEnv into cgi-data

   output "Content-type: text/html"
      || crlf
      || crlf
      || "<table border=%"1%">"

   repeat over cgi-data
      output "<tr><td>"
         || key of cgi-data
         || "</td><td>"
      submit cgi-data
      output "</td></tr>%n"
   again
   output "</table>"

find "<"
   output "&lt;"

find ">"
   output "&gt;"

find "&"
   output "&amp;"
```

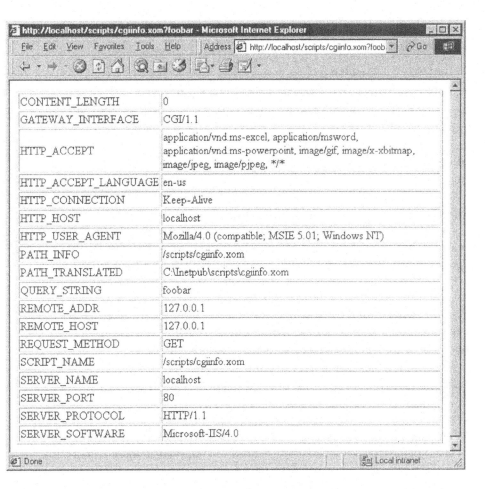

CONTENT_LENGTH	0
GATEWAY_INTERFACE	CGI/1.1
HTTP_ACCEPT	application/vnd.ms-excel, application/msword, application/vnd.ms-powerpoint, image/gif, image/x-xbitmap, image/jpeg, image/pjpeg, */*
HTTP_ACCEPT_LANGUAGE	en-us
HTTP_CONNECTION	Keep-Alive
HTTP_HOST	localhost
HTTP_USER_AGENT	Mozilla/4.0 (compatible; MSIE 5.01; Windows NT)
PATH_INFO	/scripts/cgiinfo.xom
PATH_TRANSLATED	C:\Inetpub\scripts\cgiinfo.xom
QUERY_STRING	foobar
REMOTE_ADDR	127.0.0.1
REMOTE_HOST	127.0.0.1
REQUEST_METHOD	GET
SCRIPT_NAME	/scripts/cgiinfo.xom
SERVER_NAME	localhost
SERVER_PORT	80
SERVER_PROTOCOL	HTTP/1.1
SERVER_SOFTWARE	Microsoft-IIS/4.0

The output of the CGI information program in a browser. Note that I added a query string to the URL, which showed up in the response as the QUERY_STRING parameter.

Technique

Reading data from the CGI interface

The OmniMark CGI library, "omcgi.xin", provides two functions for reading the environment data and form data. The function to retrieve the CGI environment data is CGIGetEnv. The line that invokes this function is:

```
CGIGetEnv into cgi-data
```

There are several things to explain about this line.

The first is the form of the function call. You probably expect a function call to look like this:

```
CGIGetEnv ( cgi-data )
```

But the omcgi library uses a feature of OmniMark called **heralded function arguments**. With heralded function arguments, you can dispense with the use of parentheses and commas to separate function arguments and use words as "heralds" to tell one function argument from another. This lets you use descriptive herald names to design a function call that reads like a sentence and makes the code much easier to follow.

CGIGetEnv is a function that modifies its argument rather than returning a value. Such functions are often hard to follow in code, but the use of the herald "into" makes it clear that the function will get environment data and put it into the variable cgi-data. I will discuss how to create functions with heralded arguments in a later chapter.

As you can tell from the declaration, `cgi-data` is a stream. But this stream declaration is different from the ones in earlier programs. It includes the keyword `variable`. This brings us to the subject of shelves.

Using shelves

I first talked about shelves when discussing #args in Chapter 2. A shelf is a multi-value object that, in the case of #args, acts like a simple array. But a shelf is more than a simple array, it is an associative array. That is, every item on a shelf has a textual key as well as a positional item number. You can retrieve items on a shelf either by item number or by key.

All OmniMark variables are in fact shelves, though a normal variable declaration creates a fixed size shelf with a single item on it, so the fact that it is a shelf isn't particularly important. When you declare a shelf with the keyword `variable`, however, you are creating a shelf of variable size to which you can add items in code. The initial size of a variable shelf is 0 items.

CGIGetEnv returns a shelf with one item for each CGI environment variable passed by the web server. To do so, it needs a variable shelf to which it can add items. That is why you have to declare the shelf that you pass to it as `variable`.

You know how to retrieve the items on a shelf by item number. But you need something else to handle the CGI environment data. Each CGI environment variable is a key-value pair — the variable name and its value. Fortunately, OmniMark shelves make this easy, because each item on a shelf can have a unique text key. The CGIGetEnv function reads each key-value pair from the environment and assigns the value to the item and the key to the item's key. (If you want to skip ahead and see how this is done, dig into your OmniMark installation and examine the CGIGetEnv function in the "omcgi.xin" file.)

In the next chapter, I will show you how to retrieve individual items by key. This program just prints out a list of the CGI environment variables and their values.

Repeating over a shelf

The program outputs each item on the cgi-data shelf in turn. It does this with a repeat over loop. All loops in OmniMark start with repeat and end with again. repeat over is a special loop type designed to operate on each item on a shelf in turn:

```
repeat over cgi-data
    output "<tr><td>"
        || key of cgi-data
        || "</td><td>"
    submit cgi-data
    output "</td></tr>%n"
again
```

Inside a repeat over loop, you can use the variable name cgi-data alone, without an item selector. The next item will be selected each time through the loop.

Retrieving a key

The CGIGetEnv function places the value of each CGI environment variable in a shelf item and the name of the CGI environment variable in the corresponding key. To create the table, the program outputs the CGI environment variable name stored in the key. To retrieve the key of an item it uses the expression key of cgi-data within the repeat over loop.

Escaping markup characters when generating HTML

Whenever you generate an HTML page from arbitrary data, you have to deal with the possibility that the data may contain markup characters. The markup characters you have to worry about are "<", ">", and "&".

The escaping is done very simply by submitting the value of the current shelf item each time through the loop. This invokes the three find rules at the end of the program that replace "<", ">", and "&" with the character entities "<", ">", and "&" respectively.

Syntax

These are the new syntax items introduced in this chapter.

variable

All OmniMark variables are multi-value objects called shelves. To declare a shelf with a variable number of items, use the keyword variable in your declaration:

```
local stream CGI-data variable
```

This declaration creates a shelf of type stream with 0 items on the shelf.

repeat over

You can use **repeat over** to perform the same operation on each item on a shelf. Within the body of the loop, you can use the name of the shelf alone to retrieve the current item for each iteration over the shelf.

key of

You can use **key of** to retrieve the key of an item on a shelf.

Within a repeat over loop, use the syntax:

```
output key of CGI-data
```

Outside of a repeat over loop, you need to specify the item whose key you want to retrieve:

```
output key of CGI-data[4]
```

It you do not specify the item to be used, the key of the last item will be returned.

Review

The following are the main points covered in this chapter. If you don't understand any of the statements below, go back and review the material in this chapter before you go on.

- A shelf is a multi-value object that allows you to retrieve values by item number or by key.
- Many library functions, including CGIGetEnv, require you to pass them a variable shelf on which they can place items.
- You can repeat over a shelf to access each item on the shelf in turn.
- When generating HTML, you need to escape the markup characters "<", ">", and "&" from the source data. You can do this by submitting the data to an appropriate set of find rules.

Exercises

1. Modify cgiinfo.xom to report the contents of form data as well as the CGI environment data. You will find this program a useful debugging tool for later CGI projects. You can retrieve the form data with the CGIGetQuery function. When you use the CGIGetQuery function you must also include the declaration declare #process-input has unbuffered in your program.

6: Disaster countdown

Not so long ago, there were Y2K countdown clocks everywhere on the web. Though we survived Y2K, there will be other disasters to worry about. The project for this chapter is a generalized disaster countdown clock. All the user has to do is specify the disaster they are interested in and the day that disaster is scheduled to occur and the clock will tell them how many days are left to go before the disaster.

This program introduces the handling of HTML form data. It shows you how to select an individual item from a shelf, demonstrates some new scanning tricks, and introduces data type conversion.

```
#!omnimark.exe -sb
;disaster countdown
;boom.xom
include "omcgi.xin"
include "omdate.xin"

declare #process-input has unbuffered

process
   local stream form-data variable
   local stream cgi-data variable

   CGIGetEnv into cgi-data
```

```
CGIGetQuery into form-data

output "Content-type: text/html"
    || crlf
    || crlf
    || "<HTML><BODY>"
    || "<H1>Disaster countdown</H1>"

do when form-data has key "date"
   do scan form-data{"date"}
      match
        digit{4} => year
        "-"
        digit{2} => month
        "-"
        digit{2} => day

          output 'Oh no! '
              || form-data{"disaster"}
              || ' will happen in only '
              || "d" % ymdhms-day-difference
                 (year || month || day || "000000+0000",
                 now-as-ymdhms)
              || ' days.'
              || '<p><A HREF="'
              || cgi-data {"SCRIPT_NAME"}
              || '">When will the next '
              || 'disaster strike?</A>'
   else
      output "<P>Bad input."
   done

else
    output '<P>Use this page to get the current '
        || 'countdown to the disaster of your choice.'
        || '<FORM METHOD="GET" ACTION="'
        || cgi-data{"SCRIPT_NAME"}
        || '">'
        || '<B>Name of the disaster:</B>"'
        || '<INPUT TYPE="text" NAME="disaster" SIZE=16>'
        || '<P><B>Date of disaster (YYYY-MM-DD):</B>'
        || '<INPUT TYPE="text" NAME="date" SIZE=16>'
        || '<P><INPUT TYPE="submit" VALUE="Submit">'
        || '</FORM>'
```

```
done

output "</BODY></HTML>"
```

Here's what the program looks like in action:

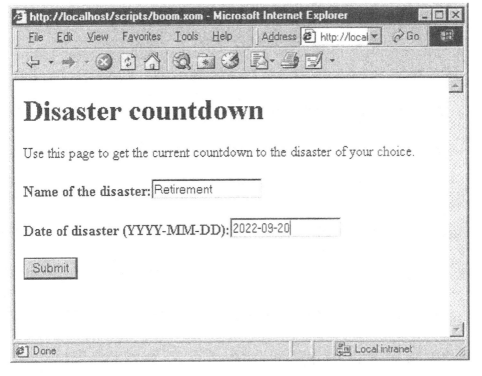

The disaster countdown entry screen.

Disaster countdown result page.

Technique

Retrieving specific items from a shelf

This CGI program needs to read data from an HTML form. It does this using the function CGIGetQuery from the omcgi library. This function works just like CGIGetEnv, which was used in the last chapter. It returns a shelf that contains one item for each field on the form.

Instead of outputting all the environment variables, like cgitest.xom, this program needs to retrieve specific items from both the CGI environment and the HTML form by name. Since the names of the CGI variables and the form files are stored in the keys of the CGI-data and form-data shelves respectively, the program retrieves the fields it needs by key. To access a shelf item by key, you specify the key inside curly braces:

```
output cgi-data{"SCRIPT_NAME"}
```

A CGI program with multiple modes

This program can be called in one of two modes. It can be called by its address alone, in which case it will return the form asking the user to enter the disaster they are interested in. If called in response to the "Submit" button being clicked, it must calculate the date and display the number of days until the disaster. This means that if it is called by its address alone, it must respond with a form whose action is to call the script again. To avoid introducing any file name dependencies into the program, it reads the script name from the CGI environment and uses it to create the form:

```
output '<P>Use this page to get the current '
    || 'countdown to the disaster of your choice.'
    || '<FORM METHOD="GET" ACTION="'
    || cgi-data{"SCRIPT_NAME"}
    || '">'
    || '<B>Name of the disaster:</B>"'
    || '<INPUT TYPE="text" NAME="disaster" SIZE=16>'
    || '<P><B>Date of disaster (YYYY-MM-DD):</B>'
    || '<INPUT TYPE="text" NAME="date" SIZE=16>'
    || '<P><INPUT TYPE="submit" VALUE="Submit">'
    || '</FORM>'
```

To distinguish which mode the script is being called in, the program examines the form-data shelf to see if it contains any form data. It does this by checking to see if it has an item with the key "date", which is the name of one of the form fields:

```
do when form-data has key "date"
    ...
done
```

The structure do when ... done is OmniMark's basic conditional structure. It is equivalent to an "if" block in other languages. As in other languages, you can have an else clause in a do when block. In this case, boom.xom uses a do when structure to control which mode the program operates in.

If the shelf form-data does have the key "date", then the program is dealing with a form submission. In that case, it needs to print out the name of the selected disaster and calculate the number of days between today and the date of the disaster. To do this it needs to get the date information into a form that can be used with the date arithmetic functions provided by OmniMark's date library, "omdate.xin".

Pulling values out of a string

In a streaming programming language, how do you analyze the content of a variable? In other languages, you would probably use a pointer or some other form of indexing into the string. But in a streaming language, you stream the content of the variable. Think of it this way: in a data structure oriented language, the data stays still and the eyes move; in a streaming language, the data moves and the eyes stay still. In OmniMark, you can use any stream variable as a scanning source.

To format the date value, the program needs to break out the year, month, and day elements of the user's input. As you would expect, it does this by scanning the value of the date field, which it retrieves with the expression `form-data{"date"}`. However, it doesn't use `submit` and find rules to do the scanning, but another scanning structure called `do scan`.

In this case, the scanning needs are very limited and specific. A single pattern will rip apart the date into its constituent year, month, and day values. That pattern will match the whole of the input in a single shot. For such a simple task, it is better to do our scanning locally.

`do scan` acts like `submit` in that it creates an input scope and initiates scanning. Unlike `submit`, it does not activate `find` rules. Instead, it uses `match` alternatives in the body of the `do` block. `match` statements are called "alternatives", rather than "rules", because they are not rules at the root level of the OmniMark program, but they are really just localized `find` rules operating in the body of the `do` block. As far as scanning is concerned, they behave in every way like `find` rules and you can apply everything you have learned about `find` rules to `match` alternatives.

`do scan` is a one-shot scanner. It looks at the data exactly once, starting from the beginning. If it matches a pattern, the data is consumed and the actions associated with the match alternative are performed. If not, the actions associated with the `else` clause are performed (if there is an `else` clause). No further attempts are made to match data. Data scanned by `do scan` does not stream through to current output so there is no role for a sponge rule in a `do scan`. (Yes, this can mean that unconsumed and unprocessed input data remains in the source. As we shall see later, this can be a very useful property of `do scan`.)

There are many important uses for `do scan`, and we'll see several of them as we go along. For now it is just used as a text ripper to shred the input date value into the pieces needed for date calculation.

```
match digit{4} => year
```

```
"-"
digit{2} => month
"-"
digit{2} => day
```

Once the year, month, and day values are split out, they are used to format a value that can be fed to the ymdhms-day-difference function of the omdate library. This library deals with dates as text strings in the form "years months days hours minutes seconds", or "ymdhms". It uses four digits for the year and two digits for the other values. It also includes a UTC offset in "+" or "-" hours and minutes. To convert the input date to this format, the program concatenates the years, months, and days and the string "000000+0000" to account for the time and UTC offset. Since the program only discriminates to the level of days, all "0"s will suffice for this. The function returns a value that is the number of days between two dates. The call (which uses plain old parentheses and comma notation) looks like this:

```
ymdhms-day-difference
  (year || month || day || "000000+0000",
  now-as-ymdhms)
```

The function now-as-ymdhms returns the current date in ymdhms format.

Converting a number to text for output

The value returned by ymdhms-day-difference must be formatted as a string for output using the format operator (%):

```
output 'Oh no! '
    || form-data{"disaster"}
    || ' will happen in only '
    || "d" % ymdhms-day-difference
        (year || month || day || "000000+0000",
        now-as-ymdhms)
    || ' days.'
    || '<p><A HREF="'
    || cgi-data{"SCRIPT_NAME"}
    || '">When will the next disaster strike?</A>'
```

The "d" here is a format string used by the format operator (%) to determine how to format the number returned by ymdhms-day-difference. OmniMark supports both template and command based formatting for a range of supported data types. We will look at more of them later.

Turning off input buffering

One other important point: If you are going to use the `CGIGetQuery` function to retrieve POST data, you must include the following declaration at the top of your program:

```
declare #process-input has unbuffered
```

CGI programs that use POST may hang if this declaration is missing. (OmniMark is trying to fill the buffer it is using for `#process-input`, but there is no more data coming from standard input.)

Syntax

These are the new syntax items introduced in this chapter.

shelves

All OmniMark variables are shelves. A shelf is a multi-value object. Each item on a shelf holds a value. Each item has a key. The key of the item can hold a unique string value. It is an error to attempt to create a key with a duplicate value.

You can create a shelf of a fixed size or of variable size. There are many options, but for 95% of your work you will need one of the two following forms:

```
local stream user-name
local stream cgi-data variable
```

The first form creates an ordinary variable (a fixed-sized shelf with one item). The second form creates a variable-sized shelf with zero items.

You can access an item on a shelf in one of three ways. The first is simply to name the variable. This is the normal form for a regular variable. If you use this form with a multi-item shelf, it will output the value of the last item:

```
output user-name
```

This code outputs the value of the second item on the shelf:

```
output CGI-Data[2]
```

This code outputs the item whose key is the string "SCRIPT_NAME":

```
output CGI-Data{"SCRIPT_NAME"}
```

You can also read the value of a key. The syntax is as follows:

```
output key of CGI-Data[3]
```

Earlier versions of OmniMark used a different syntax for accessing shelf items. These forms are supported for backward capability, but you should not use them in new code. The earlier forms of

```
output CGI-Data[2]
```

are:

```
output CGI-Data item 2
output CGI-Data @ 2
```

The earlier forms of

```
output CGI-Data{"SCRIPT_NAME"}
```

are:

```
output CGI-Data key "SCRIPT_NAME"
output CGI-Data ^ "SCRIPT_NAME"
```

You should be able to recognize these forms if you see them in code written for earlier versions of OmniMark.

has key

You can test to see if a shelf has an item with a particular key using the test expression has key. You can use it as part of a conditional expression such as do when:

```
do when form-data has key "date"
    . . .
done
```

format operator (%)

You can use the format operator (%) to determine how a string or numeric value is output. The form of a format expression is:

<format string> % <value to be formatted>

The format string is a text string in which each character gives some instruction on how the value to be formatted is to be displayed. There are many different format strings, but by far the most common is "d", which causes a numeric value to be formatted as a simple set of decimal digits. Thus the expression:

```
output "d" % (2 + 2)
```

will cause the character "4" to be output.

do when

do when is OmniMark's "if" statement. You will notice that all block statements in OmniMark start with do and end with done. Similarly, all loops begin with repeat and end with again.

do when blocks take the forms you would expect:

```
do when <condition>
    <actions>
done
```

and

```
do when <condition>
    <actions>
else
    <actions>
done
```

and

```
do when <condition>
    <actions>
else when <condition>
    <actions>
else when <condition>
    <actions>
else
    <actions>
done
```

Visual Basic programmers should take care to remember that in OmniMark do is always a block structure, never a loop structure as it is in Basic.

do scan

All do constructs in OmniMark are blocks, not loops. So do scan is a one-shot scanner. It tries to match the input data against each of its match alternatives exactly once. If no data matches, the else clause is executed (if there is one). Then the block ends.

The forms of do scan blocks are as follows

```
do scan <condition>
  match <pattern>
```

```
      <actions>
   match <pattern>
      <actions>
   match <pattern>
      <actions>
done
```

and

```
do scan <condition>
   match <pattern>
      <actions>
   match <pattern>
      <actions>
   match <pattern>
      <actions>
   else
      <actions>
done
```

match

When you scan data locally within the body of a single OmniMark rule, using
do scan or repeat scan (which we will meet later), you use match alternatives
instead of find rules to define the patterns to match. Anything you can do in
a find rule, you can do in a match alternative.

Review

The following are the main points covered in this chapter. If you don't understand
any of the statements below, go back and review the material in this chapter before
you go on.

- You can retrieve an item from a shelf by its item number.
- You can retrieve an item from a shelf by its key.
- A CGI program that receives form data via the POST method must include
  the declaration declare #process-input has unbuffered.
- You can use do scan and match to scan text locally without using find rules.
- do scan is a one-shot scanner.
- You can use do scan as a text ripper to pull multiple values out of a string.
- You must convert a number to a string for output.

- OmniMark's "if" statement is do when.
- do constructs are always blocks.
- repeat constructs are always loops.

Exercises

1. Rewrite boom.xom to report the time to the disaster in seconds. Require the user to input the date of the disaster to the second.
2. Improve the error checking and reporting in the case of bad input. Give the user a way to correct the error and continue without having to hit the browser Back button.

7: Hit counter

Even a streaming language needs variables. We have already seen the stream data type. In this chapter we will look at integers. We will also take a further look at OmniMark's abstraction of data sources and destinations. In this case, it will allow us to read a textual representation of a number into an integer variable in a single operation.

The project for this chapter is one of the most basic CGI programs, a hit counter:

```
#!omnimark -sb
;hitcount.xom
process
   local integer hits initial {0}
   set hits to file "hits.txt"
   increment hits
   set file "hits.txt" to "d" % hits
   output "d" % hits
```

The idea here is simple. Read the last hit count from a file. Increment it. Write it back to the file, and output it.

A hit counter does not return a whole page, just a hit count. It is typically called from within an HTML page using a server-side include. Since it requires no information from the CGI interface, you don't need to set it up on your web server to see it work, you can run it in the IDE. First, though, you will need to give it a file to work with. Create a text file in the current working directory with the name "hits.txt", and place the digit 0 in that file. Then run the program from the IDE. It will output "1". The next time you run it, it will output "2", and so on.

If you want to run it on your web server, you can call it as a server-side include from the page whose hits you want to count. Here's a sample:

```
<HTML><BODY>
<P>This boring page has been viewed
<!--#exec cgi="/scripts/hitcount.xom" -->
times. Imagine if it were interesting!
</BODY></HTML>
```

You can use this page to try out the counter program. You will need to give it a name that your web server will recognize as a page that uses a server-side include. The usual convention is that such files must have an extension of ".shtm" or ".shtml".

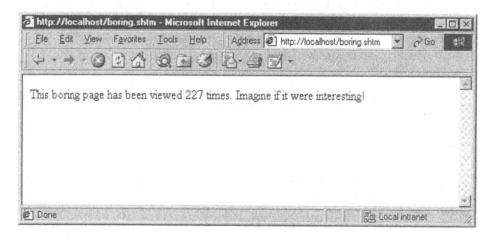

The hit counter at work.

Technique

hitcount.xom packs a lot of new material into eight lines. It introduces a new data type and a new way of manipulating values.

The integer data type

This program introduces a new type of variable, an integer. (In case you were wondering, the value returned by the ymdhms-day-difference function that was used in the last chapter was of type integer.)

In many older OmniMark programs, you will see a variable type called counter. This was also an integer type. It is no longer used.

Setting the value of a data destination

The set action is used to assign the value of a data destination. In other languages, we would simply say it was used to set the value of a variable. But in OmniMark, a variable is just another data destination and all data destinations are treated alike. So are all data sources. So if you want to set the value of the variable "hits" to a value found in a file "hits.txt", you can do it very easily:

```
set hits to file "hits.txt"
```

This statement does a lot of work. In a single line, it sets the value of the variable hits to the value found in the file "hits.txt". You don't go to all the fuss of opening the file. (You never actually open or close a file in OmniMark, you deal strictly with sources and streams.) In this case, the source file "hits.txt" is streamed directly into the variable hits. The text value of the source is converted automatically into an integer value. (OmniMark coerces text to integer values automatically.)

The variable hits is incremented with the line:

```
increment hits
```

and the incremented value is written back to the file with:

```
set file "hits.txt" to "d" % hits
```

This line again illustrates how OmniMark abstracts sources and destinations of data. Here the value of a file is set to the value of a variable. Variables and files are just places to keep data, so it is natural that we should treat them as the same sort of thing. You will see this over and over again in OmniMark programming. To OmniMark, all data sources are alike and all data destinations are alike. You just need to know how to attach to them.

This line of code, however, does have one complication. In this line, the integer value must be converted into a string value before it is written to the file. This is done with the format operator. The string "d" is a formatting instruction used to convert an integer value to the equivalent string value. `"d" % hits` is an expression that returns the string equivalent of the value of the integer `hits`.

After this, it is just plain old output. The format operator is used again to format the number for output.

Streams as strings

Though it is a trivial cost here, the program is formatting the value of "hits" twice. It is usually a good idea to do calculations once and store the value, rather than to do the calculation multiple times. This can be done by introducing another variable:

```
#!omnimark -sb
;hitcount2.xom
process
   local integer hits initial {0}
   local stream hits-text
   set hits to file "hits.txt"
   increment hits
   set hits-text to "d" % hits
   set file "hits.txt" to hits-text
   output hits-text
```

Here the text equivalent of "hits" is calculated and stored in the stream variable "hits-text". You were probably expecting a string variable, but in OmniMark stream variables do double duty. Not only are they used for directing output, they are also used to hold string values in a program.

This use of stream variables is in fact quite consistent with their primary purpose. After all, a variable is simply an area of memory where you can put data. As such, it is a data destination, and, as we have seen, all data destinations are alike to OmniMark.

Finally, here is a slight variation on the program:

```
#!omnimark -sb
;hitcount3.xom
process
   local stream hits
   set hits to "d" % (file "hits.txt" + 1)
   set file "hits.txt" to hits
   output hits
```

Here the economy with which OmniMark lets you read sources and use the data is even more pronounced. The expression `file "hits.txt"` is used as a numerical expression in the mathematical operation `(file "hits.txt" + 1)`, which is the argument of the format operator (%), which is used to assign the text value of the stream variable `hits`. Study this program and make sure you understand what is going on. If you understand the generality of OmniMark's handling of data sources and destinations, you will be able to write some very elegant and efficient code.

Syntax

These are the new syntax items introduced in this chapter.

set

`set` assigns a value to a data destination. The destination may be a variable or any other type of destination. The value may be a literal, the value of a variable, or the data from any other type of source.

You can think of `set` as a variable assignment statement if you like. But it really does more than that. It moves data from a source to a destination just as you can with `using input as`, `using output as`, `submit`, and `output`. The only difference is that `set` provides no opportunity to process the data in transit. If you want to copy one file to another, the easiest way in OmniMark is with `set`:

```
set file "foo.txt" to file "bar.txt"
```

integer

An integer is a signed 32-bit integer value. Integer variables default to 0.

initial

You use the keyword `initial` to initialize a variable when you declare it. The value is given in curly braces:

```
local integer hits initial {0}
```

You can provide multiple initial values for a variable shelf:

```
local stream animals variable initial {"cat", "dog", "cow"}
```

This creates a variable-sized shelf with an initial size of three items. Item one is initialized to "cat", etc.

You can also assign initial keys to shelf items:

```
local stream animals variable initial
    {"cat" with key "Boots",
     "dog" with key "Rex",
     "cow" with key "Bessie"}
```

increment

increment increases the value of an integer by one. Its companion, decrement, decreases the value of an integer by one. You can also increment or decrement by a specific amount:

```
increment hits by 2
increment blows by hits
```

Review

The following are the main points covered in this chapter. If you don't understand any of the statements below, go back and review the material in this chapter before you go on.

- integer is a 32-bit signed whole number.
- The set command allows you to set the value of variables.
- Because of the abstraction provided by OmniMark streams, you can also use set to read and write the content of files or any other data source or destination.

Exercises

1. Write a program to print the date last accessed on a page. To get the current date and time, use the expression date "=xY-=M-=D =H:=m:=s".

8: Database to XML

Many people are looking to XML as a means to transport data held in relational databases. Here is a simple OmniMark program that takes an arbitrary SQL query and outputs an XML document containing the data returned from the query:

```
;db2xml.xom
include "omdb.xin"

process
   local stream dsn
   local stream query
   local dbDatabase db
   local dbField current-record variable

   do unless number of #args = 2
      output "Usage: omnimark -s db2xml <dsn> <query>"
      halt
   done

   set dsn to #args[1]
   set query to #args[2]

   output '<?xml version="1.0">'
       || "<db2xml-table>"
```

```
set db to dbOpenODBC dsn
dbQuery db sql query record current-record

repeat
   exit unless dbRecordExists current-record
   output "<db2xml-record>"
   repeat over current-record
      output '<db2xml-field name="'
         || key of current-record
         || '">'
      submit dbFieldValue current-record
   always
      output "</db2xml-field>"
   again
always
   output "</db2xml-record>"
   dbRecordMove current-record
again

catch #external-exception message the-problem
   output "<db2xml-error>"
   submit the-problem
   output "</db2xml-error>"

always
   output "</db2xml-table>"

find "<"
   output "&lt;"

find ">"
   output "&gt;"

find "&"
   output "&amp;"
```

Technique

Accessing databases

OmniMark's high-level database library, omdb, provides a pair of OMX components for accessing databases, dbDatabase and dbField. If you are familiar with Microsoft's DAO or other high-level database libraries, you may be expecting a recordset object as well. However, omdb does not need a recordset object. Instead, it uses an ordinary OmniMark shelf to represent a record. That shelf, called `current-record` in the program above, is a shelf of type `dbField`. In other words, it is a shelf of `dbField` variables, each one of which represents one field in the record. As you would expect, the key of each item is the name of the field.

To connect to a database, you use the `dbOpenODBC` function which returns a dbDatabase variable. The dbOpenODBC function takes one parameter, an ODBC "DSN" (Data Source Name).

The `dbOpenODBC` function connects to an ODBC data source. (Later versions of the library may support other types of database access, but ODBC will get you access to most databases.) To access an ODBC data source, you must set up an ODBC driver manager on your machine and create a connection to the database of your choice. In doing so you will assign a local name to that data source: its DSN. `dbOpenODBC` uses the DSN to talk to the ODBC driver manager and negotiate a connection to the database.

Once you have access to a database, you can query it to retrieve information. You do this with the `dbQuery` function. The `dbQuery` function takes three parameters: a dbDatabase variable, a database query in the form of an SQL statement, and a variable shelf of type dbField.

If the query is successful, you can access the result set using the `current-record` shelf. Each item on the shelf is a dbField OMX variable. The `dbFieldValue` function returns an OmniMark source for the field data:

```
submit dbFieldValue current-record
```

Once you have a source, you can process the data just like any other source in an OmniMark program.

To move to the next record, you use the `dbRecordMove` function with the `current-record` shelf as a parameter:

```
dbRecordMove current-record
```

Generating XML

One of the things you must do when using XML as a transport medium is escape the characters "<", ">", and "&" in the data, just as we do when generating HTML. We do this very simply by submitting the content of each field and letting the find rules at the end of the program do the required translations.

One thing you need to be concerned with in generating XML to transport database data is the management of white space. When you are creating HTML, you could freely throw in "%n" to make the resulting HTML code easier to read. You can do this because you know that line feeds are ignored by HTML browsers. In transporting database data, however, we cannot cavalierly introduce line feeds into the data. Instead, you need to make sure there is nothing between the beginning and end field tags except the data from the database.

To ensure this, the program does no pretty printing of the XML. (It is meant for machine consumption, not human consumption anyway.) This way, all carriage returns that end up in the file are known to belong to the data. The application that is processing the received XML must treat all carriage returns in the data as significant. By the way, it is not necessary to use the xml:space attribute specified by the XML 1.0 specification to control the interpretation of white space. A processing application designed to work with the markup produced by this program already needs to know the rules for reading this data, and telling it again won't help.

Handling errors

This program depends on several external pieces of software in order to retrieve information from the database. What happens if there is an error in one of these external systems? The database library, which is responsible for managing the relationship with those external systems, will throw an external exception if an error occurs while accessing the database.

Unless the program does something about it, this external exception will result in a run time error and the program will halt. This will result in the user receiving an incomplete XML document.

To avoid this, the program provides a catch point for external exceptions with the code:

```
catch #external-exception message the-problem
      output "<db2xml-error>"
      submit the-problem
      output "</db2xml-error>"
```

What happens if there is an error while attempting to access the database? OmniMark will generate a throw to #external-exception. The throw will be caught at the line catch #external exception. That is to say, program execution will pass to that line. As execution is passed to that line, the scope in which the throw occurred is collapsed and any local variables are cleaned up automatically.

All intervening scopes are also collapsed. Execution then continues with any statements under the catch.

The statements under the catch in this program output XML tagging around a description of the error that occurred. I submit the error message to the find rules for XML escaping, just as I did with any other text that I inserted into the XML document.

You can retrieve the identity, message, and location of the external exception by specifying the appropriate heralds and suitable variable in the catch statement. In this case I just want the message, so I specify the herald message and provide the variable the-problem to receive the message text.

Using always to ensure a valid document is returned

This program uses catch and throw to detect errors and uses the catch block to add the error report to the XML data stream sent back to the user. However, catch and throw collapses the scope in which the error occurs, and all scopes up to and including the scope in which the catch occurs. In this program, those scopes have an important task to perform whether or not an error occurs: they have to output an end tag for the element they are creating. It the end tags are not sent, the client will not received a well formed XML document and may have difficulty processing the response.

To ensure that the end tag is output even if an error occurs, I place the statement that outputs the end tag in an always block:

```
always
    output "</db2xml-table>"
```

Code in an always block is always executed, even if the scope in which it occurs is collapsed as a result of a throw. As a result, my end tags will always be output no matter what happens.

Syntax

These are the new syntax items introduced in this chapter. This chapter introduces functions from the database library. To use the database library in your code, you must include the file "omdb.xin"

catch

You can use **catch** to establish the point where program execution will resume following an exception or program error. OmniMark's catch and throw mechanism is a structured and highly safe flow control mechanism. It has none of the frailty that makes catch and throw so precarious in languages such as C++.

When an error occurs in an OmniMark program, OmniMark looks for a **catch #program-error** statement in a currently executing program scope. If it finds one, it initiates a throw to that statement. If it does not find one, the program terminates.

As we will see in a later chapter, you can also create your own throws and catch them with a **catch** statement.

When a throw is made, local scopes are closed and cleaned up systematically, up to and including the scope containing the **catch #progam-error** statement. Any actions associated with the catch are then executed. (We will see actions associated with a catch in a later chapter).

#external-exception

#external-exception is a catch name that is used by OmniMark and OMX components whenever an error occurs that is external to your program itself. Failures to open a file or to connect to a database are examples of external exceptions.

You cannot generate a throw to **#external-exception** yourself, but you can catch **#external exception**:

```
catch #external-exception
```

Three parameters are included in a throw to **#external-exception**:

- **identity**, a stream that contains an identifying error code
- **message**, a stream that contains a description of the error
- **location**, a stream that contains the location of the error in the OmniMark source code

You can receive these parameters by specifying their heralds and supplying variables to hold their values:

```
catch #external-exception
 identity id
 message msg
```

```
location loc
   output "An error occurred at "
       || loc
       || ". The code is "
       || id
       || " and the message is %""
       || msg
       || "%"."
```

It is a program error if there is a throw to **#external-exception** that is not caught. This means that a throw to **#external-exception** will always produce a throw to **#program-error** if it is not caught.

number of

You can use the **number of** operator to return the number of items on a shelf:

```
process
   local integer number-of-arguments
   set number-of-arguments to number of #args
```

dbOpenODBC

You can use the dbOpenODBC function to connect to an ODBC data source. The function takes three parameters:

- the DSN (Data Source Name, established by the ODBC driver manager on the host machine)
- the user name (optional), heralded by **user**
- the user's password (optional), heralded by **password**

The function returns an OMX variable of type dbDatabase.

Here is a sample call to dbOpenODBC:

```
include "omdb.xin"

process
   local dbDatabase database
   set database to dbOpenODBC "DatabaseDemo"
       user "Fred Flintstone"
       password "Yabba Dabba Doo"
```

dbQuery

Once you have established a connection to a database, you can retrieve data by sending an SQL query to the database. You do this with the dbQuery function. The dbQuery function takes three parameters:

1. the dbDatabase variable for the database you want to connect to
2. the SQL query string, heralded by SQL
3. a variable shelf of type dbField, heralded by record

The dbQuery function modifies the dbField shelf, creating one dbField object for each field in the record set returned by the query.

Here is a sample call to dbQuery:

```
dbQuery db
 sql query
 record current-record
```

dbFieldValue

To access data from a field, you use the dbFieldValue function to access an item on the record shelf (the shelf of dbField objects that you passed to the dbQuery function). The dbField function takes two parameters:

1. the dbField variable to access (this is an item on the record shelf)
2. the string to be returned if the field value is null (optional), heralded by null

The dbFieldValue function returns an OmniMark source containing the data in the field.

Here is a sample call to dbFieldValue:

```
submit dbFieldValue current-record[3] null "-null-"
```

dbRecordMove

You can use the dbRecordMove function to make the record shelf access a new record in the record set returned by dbQuery.

The dbRecordMove function takes two parameters:

1. the record shelf
2. either an integer indicating the size and direction of movement (optional), heralded by by; or an integer indicating the absolute position from the beginning or end of the record set (optional), heralded by to

The default movement is one record forward.

Specifying a positive number with the herald **by** moves forward by that number of records. Specifying a negative number with the herald **by** moves backward by that number of records.

Specifying a positive number with the herald **to** moves to the record that number from the beginning. Moving **to** 1 moves you to the first record. Specifying a negative number with the herald **to** moves to the record that number from the end. Moving **to** -1 moves you to the last record.

It is an error to specify both an absolute and a relative movement.

You will normally call dbRecordMove within a repeat loop so as to process each record of the record set in turn. Here is a sample call to dbRecordMove:

```
repeat
        exit unless dbRecordExists current-record
        output "<db2xml-record>"
        repeat over current-record
            output '<db2xml-field name="'
                || key of current-record
                || '">'
            submit dbFieldValue current-record
            always
                output "</db2xml-field>"
        again
        always
            output "</db2xml-record>"
        dbRecordMove current-record
again
```

dbRecordExists

Before making a call to dbFieldValue, you should check that the record shelf is pointing to a valid database row. You can do this with the dbRecordExists function.

The dbRecordExists function takes a single argument, the record shelf.

The dbRecordExists function returns true if the record shelf is pointing to a valid database record and false if it is not.

You will frequently call `dbRecordExists` as an exit condition for the repeat loop that processes the record set, as in the example above.

always

The keyword `always` introduces a code block that will be executed even if the scope in which it occurs in collapsed by a throw.

When a throw occurs, code is executed in this order:

1. The `always` block in the scope of the `throw`
2. The `always` block in intermediate scopes
3. The `catch` block in the scope of the `catch`
4. The `always` block in the scope of the `catch`.

An `always` block must always be the last code in a lexical scope and must follow the `catch` block for that scope, if there is one.

number of

The `number of` operator returns the number of items on a shelf. Do not confuse it with `length of`, which returns the number of characters in a string.

halt

The `halt` statement terminates the execution of an OmniMark program. OmniMark attempts to do as much cleanup as possible when executing a `halt` statement. To terminate a program immediately and without any cleanup you can use `halt-everything`.

Review

The following are the main points covered in this chapter. If you don't understand any of the statements below, go back and review the material in this chapter before you go on.

- You can access ODBC databases from an OmniMark program using the omdb database library.
- The dbDatabase OMX provides access to databases. The dbField OMX provides access to the data in individual fields.
- A database record is represented by a shelf of type dbField, with each item on the shelf representing a field in the record.

- When generating an XML file from a database query, you must escape markup character found in the data. For element content, you must escape "<", ">", and "&". For attribute content, you must escape the quotation mark character as well.

Exercises

1. As it stands, the program makes no distinction between empty fields and null fields. This distinction is important, and it would be useful to support it.

9: A game of hangman

Streaming and scanning are not just techniques for handling initial I/O.
They also provide elegant means for implementing many algorithms that you
might implement with pointers, offsets, or arrays in other languages. In this chapter
we will explore scanning as a data manipulation technique with many applications.

The project in this chapter is a simple game of hangman. (For those who don't know
it, hangman is a word guessing game in which the player is told how many letters are
in the word. The player must discover the word by guessing letters one at a time.
Each correctly guessed letter is added to the word. On each wrong guess, a body part
is added to a picture of a hanged man. Once the hanged man is complete, the player
loses the game. I don't implement the graphic portion of the game here. I just report
the number of remaining chances.)

Hangman presents a number of string manipulation problems that will let us explore
some of the functions you can perform with scanning. The program also illustrates
the use of catch and throw as an efficient means of flow control.

Perhaps the most difficult, or at least tedious, part of developing a game of hangman
is coming up with the list of words for people to guess. This hangman game puts
the onus on the users themselves. In order to play the game, the user is required to
supply a new word to add to the word list. I probably wouldn't implement this

feature on a publicly available game, but here it gives us the opportunity to study some useful programming techniques.

The program is too long to list here. You will find the full program in Appendix 3 and in the examples collection.

The basic structure of the program is as follows:

The process rule sets up the CGI environment and selects a function to perform based on extra path information.

There are three functions, new-page, login-page, and guess-page.

new-page is called when the player first connects. It displays the initial page that asks the player for a word to add to the dictionary.

login-page is called when the player supplies a new word. It performs the following tasks:

1. Choose a word for the player to guess by calculating an offset into the word list file. It does this by consulting the file that specifies the number of words in the dictionary and generating a random number between 1 and the number or words in the file.
2. Scan the word file. Check the user's word against each word in the file to make sure the new word is original. If not, ask for another word. When it reaches the offset calculated in step one, store the word for game play.
3. Add the user's supplied word to the word file and update the word count file.
4. Output the page that begins the game by asking the player to guess the first letter. The game word is stored in the hidden field "word". The number of wrong guesses allowed is stored in the hidden field "chances".

guess-page plays the rest of the game, accepting each guess and updating the guess page accordingly. It performs the following tasks:

1. Retrieve the values for the game "word", for the previous "right" and "wrong" guesses, for the current "guess", and for the remaining number of "chances" from the form data.
2. Create a list of the letters in the game word (eliminating duplicates).

3. Check the current guess against the game word to see if it is a good guess. If it is, add the letter to the right-guesses list and compare the length of the right-guesses list to the list of letters in the game word. If they are the same length, the player has won the game. On a win, throw you-win. If it's a wrong guess, add the letter to the wrong-guesses list. Decrement remaining chances. If there are no chances left, throw game-over.

4. Output the appropriate message depending on whether the guess was right or wrong.

5. Print out the game word with the guessed letter shown and the not-guessed letters replaced by hyphens.

6. Print the alphabet with all the guessed letters replaced by asterisks.

7. Output the guessing form, updating the hidden fields as appropriate.

8. Catch game-over and print an appropriate message.

9. Catch you-win and print an appropriate message.

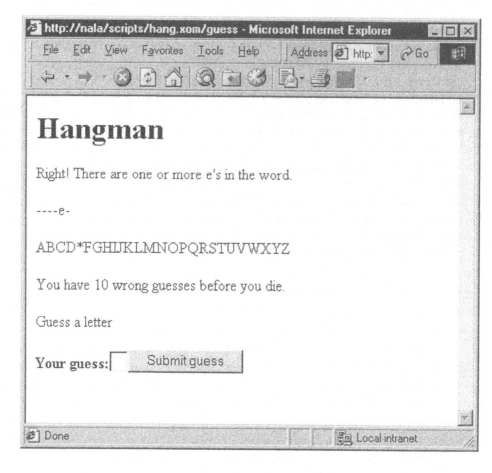

The guess page of the hangman game. The player has already correctly guessed "e". The letter "E" has been replaced by an asterisk in the alphabet listing and the "e" appears in the display of the word to be guessed.

The program remembers the word the player is trying to guess and the letters they have already guessed using hidden fields on the form. This makes it very easy to cheat, so you may want to adapt the program to use a more secret method.

Technique

This is the longest program we have looked at so far, and it is capable of responding to the user in a number of different ways based on the input it receives. There are a number of things to look at here:

- scanning as a programming technique
- flow control in a streaming program
- guarding statements
- basic error reporting

Scanning as a programming technique

All the algorithms used to play the hangman game are implemented using scanning techniques. You probably would not think of implementing these algorithms this way in other languages, which is a very good reason to study how scanning is used to implement them here.

In the examples that follow, note that one of the advantages of these algorithms is that they don't build intermediate data structures. They output text directly as it is generated.

One of the tasks of the **guess-page** function is to print out the alphabet with the letters that have already been guessed replaced by asterisks. I do this by scanning the alphabet and matching each letter against the previous guesses:

```
repeat scan "ABCDEFGHIJKLMNOPQRSTUVWXYZ"
match any => the-letter
    do unless guesses matches any** ul the-letter
        output the-letter
    else
        output "*"
    done
again
```

This code introduces two new scanning tools, **repeat scan** and **matches**. It is also the first time we have seen the zero-or-more-upto repetition indicator (******) in action.

repeat scan is structured like **do scan**, with one important exception: it is contained in a repeat loop instead of a do block. Unlike **do scan**, which is strictly a one-shot scanner, **repeat scan** continues scanning the input for as long as it continues to match data. You can use **repeat scan** locally instead of using **submit** and find rules. There is only one major difference between **submit** and **repeat**

scan: a repeat scan runs only so long as it continues to match data. Unmatched data does not stream through to output as it does with submit. If you want to ensure that a repeat scan runs to the end of the data, you must make sure that it has a match alternative for every byte in the input data. This repeat scan accomplishes this because it simply matches one character at a time:

```
match any => the-letter
```

Once I have a letter, I use matches to determine whether that letter has been guessed or not. The letters that have been guessed are listed in the stream variable guesses. I use the matches operator to see if the letter I am looking at matches any of the letters in the guesses stream.

The matches operator works like a do scan with a single match alternative, and it returns a Boolean value depending on whether or not the pattern matched. In this case, guesses is the input to be scanned and any** ul the-letter is the pattern to match. The any** part skips over any letters before the one we are looking for. The matches test succeeds if the letter occurs in guesses, and fails otherwise. So the program outputs each letter of the alphabet, unless it has been guessed, in which case it outputs an asterisk.

I use matches in the same way to determine if a guess is correct. Here word is a stream variable containing the game word, and guess is a stream containing the current letter guess:

```
do when word matches any** guess
```

The expression word matches any** guess returns true if the stream word contains zero or more characters followed by the contents of the guess stream.

To print out the word the user is trying to guess, I use the same scanning technique I used to print the alphabet. I scan the variable word, which contains the game word, and match each letter against the set of correct guesses contained in the variable right-guesses. For letters that have been guessed, I output the letter. For letters that have not been guessed, I output a dash:

```
repeat scan word
   match any => the-letter
      do when right-guesses matches any** the-letter
         output the-letter
      else
         output "-"
      done
again
```

I also use `repeat scan` and `matches` to create a list of letters in the word:

```
repeat scan word
   match any => the-letter
      do unless word-letters matches any** the-letter
         set word-letters to word-letters || the-letter
      done
again
```

This list is used to determine if the player has won the game. If the list of correct guesses is the same length as the list of letters in the word, the game is won. I also use `matches` to determine if a guess is correct:

```
do when word matches any**  guess
   ; good guess
   set right-guesses to right-guesses || guess
   throw you-win
    when length of right-guesses = length of w  d-letters
```

Flow control in a streaming program

I use three different methods for flow control that are worth discussing:

- `do scan` as a flow control device
- functions to encapsulate processing logic
- `catch` and `throw` to handle exceptional cases

Using do scan for flow control

We have already seen `do scan` used as a text ripper to break up a string and grab the parts. Here I use it as a "select" statement for text values. (OmniMark does have a select statement, `do select`, for use with numeric values.) Since `do scan` is a one-shot scanner, it will scan the string, select one alternative, and perform the associated actions.

```
do scan cgi-data{"PATH_INFO"}
    drop ~cgi-data{"SCRIPT_NAME"}
      match "/login" =|
         login-page
      match "/guess" =|
         guess-page
      else
         new-page
   done
```

In the **do scan**, I guard each match pattern with the =| (**value-end**) positional pattern. This makes sure that I don't accidentally match an erroneous value. Without the =| sub-pattern, the pattern "guess" by itself would happily match a rather dubious value like "guess-whos-coming-to-dinner". Whenever you use do scan as a select statement, end all the alternatives with =| to ensure you match the whole of a value and not just part of it.

The program uses the extra path information contained in a URL to select program mode. (Extra path information is any path-like characters following the name of the script in the URL.) The omcgi library does not provide the extra path information directly, but you can get it using two CGI variables. The CGI variable "PATH_INFO" contains the complete path information passed to the program in the URL. (That is, everything from the end of the domain name up to the first "?" or "#" character.) The "SCRIPT_NAME" variable contains the actual name of the script, with path, from the URL. The extra path information is everything in "PATH_INFO" that is not in "SCRIPT_NAME".

How do you get at everything in "PATH_INFO" that is not in "SCRIPT_NAME"? You do it by dropping the value of SCRIPT_NAME from the value of PATH_INFO using **drop**:

```
cgi-data{"PATH_INFO"} drop ~cgi-data{"SCRIPT_NAME"}
```

The **drop** operator is yet another scanning tool. It matches a pattern at the beginning of a source and returns the remainder of the source. (It has a partner, **take**, that returns the data matched by a pattern.)

What is the "~" character before the reference to **cgi-data{"SCRIPT_NAME"}**? It is the identity operator. It is used here to make it clear that **cgi-data{"SCRIPT_NAME"}** is a reference to an item on a shelf and not a pattern followed by an occurrence indicator. Both square brackets and curly braces play two roles in OmniMark. They are used for shelf indexing and for creating character classes and repetition indicators in patterns. Therefore, any reference to a shelf item in a pattern must be preceded by the identity operator to make sure it is interpreted properly.

Having stripped the "SCRIPT_NAME" from "PATH_INFO", the program can now use **do scan** to scan the extra path information:

```
do scan cgi-data{"PATH_INFO"} drop ~cgi-data{"SCRIPT_NAME"}
```

After that, it simply uses each **match** alternative to call a different function. The code for each of the program's modes is contained in the functions.

Encapsulating logic with functions

The principal use of functions in a programming language is to encapsulate code that is used frequently. Here I am using them simply to break the code into more readable pieces and to avoid putting all the response code into the do scan block that selects the mode the program will operate in. This gives us a chance to look at how to define functions in OmniMark.

The first thing to notice is right at the top of the program where I define three function templates:

```
define function new-page elsewhere
define function guess-page elsewhere
define function login-page elsewhere
```

This does not actually define the functions. That is done "elsewhere". It simply defines the function template. The function template must be defined before the function is referred to in the code. You can do this by defining the entire function before it is called, or by defining just the template with the keyword elsewhere, then defining the functions later. I find it easier to read a program if the process rule is the first executable thing in the file, so I use the elsewhere form frequently.

To define the actual function, I define the template again followed by the keyword as:

```
define function guess-page as
```

This is followed by the statements that make up the body of the function. You can do anything in a function that you can do in a rule. What you cannot do in a function is define a rule or a function.

You don't have to mark the end of a function. The function ends at the next declaration, rule, or function definition.

Using exceptions for exceptional cases

Catch and throw is an exception handling mechanism. In many languages, exception handling means handling catastrophic errors and not much else. The exception handling mechanisms that many languages provide are simply not structured and reliable enough for any other use. In OmniMark, exception handling is an integral, structured, and safe part of the language. You can and should use it for handling many types of exceptions, including the coding of exceptional cases.

In many processing problems, the exceptional cases are the most interesting. That is certainly true in the case of the hangman program. To play, the user has to provide a new word to add to the dictionary. In most cases that word given will not be in the dictionary already, but occasionally it will be. This exceptional circumstance needs to be handled differently. Similarly, winning the game and losing the game are exceptional cases requiring different handling. I use catch and throw to deal with all three of these exceptional circumstances.

The first case is the check to make sure that the word the user submitted is not in the current dictionary. I do this by scanning the dictionary file and comparing each word to the word the user submitted:

```
repeat scan file "words.txt"
    match any-text+ => current-word
       throw unoriginal-new-word
        when form-data{"new_word"}
        matches ul current-word =|
       set chosen-word to current-word
        when words-seen = chosen-word-offset
       increment words-seen
    match "%n"
  again
```

If the user's word does match one of the words in the dictionary, the match alternative succeeds and the line throw unoriginal-new-word is executed.

unoriginal-new-word is a catch name. It was declared as such at the beginning of the program with the line declare catch unoriginal-new-word. A catch name must always be declared before it can be used.

When you tell OmniMark to throw to unoriginal-new-word, it does a clean jump to the line catch unoriginal-new-word. What do I mean by a "clean jump"? A clean jump is one that leaves your program in a stable and workable state and does not create any garbage such as leftover local variables. You can think of catch and throw as a long exit mechanism. You can only use it to exit out of nested program scopes to scopes at a lower level of nesting.

Just as the exit statement will let you exit a repeat loop, and will properly clean up any local variables used in the repeat loop, so catch and throw will let you exit from any number, and any combination, of nested do blocks, repeat loops, find rules, or function calls, cleaning up each level of nesting as it goes. But it can never jump into a new scope that was not part of the current call stack.

In this program the jump is a fairly simple one, and the whole thing could have been coded as nested **do when else done**. However, even in simple cases, nesting can get to be confusing and the cascade of **done**'s at the end of such a structure is so far removed from the start of all the **do when** blocks as to be downright mysterious. Using catch and throw makes for cleaner, more readable code.

Guarding statements

There is another interesting technique in the lines just quoted:

```
throw unoriginal-new-word
 when form-data{"new_word"}
 matches ul current-word =|
```

You might have expected this statement to take the form of a **do when** block:

```
do when form-data{"new_word"}
 matches ul current-word =|
    throw unoriginal-new-word
done
```

But in OmniMark you can place a guard on any statement simply by following the statement with **when** or **unless** followed by the condition. This form is more compact and economical than wrapping a single statement in a **do when** block, and it reads better.

Basic error reporting

This program is sufficiently complex that errors can occur that I have not provided for. I don't do full error checking and recovery at all the potential error points. For instance, I don't have a specific check to make sure that the dictionary file is opened successfully. (You can add any error checking you feel is appropriate.)

I have added an error catch and reporting point at the end of the process rule in the form of a catch of **#program-error**. In the last chapter I used catch **#external-exception** to catch error originating outside the program. **#program-error** is used to catch errors originating within the program. However, because the failure to catch any other kind of throw is itself a program error, a catch of **#program-error** can be an effective catch all.

Since the entire program runs in the execution scope of the process rule, any throw that occurs anywhere in the program will be caught here if it is not caught elsewhere. The catch prints out a message describing the error that has occurred. Simply printing out the error message is more useful for debugging than for production code, but it lets me show you how to retrieve information about the error that caused a throw to #program-error. This is the catch statement:

```
;catch any unanticipated errors and report them
catch #program-error
 code c
 message m
 location l
   output "<P>We're sorry, an error occurred.%n"
      || "<p>%d(c)%n<p>%g(m)%n<p>%g(l)"
```

Three pieces of information are passed with every throw to #program-error; the error code, the error message, and the location. To receive these parameters, you must specify the appropriate heralds and supply variable names in the catch statement. The required heralds are code, message, and location. The variable names I have used here are c, m, and l, though you can supply any names you like.

The output statement forms the body of the catch block. Up to now, we have not seen actions associated with a catch.

In the output statement, %d and %g are *format items*. Format items are shortcuts embedded in strings that perform a number of different jobs in OmniMark. These two let you format integer and string values (respectively), without having to use the format operator (%), and concatenate the results. The string "<p>%d(c)%n<p>%g(m)%n<p>%g(l)" is a shortcut form of the following:

```
   "<p>"
|| "d" % c
|| "%n<p>"
|| g % m
|| "%n<p>"
|| g % l
```

You can use format modifiers on %g to change how a string is displayed. Here, it is used simply as a way to in-line the reference to the variables m and l to avoid the need for the concatenation operator.

Using reopen to append data to a file

If you open a stream with the open command, any data in the attached file is overwritten by the data you stream to it. To add data to an existing file, you must use the reopen command instead. Because you want to append to a new word to the word file, rather than replace its contents each time you add an entry, this program uses the keyword reopen instead of open to open the words-file stream:

```
; update the words file
```

```
reopen words-file as file "words.txt"
using output as words-file
 ; force the word to lowercase
 output "lg" % form-data{"new_word"} || "%n"
close words-file
```

Note that when you open a stream to a network destination, the distinction between open and reopen is usually moot. You are sending information to a system which has its own ideas about what to do with it and the append/replace distinction is either meaningless or is handled by some other protocol.

Syntax

These are the new syntax items introduced in this chapter. This chapter uses functions from the system utilities library. To use function from the system utilities library, you must include the file "omutil.xin" in your program.

reopen

The reopen action allows you to open a file and append data to it. You can also use reopen to append data to a buffer or a referent (concepts we'll cover later). For most network data destinations the difference between open and reopen is moot since it is not usually possible to do anything other than append data to them. (That is, you simply send them data. It is usually not meaningful to ask whether or not that data replaces other data at that destination.)

You can also use reopen to reopen a stream that is already attached to a destination but that is currently closed. To do this, you use reopen and the stream name without an as clause:

```
reopen log-file
```

format items

A format item is an escape sequence in a text string. You can use format items for a variety of purposes. The most common include the static format item "%n", which outputs a line feed character; the dynamic format item "%d(<numerical-variable>)" which outputs a string representation of a numerical value; and "%g(<stream-variable>)" which outputs the contents of a stream variable.

The principle difference between using an inline format item and using the % operator is that the format item can only take single numerical or stream variables, not numeric or string expressions, and not shelf expressions with indexers.

#program-error

#program-error is a catch name that is used by OmniMark whenever a program error occurs.

You cannot generate a throw to #program-error yourself, but you can catch #program-error:

```
catch #program-error
```

Three parameters are included in a throw to #program-error:

- code, an integer that contains an identifying error code
- message, a stream that contains a description of the error
- location, a stream that contains the location of the error in the OmniMark source code

You can receive these parameters by specifying their heralds and supplying variables to hold their values:

```
catch #external-exception
 code id
 message msg
 location loc
   output "An error occurred at "
       || loc
       || ". The code is "
       || "d" % id
       || " and the message is %""
       || msg
       || "%"."
```

when and unless

The keyword when and its companion unless are guards. A guard allows you to make any OmniMark statement conditional. You can guard any OmniMark statement by following the statement with when or unless and a test expression:

```
close log-file when log-file is open
```

```
set a to b / c unless c = 0
```

You can make a rule conditional in the same way:

```
find letter+ when x = 2
```

This rule will only fire if the value of x is 2.

repeat scan

`repeat scan` is a scanning operation that uses match alternatives to scan the input data. Scanning continues until the input is exhausted or the current input data cannot be matched. The general form of a repeat scan is as follows:

```
repeat scan <source>
   match <pattern>
      <actions>
   match <pattern>
      <actions>
   match <pattern>
      <actions>
again
```

As with find rules, each match alternative is tried in turn until a match is found. Once the matched text is found, the actions associated with the match alternative are performed and scanning resumes with the next piece of input data.

Unlike find rules, unmatched data does not fall through a repeat scan to the current output scope. Instead, the repeat scan exists if it encounters any data that cannot be matched by any of its match alternatives.

any**

The zero-or-more-upto (**) and one-or-more-upto (++) occurrence indicators play a special role in OmniMark patterns. First, there must be a following pattern. ** and ++ match up to a following pattern. If a following pattern is not specified, you will get a compile time error.

Second, these occurrence indicators can only be used on character classes, not literal strings. If you think about it you will realized that there is no functional difference between:

```
"elephant"+ "hippopotamus"
```

and

```
"elephant"++ "hippopotamus"
```

The second form is not allowed and will cause an error.

In practice, ** and ++ are almost always used to modify the character class any, and provide a way to match any number of characters up to a certain delimiter. One use for this is when the pattern you want to match occurs in the middle of a data stream, rather than at the beginning. Thus you can determine if the letter "x" occurs anywhere in the variable foo with the expression:

```
do when foo matches any** "x"
```

Be careful when deciding whether to use ** or ++. Because ** matches zero or more characters up to the next pattern you may get more matches than you bargained for. For example, the rule:

```
find any** lookahead "</table>"
```

Will always match twice if there are any characters in current input before the string "</table>". This is because the first attempt at the rule matches the characters up to "</table>", leaving "</table>" the next string in current input. The next attempt at the rule matches zero characters (which is allowed by zero-or-more) up to "</table>". The rule fires again, with "</table>" still the next string in current input. The next try fails, however, because OmniMark does not allow two zero-length matches at the same spot in the input.

To avoid the rule firing twice, you can use ++ instead of **:

```
find any++ lookahead "</table>"
```

Notice that this rule will not fire even once if the next string in current input is "</table>", since it must match at least one character before "</table>". This is probably the behavior you want, since you probably don't want this rule to fire at all if there is no data before "</table>".

=|

=| is the short form of the positional pattern value-end. One of the most important uses of =| is to ensure that a match or matches expression matches a whole value rather than just the start of a value.

The expression x matches y =| is equivalent to the expression x = y. Without the =|, the expression x matches y will return true if the beginning of x matches y, even if x is longer then y.

declare catch

Every catch has a name and every name introduced into your program must be declared. Therefore you need a declare catch statement for every catch name you use in your program. You can also pass parameters to a catch, as we shall see later. Parameters must be declared in the catch declaration.

catch

The catch keyword introduces a named catch point in your program. It may also introduce a block of code that is executed when a throw is caught by this catch. You can also pass parameters to a catch, as we shall see later.

Note that a catch is not a label. Execution does not fall through a catch statement. The code in a catch block is executed only if the catch catches a throw.

throw

The keyword throw initiates a transfer of execution to the named catch.

This is what happens when a throw is executed:

1. OmniMark searches the current scope for a catch statement with the same name as the throw. If none is found, it keeps searching each wider scope until the named catch is found. If the named catch is never found, a runtime error occurs.
2. OmniMark shuts down and cleans up local scopes in turn, up to the scope of the catch. It executes any always blocks found in those scopes before shutting them down.
3. OmniMark executes the catch block associated with the catch.
4. OmniMark executes any always blocks in the scope of the catch.
5. OmniMark shuts down the scope in which the catch occurred.
6. Execution resumes in the next highest scope.

Note that throw is not a "go to". There is no going back. Once you throw, the program scope in which you executed the throw is shut down. You have exited to the point in your program immediately after you created the program scope that caught the throw. Using throw and catch in this way is a safe and appropriate programming practice.

You can also include parameters in a throw in order to pass parameters to the catch block. We will see this in a later chapter.

~ (identity)

The identity operator (~) is used in patterns to force OmniMark to recognize an expression as a value-returning expression instead of as a pattern. For instance, consider this find rule:

```
find foo{"5"}
```

Remember that string expressions are coerced to numbers in the appropriate context, and then ask yourself if the pattern above means match the item on the shelf foo with the key "5" or if it means five repetitions of the variable foo. The confusion arises because the symbols { and } are used to define occurrence indicators in patterns and for shelf indexing by key in other contexts. Similarly, [and] are used for defining character classes in patterns and for shelf indexing in other contexts. The identity operator (~) removes the ambiguity by forcing the item it precedes to be read as an expression rather than a pattern. The value returned by the expression is then incorporated into the pattern.

Removing ambiguity over the meaning of braces and brackets is not the only use of the identity operator in a pattern. It forces any expression occurring in a pattern to be evaluated, including Boolean expressions. Thus you can write a pattern like this:

```
find digit+ => quantity ~(quantity > 50)
```

This pattern means, match a string of digits if that string of digits represents a number greater than 50.

drop (and take)

The keyword drop, and its partner take, provide the streaming language equivalent of a substring expression. While substring expressions in other languages work by specifying offsets, take and drop work by scanning the data with a pattern. The drop keyword returns a source representing the data not matched by the pattern. Thus the following expression returns "DEF":

```
"ABCDEF" drop "ABC"
```

The take keyword returns the matched data. Thus the following expression returns "ABC".

```
"ABCDEF" take letter{3}
```

modulo

The modulo operator returns the remainder of the division of two numeric values:

```
set chosen-word-offset to (rnd modulo num-words) + 1
```

define function

You can define a function in OmniMark using `define function`. A function must be defined before it is used. You can define the function template at the top of the program and define the full function later.

To define a function template you use the keyword `elsewhere`:

```
define function newpage elsewhere
```

To define the function itself, use the keyword **as**, followed by the body of the function:

```
define function newpage as
    <local declarations>
    <actions>
```

There is no keyword to end a function definition. The function ends at the next rule, declaration, group statement, or function definition.

The functions defined here do not take argument or return values. We will examine the syntax for defining function arguments and return values in later chapters.

matches

The keyword `matches` is a Boolean operator that you can use to test whether or not a pattern occurs in a string. You can use it as a string comparison, to test if two strings are identical, but `matches` is much more powerful than a simple string comparison. For instance, you can use it to verify the format of a value such as a telephone number:

```
do when telephone-number matches ("(" digit{3} ")" digit{3} "-"
digit{4})
```

Note that `matches` takes a simple pattern. That is, a pattern with multiple parts, such as the one above, must be placed in parentheses to make it a single group.

Like any other pattern matching operation, `matches` consumes the data it matches.

While you can capture data matched by `matches` to a pattern variable, you cannot use that pattern variable outside the body of the `matches` pattern itself. This is because, unlike do `scan` and repeat `scan`, `matches` does not introduce a code block of its own. It is just a test attached to an ordinary statement. Any pattern variables created in the course of executing that test are out of scope as soon as the test returns its true or false value. They are not available in the body of the do block.

UTIL_rand

You can use the UTIL_rand function to generate a random number. UTIL_rand is found in the system utilities library. To use it you must include the file "omutil.xin" in your program.

UTIL_rand returns a random number between 0 and 32767.

You can seed the random number generator using UTIL_srand. UTIL_srand takes an integer value that is used to seed the random number generator. The function UTIL_ GetMilliSecondTimer returns a system-dependent timer value that is ideal for seeding the random number generator. Thus, the following lines will provide a random number between 0 and 32767:

```
UTIL_srand(UTIL_GetMilliSecondTimer)
set rnd to UTIL_Rand
```

global

The keyword global declares a global variable.

Review

The following are the main points covered in this chapter. If you don't understand any of the statements below, go back and review the material in this chapter before you go on.

- Data streaming and scanning is a useful approach to solving a wide variety of problems.
- You can use do scan as a flow control mechanism, essentially as a select statement for text values.
- You can also use do scan to access substrings.
- You can encapsulate program logic with functions.
- You can use catch and throw for exception handling. This means handling any exceptional case which arises in a program, not just an error. Often, the exceptions are the most interesting cases.
- When a throw is executed, OmniMark cleans up the exited scopes and frees resources. OmniMark throws are a safe and structured flow control mechanism suitable for a wide range of programming tasks.

Exercises

1. The word list in the current program will grow bigger and bigger, slowing down

the program and making it harder for users to come up with new words. Adapt the program so that once the dictionary reaches a certain size, the chosen word is dropped from the dictionary after it is used. This way the dictionary will remain a constant size but will always be changing. This is just as good as having a large dictionary.

2. Add checking to make sure that the string the player enters is really a word, and that letter guesses are really letters.

3. Adapt the program to use a database, instead of a file, to store its dictionary.

10: Using formatting templates

The hangman program works, but it isn't pretty. If you want to add some graphic design pizzazz to the game, you have two choices. The first is to add additional HTML coding to the program. This is not an attractive option. It means you have to change the code every time you change the look and feel of your site. A better option is to separate the look of the page from the program logic by using template files for the pages. Template processing is a perfect application of the streaming programming model. You simply stream your template and make the appropriate substitutions.

Here is what a template file might look like for the hangman page that asks you to guess a letter. I haven't actually added any pizzazz to the design. I leave that for you to do:

```
<HTML><BODY>
<H1>Hangman</H1>
<<<Result>>>
<P><<<WordMask>>>
<P><<<AlphabetMask>>>

<P>You have <<<Chances>>> wrong guesses before you die.
<P>Guess a letter
<FORM METHOD="POST" ACTION="<<<Action>>>">
<B>Your guess:</B>
```

```
<INPUT TYPE="hidden" NAME="word" VALUE="<<<Word>>>">
<INPUT TYPE="hidden" NAME="wrong" VALUE="<<<Wrong>>>">
<INPUT TYPE="hidden" NAME="right" VALUE="<<<Right>>>">
<INPUT TYPE="text" NAME="guess" SIZE="1">
<INPUT TYPE="submit" VALUE="Submit guess">
</FORM>
</BODY></HTML>
```

It looks like an ordinary HTML file except for the tags in the triple angle brackets such as "<<<Action>>>" and "<<<WordMask>>>". These tags are the placeholders for the information that the program will generate. The form these tags take doesn't matter much, since they will not be in the file by the time it reaches the web browser. All that is needed is to make reasonably sure that the program isn't going to confuse other parts of the document with the template tags. If someone did want to put "<<<" into an HTML file, they would almost certainly write it "<<<", so "<<<" seems pretty safe to use for the template tags.

The other template pages as well as the program itself are in Appendix 3 and in the examples collection.

Technique

In this program, I replace the logic that builds the page with logic that scans a template file, finds placeholders, and puts out the appropriate data for that placeholder. Thus the new-page function looks like this:

```
define function new-page as
    repeat scan file new-template
        match any++ => stuff lookahead ("<<<" | =|)
            output stuff
        match "<<<Action>>>"
            output cgi-data{"SCRIPT_NAME"}
                || "/login"
    again
```

This function uses a **repeat scan** to stream the template file. There is only one placeholder in the new-page template, the "<<<Action>>>" placeholder. This is used to dynamically set the URL of the script, making the whole system more portable than if paths were encoded in the templates. The code simply matches the text of the placeholder and outputs the appropriate URL based on the SCRIPT_NAME parameter from the CGI environment.

What about the rest of the template? Because there is no stream-through in a repeat scan, I have to explicitly capture the template contents and output them. I do this with a match alternative that is designed simply to capture this data and output it again unchanged. I call this kind of match a "bucket match". The idea of a bucket match is very similar to the sponge matches we looked at earlier. The only difference is that a bucket match captures and outputs the data it matches.

An optimized bucket match

Both sponges and buckets can be optimized. There are two things you want to do when optimizing a bucket or a sponge. First, you want to move it from the last position to the first position. Since match alternatives are tried in order, putting the bucket match first reduces the amount of pattern matching that takes place for any given piece of input. Second, you want the bucket match to take as many characters as possible in a single match. This reduces the number of times the program goes round the loop.

In this case it is easy to optimize the bucket match because all the other alternatives start with the same pattern: "<<<". This makes it easy to move the bucket match ahead of the other alternatives by ensuring that it never matches a pattern beginning with "<<<".

Actually, we discussed the necessary technique back in Chapter 3 where we discussed matching up to a multi-character delimiter. The pattern required is any++ lookahead "<<<". There is just one problem with this pattern. It won't match any characters between the last placeholder and the end of the file because there is no concluding "<<<". So the pattern needs to look ahead for either "<<<" or the end of the file. You can represent the end of the file with the value-end positional pattern: =|. This gives the pattern any++ lookahead ("<<<" | =|). Because the bucket match needs to grab and output the material matched by any++, I inserted a pattern variable, stuff, giving a complete bucket match:

```
match any++ => stuff lookahead ("<<<" | =|)
        output stuff
```

Using an argument file to parameterize a program

Using template files greatly simplifies the creation of dynamic web pages, but it introduces dependencies between your template files and your program file. Rather than hard-coding the paths to the template files into your program, it is preferable to be able to parameterize your program with the appropriate file names for the system on which it is installed.

OmniMark makes this particularly easy because it allows you to override the initial value of a variable from the command line.

To set the value of a global stream from the command line, you would include the following in the command line used to run the program:

```
-define new-template "hang\new.htm"
```

You may want to parameterize a couple of aspects of this program differently in different circumstances. First, there is the number of guesses the user gets before they die. You can make the game harder or easier by playing with this number. Then there is the location of the template files. If the program is going to be installed on different systems, you may need to change the location of the template files.

The number of guesses and the paths to the template files are handled by global variables that are given initial values at the start of the program. Unfortunately, the command line needed to set all the variables we are interested in would be very long, and the CGI interface makes it very difficult to manipulate the command line of a CGI program. Fortunately, OmniMark provides a solution in the form of argument files. An argument file is simply a text file containing command-line arguments for an OmniMark program.

To enable us to use argument files to set the value of global variables, you need to add a new entry to the mapping table for the scripts directory of your web server. The conventional file extension for an OmniMark argument file is .xar, so we need to set up the web server to run .xar files. See Appendix 2 for the procedure.

Now that you have the ability to run OmniMark CGIs from argument files, you can consolidate all the files used for hangman in their own directory instead of leaving them scattered about the scripts directory.

The following argument file sets all the program paths to use a directory off the scripts directory called "hang". It also makes the game harder by changing the number of guesses from 10 to 7:

```
;hangman.xar
-sb hang3.xom
-define num-chances "7"
-define new-template "hang\new.htm"
-define guess-template "hang\guess.htm"
-define unoriginal-new-word-template "hang\unoriginal.htm"
-define lose-template "hang\lose.htm"
-define win-template "hang\win.htm"
-define words-file-name "hang\words.txt"
-define numwords-file-name "hang\numwords.txt"
```

Notice that you must include the -sb command in the argument file.

Here's how to run the program using the argument file:

1. Configure your web server to run .xar files.
2. Create the argument file above in your scripts directory and call it "hang3.xar".
3. Create the directory "hang" and place in it all the hangman-related files except the hang3.xom and hang3.xar.
4. Change your URL for running hangman to hang3.xar.
5. Use your browser to access the program.

Centralizing template processing

One problem with the program as written is that the basic template processing logic is repeated every time a template is used. This creates several problems in terms of readability and maintainability, and it makes it difficult to provide effective template error handling.

You can improve things by centralizing template handling, as in the hangman3.xom, which you will find in Appendix 3 and in the samples collection.

Since this requires the use of functions that take parameters, I have rewritten other parts of the code to use parameterized functions:

The template processing function

In order to centralize template processing, you need to be able to pass placeholder names and the equivalent values to the template processing function. This program does this by passing in a shelf in which the placeholder names are keys and the values are the values of the shelf items. Here is the definition of the template-processing function:

```
define function process-template
   value stream template-file
   using read-only stream substitutes
   as

   repeat scan file template-file
      match any++ => stuff lookahead ("<<<" | =|)
         output stuff
      match "<<<" letter+ => placeholder ">>>"
         do when substitutes has key placeholder
            output substitutes{placeholder}
```

```
        else
           throw invalid-template
        done
     match any ;this should never fire
        throw invalid-template
  again
```

This is the first program in the book that contains a function with arguments. I have already discussed calls to functions with arguments, and you have seen how OmniMark allows the use of tokens as heralds for function arguments, as well as the conventional parenthesis and comma form. This function uses the herald using between the first and second arguments so that a call to the function will read almost like a sentence:

`process-template new-template using substitutes`

The first argument is the name of the template file to use. The declaration of the argument looks like this:

`value stream template-file`

The word value declares how the argument is passed to the function, in this case, it is the value of the argument that is passed. The word stream is the data type of the argument. The word template-file is the variable name assigned to the argument within the function.

The second argument is the shelf of substitute values to be used to replace placeholders. The declaration of this argument looks like this:

`using read-only stream substitutes`

Here the word using is the herald. The word read-only declares the method by which the argument is passed. In this case the function gets read-only access to the entire shelf. The words stream and substitutes are the data type and variable-name respectively. Note that the shelf is not actually copied to the function. The function is allowed to access the passed shelf, in a read-only manner, using the variable name substitutes. The fact that this is also the variable name used in the function call is, of course, purely coincidental.

The template processing function uses the same kind of repeat scan as was used in the original program, except that instead of matching specific placeholders, it matches anything that looks like a placeholder, and then uses the has key test to see if there is a match for the placeholder in the shelf it has been passed.

```
do when substitutes has key placeholder
   output substitutes{placeholder}
else
   throw invalid-template
done
```

If the placeholder exists, it is used as the key to access the appropriate value to output. If not, the program throws invalid-template.

The logic for building a page now consists of building a shelf with the appropriate placeholders and values and then calling the process-template function:

```
set new substitutes{"Word"}
 to form-data{"new_word"}

set new substitutes{"Action"}
 to cgi-data{"SCRIPT_NAME"} || "/login"

process-template unoriginal-new-word-template
 using substitutes
```

Handling template errors

Two kinds of errors can occur in a template. The first is that the program may not recognize the placeholder name. The second is that a placeholder may be malformed.

To handle unrecognized names, the program checks the substitutes shelf to make sure it has a key with the placeholder name. If it doesn't, it throws invalid-template.

Our first two match alternatives should capture every part of a valid template file. But if a placeholder is malformed, the third match alternative will fire and throw invalid-template. A placeholder could be malformed by having a space between the name and the closing ">>>", by having a space in the name, or by missing all or part of the closing ">>>". The following are all malformed placeholders:

```
<<<Action >>>
<<<Word Mask>>>
<<<word>>
```

When a template error occurs, the program must inform the user and exit gracefully. To do this, it catches invalid-template at the end of the process rule and outputs an appropriate message.

Syntax

These are the new syntax items introduced in this chapter. The descriptions cover the syntax as used in this chapter, with some hints on general usage, but do not necessarily represent all the varieties of syntax present in the language. Please see the OmniMark documentation for complete information.

define function (with arguments)

You can define a function that takes arguments. For each argument you must specify:

- the argument separators that divide one argument from another
- the method used to pass the argument to the function
- the type of the argument
- the variable name assigned to the argument inside the function

You can choose from two styles of argument dividers: heralds, or parentheses and commas. A function definition with parentheses and commas looks like this:

```
define function process-template
   ( value stream template-file,
     read-only stream substitutes
   ) as
```

A function definition with heralds looks like this:

```
define function process-template
   value stream template-file
   using read-only stream substitutes
   as
```

In this definition, the first argument has no herald (it is effectively heralded by the function name). The second argument has the herald using. It is possible to specify a herald for the first argument:

```
define function process-template
   template value stream template-file
   values read-only stream substitutes
   as
```

In this defintion, the first argument has the herald template and the second argument has the herald values.

When passing argument to a function that uses parentheses and commas, you can use complex expressions as arguments, but with heralds you must enclose complex arguments in parentheses, as in the following example:

```
define counter function sum
 ( value integer x,
   value integer y
 ) as
  return x + y

define counter function add
 value integer x
 to value integer y
 as
   return x + y

process
    output "d" % sum(2 * 3, 7 - 2)
    output "d" % add (2 * 3) to (7 - 2)
```

If the call to the **add** function were written 2 * 3 to 7 - 2, without the parentheses, OmniMark would report a syntax error.

There are three ways to pass an argument to a function:

- value
- read-only
- modifiable

A **value** argument passes a single value to the function. When you call the function, the argument can be any expression that returns a value of the appropriate type.

In order to pass a whole shelf to a function, you must declare the function argument to be **read-only** or **modifiable**. The difference is that a read-only argument is read-only within the function, while a shelf passed as a modifiable argument can be modified inside the function, and the modification will affect the shelf in the calling scope. For example, the **cgiGetEvn** function that we have used since Chapter 1 modifies the shelf that is passed to it.

The type of the variable can be any internal or OMX variable type. You must include the appropriate function library to support the OMX types used in your functions.

The variable name used for the argument can be any valid OmniMark name. As with any other local variable, the name of a function argument variable will hide any global variable of the same name.

has key

You can test to see whether a shelf has a key of a certain value before attempting to use that key:

```
do when rhymes has key "Mary"
   output rhymes{"Mary"}
done
```

This is useful, since it is an error to attempt to use a key that does not exist on the shelf.

key of

You can access the key corresponding to an item on a shelf using key of:

```
output key of rhymes[2]
```

By default, key of refers to the current item on the shelf, so, for example, you can use it in a repeat over without specifying the item:

```
repeat over rhymes
   output key of rhymes
again
```

set new

The set new statement creates a new item on a variable-sized shelf and gives that item a value. It combines the actions of the set statement, which you know, and the new statement. The new statement can be used alone like this:

```
new substitutes
set substitutes to "hello"
```

If you don't specify a key or item when dealing with a shelf, OmniMark acts on the last item on the shelf, so this code will give the new item the value "hello".

Bringing the two statements together into one set new statement results in a line of code that looks like this:

```
set new substitutes to "hello"
```

If you are using keys, you assign the key as part of the set new:

```
set new substitutes{"word"} to "hello"
```

New items are added to the end of a shelf. If you are using keys, you probably don't care where an item is on the shelf because you will retrieve it by key, not position. If you are not using keys, you may want to put the new item in a particular place on the shelf. You can do this using `before` and `after` to modify the `set new` statement. These keywords let you insert the new item before or after another item. Sample uses include the following:

```
set new substitutes after [2] to "hello"
set new substitutes before {"fred"} to "goodbye"
set new substitutes before lastmost to "penultimate"
```

Perl programmers should note that OmniMark is much stricter in its control of the creation of items on a shelf than Perl is in adding items to a hash. In Perl the expression:

```
$foo{"x"} = "y"
```

will create an item in foo with the key "x" and the value "y", whether or not there is already an item with the key "x". If an item with the key "x" already exists it is overwritten.

While Perl is, by design, a free-and-easy language, OmniMark is a safety-first language, and won't let you accidentally clobber a value in this way. In OmniMark, therefore, you must explicitly say:

```
do when foo hasnt key "x"
    set new foo{"x"} to "y"
else
    set foo{"x"} to "y"
done
```

If you attempt to create a new item with a key that is already in use, OmniMark will throw a program error.

Review

The following are the main points covered in this chapter. If you don't understand any of the statements below, go back and review the material in this chapter before you go on.

- You can add flexibility to your web applications by using templates to separate appearance from program logic.
- Choose a markup for your template language that will not occur in the HTML portion of the template file.
- You can optimize bucket and sponge matches and find rules by moving them to

the top of the list of rules or alternatives, by making them match as much data as possible in a single match, and by minimizing the use of lookahead. In order to move a bucket or sponge match to the first position, you must make sure it does not catch any of the data you are looking for in the other matches.

- You can use an argument file to parameterize a program by setting the values of global variables from the argument file.
- You can use a generic template processing function to centralize template processing.
- You can pass a whole shelf of data to a function using a **read-only** or **modifiable** argument.

Exercises

1. Rewrite the disaster countdown program using templates.
2. By preparing different template files and using a different argument file, implement a celebration countdown. You should not have to change any code from your template-based disaster countdown.

11: An embedded language interpreter

The templates used in the last chapter used simple placeholders. The program looked up the placeholder name and output a value to replace it. But it is possible for templates to contain more sophisticated placeholders that can contain multiple parameters. This allows you to develop a sophisticated template language.

Active Server Pages and ColdFusion both offer an alternative to CGI in the form of interpreters that can read an HTML page and interpret special tags. These special tags contain instructions to generate dynamic data. This can be a useful approach to web development, but unfortunately, these shrink-wrapped systems restrict you to the functions supplied by the manufacturers. In this chapter, I'll start to build an embedded language interpreter that you can extend whenever and however you like. In the spirit of naming these things after improbable scientific discoveries, I'll call this system "Perpetual Motion".

It is not the purpose of this chapter to work out a complete Perpetual Motion command language, only to show you how to go about building an interpreter for such a language using OmniMark. If you need something like Perpetual Motion, it will be to suit your own particular processing needs, and you should invent the specific vocabulary for yourself.

Here is the OmniMark code for a basic Perpetual Motion processor. It implements only two simple Perpetual Motion commands, "test" and "form":

```
#!omnimark.exe -sb
;pmo.xin
;perpetual motion
;(in the spirit of naming these things
;after improbable scientific discoveries)
include "omcgi.xin"

;declarations required by the CGI library
declare #process-input has unbuffered
declare #process-output has binary-mode

;function predefinitions
define function action-test
 read-only stream argument
 elsewhere
define function action-form
 read-only stream argument
 elsewhere

;global variables
global stream form-data variable
global stream cgi-data variable

process
   CGIGetEnv into cgi-data
   CGIGetQuery into form-data
   output "Content-type: text/html"
       || crlf
       || crlf
   submit file #args[1]

; find pmo tags and let everything else stream through
find "<pmo" white-space* letter+ => command
   local stream argument variable
   repeat scan #current-input
     match
      white-space+
      letter+ => arg-key
      white-space* "=" white-space*
      ["'%'""] => delimiter
      any** => arg-value
      delimiter
```

```
              set new argument{arg-key}
                 to arg-value
           match white-space* ">"
                 exit
      again

      ;use do scan as a switch statement for text values
      do scan command
         match "test" =|
            action-test argument
         match "form" =|
            action-form argument
         else
            output "<b>[Perpetual Motion Error: "
               || "Unknown command %""
               || command
               || "%"]</b>"
      done

      catch #program-error
      output '<b>[Perpetual Motion Error: '
         || 'Error in command "'
         || command
         || '"]</b>'
; "test" command
define function action-test
 read-only stream argument
 as
      output "<p><b>[Perpetual Motion Test: "
      repeat over argument
         output key of argument
            || "=%""
            || argument
            || "%" "
      again
      output "]</b></p>"

; "form" command
define function action-form
 read-only stream argument
 as
      do scan argument{"action"}
         match "show"
```

```
        output form-data{argument{"field"}}
done
```

Here is a pair of perpetual motion files that can be used to test the Perpetual Motion interpreter. The first file contains a number of perpetual motion tags, some of which are not supported (which allows us to test the error handling capabilities of the interpreter). It also contains a conventional HTML form with one hidden field and one input field. The action parameter of this form points to the second test file.

```
<HTML>
<BODY>
<H1>This is a test of Perpetual Motion</h1>
<p>Here is the first pmo tag:
<p><pmo test one="one" two='two'>
<p>Here is the second pmo tag:
<p><pmo other one="one" two='two'>
<p><pmo fred one="one" two='two'>
<P>this is a form<p>
<form action="http://nala/scripts/test2.pmo" method="POST">
<B>Your guess:</B>
<INPUT TYPE="hidden" NAME="word" VALUE="which">
<INPUT TYPE="text" NAME="guess" SIZE="1">
<INPUT TYPE="submit" VALUE="Submit guess">
</FORM>
</body>
</html>
```

The second test file contains a perpetual motion tag for handling form data. When it sees this tag, the interpreter will look for the form data and process it according to the instructions in the perpetual motion tag.

```
<HTML>
<BODY>
<H1>This is a test of Perpetual Motion</h1>
<p>Here is the first pmo tag:
<p><pmo test one="one" two='two'>
<p>Here is the second pmo tag:
<p><pmo other one="one" two='two'>
<p>The value of the field "word" is
<pmo form field="word" action="show">
<p>The value of the field "guess" is
<pmo form field="guess" action="show">
</body>
```

```
</html>
```

In order to make Perpetual Motion work, you need to set up your web server to recognize the .pmo extension and to launch the perpetual motion interpreter. See Appendix 2 for instructions.

The syntax of a Perpetual Motion tag is pretty simple. It starts with "<pmo ", followed by a single word command that must consist entirely of letters. This is followed by zero or more attributes, which provide parameterization for the command. It ends with ">". Here's an example:

```
<pmo form field="word" action="show">
```

This style, with the command standing by itself, is perfectly good SGML, with the appropriate definition in the DTD. It is not allowed in XML, so if you want your version of Perpetual Motion to conform to XML, you will need to change the syntax so that the command is contained in a regular attribute:

```
<pmo command="form" field="word" action="show">
```

In either case, the Perpetual Motion interpreter is not going to use either the XML or SGML parsers to process the file, since this would require us to deal with all the markup in the file and the interpreter only cares about the pmo tags.

Technique

The processing here is not fundamentally different from the template processing we looked at earlier. The approach is to submit the .pmo file, find and process the pmo tags, and let the rest of the file stream through to output. The biggest difference is that the Perpetual Motion interpreter does not know the names of the template files the way the template-based programs did. Instead, this program is a generic interpreter that has to handle any perpetual motion file. The file to process will be passed on the command line. Since all the logic is contained in the code that interprets the pmo commands, the process rule is very simple:

```
process
    CGIGetEnv into cgi-data
    CGIGetQuery into form-data
    output "Content-type: text/html"
        || crlf
        || crlf
    submit file #args[1]
```

Processing the file using nested pattern matching

The effect of submitting the pmo file passed on the command line is that it will be streamed to output. A single find rule will catch the pmo tags and interpolate the appropriate data into the output stream:

```
find "<pmo" white-space* letter+ => command
   local stream argument variable
   repeat scan #current-input
     match
      white-space+
      letter+ => arg-key
      white-space* "=" white-space*
      ["'%'"'] => delimiter
      any** => arg-value
      delimiter
        set new argument{arg-key}
          to arg-value
      match white-space* ">"
          exit
     again
```

This find rule is an example of a technique called *nested pattern matching*. The technique is simple to understand. You initiate scanning of the current input source with one of the scanning actions such as `submit` or `repeat scan`. This creates a scanning process. At some point in this process, you detect a context change in the data you are scanning. You then create another scanning process, using any one of the scanning actions, with `#current-input` as the source.

We last looked at `#current-input` in Chapter 2 as a way of initiating scanning of a source that had been established as the current input scope by `using input as`. In that case, `#current-input` referred to the whole input source. But that was only because no processing had been done on current input and therefore no data had been consumed. In fact, `#current-input` always represents the unconsumed data in the current input scope.

This new scanning process takes over the scanning of the current input source at the current point. The new process is responsible for processing the data in the new context. When it detects the end of the context in the data, it exits, allowing the original scanning process to resume scanning the input source at the current point.

In this case, the first scanning process is initiated by the `submit` in the process rule. The find rule captures the start of a pmo tag and captures the pmo command into the pattern variable `command`:

```
find "<pmo" white-space* letter+ => command
```

In entering the pmo tag, the program has entered a different context, one that began with "<pmo" and will end with the concluding ">" at the end of the tag. In this context the program needs to capture zero or more attributes that are the arguments of the pmo command. To do this, the program initiates a new scanning process on the existing input source. Since there may be more than one attribute to find, the new scanning process is a `repeat scan`:

```
repeat scan #current-input
    match
     white-space+
     letter+ => arg-key
     white-space* "=" white-space*
     ["'%'""] => delimiter
     any** => arg-value
     delimiter
        set new argument{arg-key}
        to arg-value
     match white-space* ">"
        exit
   again
```

This repeat scan has two jobs to do. First, it must find any attributes within the pmo tag. Second, it must detect the end of the pmo tag, which consists of a ">" character occurring outside of an attribute value. Any process that is initiated to handle a particular context always has the responsibility of detecting the end of the context and of handing control back to the parent process.

The first match alternative of the repeat scan has the job of finding an attribute name followed by an "=" sign followed by the attribute value in double or single quotes. The rules for pmo attributes are a little stricter than for general XML/HTML attributes. The names must consist entirely of letters. The pattern `letter+ => arg-key` therefore takes care of matching and capturing the attribute name.

The pattern `white-space* "=" white-space*` takes care of the "=" sign. Note that it is important to allow for white space in your patterns anywhere an author might include it in a file.

The patterns that captures the attribute value illustrates a useful pattern matching technique:

```
["'%'""] => delimiter
any** => arg-value
delimiter
```

The attribute value can start with either a double or single quote, and must end with the same type of quote as it began. If the delimiter is a double quote, the single quote is allowed in the string, and vice versa. In previous programs I have addressed this problem with multiple rules for each quoting style, or with elaborate macros. Here I simply capture the opening delimited to the pattern variable delimiter and then use that pattern variable as part of the subsequent pattern: any** => arg-value delimiter. Using a pattern variable as a pattern expression later in the same pattern is a useful technique in many situations.

The second match alternative has the job of detecting the end of the pmo tag context. Once it finds the closing ">", it exits the repeat scan. This allows the original submit to resume scanning where the repeat scan left off.

Note how the nested pattern technique works. I do not capture the whole tag in a find rule and then re-scan it with a repeat scan. I detect the beginning of the tag with a find rule. I then invoke repeat scan scanning for the current input. The repeat scan picks up at the current point in the current input stream. Inside the repeat scan, I match the end of the tag structure and exit the repeat loop. Find rule scanning resumes at the current point in the current input stream. The input data stream is processed only once, without buffering the input and re-scanning it.

Notice that one of the benefits of nested pattern matching is that it allows us to temporarily switch from find-rule-based scanning to repeat-scan-based scanning. This is a very important technique. The question of whether find rules or repeat scan is the best scanning approach is not always a global one. It is often the case that find rules work best at the large scale and repeat scan works best for the details. You can plan your application using find rules for the large scale processing and then use repeat scan #current-input in a find rule to switch to repeat scan for interesting details such as tables.

Nested pattern matching is an enormously valuable technique in OmniMark. It allows you to break problems down into manageable pieces, and it gives you an elegant way to manage context in a pattern matching operation. The greatest obstacle many people encounter in trying to use this technique is to fall victim to a false sense of symmetry. They expect that the same process that finds the beginning of a context should also be responsible for finding the end of that context. But this is not the case. It is the job of the parent process to find the beginning of a new context. It is the job of the child process to find the end of the context. A simple analogy will illustrate this point. Finding the entrance to a building is a task you do on the outside. Finding the exit is something you do on the inside. So it is with managing contexts in data.

Implementing the commands

Each perpetual motion command is implemented using a function. As I analyze each pmo tag, I build a shelf on which the attribute names are keys and the attribute values are values:

```
set new argument{arg-key}
  to arg-value
```

Once the repeat scan has collected all the attributes onto the argument shelf, the find rule uses do scan as a selection mechanism to call the appropriate function, based on the value of the command pattern variable. The argument shelf is then passed to the appropriate function:

```
do scan command
     match "test" =|
        action-test argument
     match "form" =|
        action-form argument
     else
        output "<b>[Perpetual Motion Error: Unknown command %""
           || command
           || "%"]</b>"
   done
```

The command functions then perform whatever logic is required to implement the particular command. The action-form function implements the "form" command. The "form" command takes a parameter "action". The function uses do scan to select the appropriate action to take for each value of the action parameter. In this example, only a single value of this attribute has been implemented – "show":

```
define function action-form
 read-only stream argument
 as
   do scan argument{"action"}
      match "show"
         output form-data{argument{"field"}}
   done
```

The "show" action uses a second parameter "field" to find out which field of the form to show. It then outputs that value from the form-data shelf.

What each command function does then depends on how the command is interpreted. Whatever content the command functions generate, they simply output, and it is streamed into the resulting HTML file in the proper place.

All you need to do to extend Perpetual Motion is to design a new command and to write a command function to handle it.

Syntax

These are the new syntax items introduced in this chapter.

#current-input

We met #current-input back in Chapter 2, where I observed that it represented the current input source. Here we discover another very important aspect of #current-input. Once scanning has begun, #current-input represents the current input scope in its present state. Any data that has been processed is consumed and cannot be matched again.

This means that when you scan #current-input, using any of the scanning methods, you start at the place the current or last scan left off, not back at the beginning of the original source. This lets you use #current-input to implement nested pattern matching.

Review

The following are the main points covered in this chapter. If you don't understand any of the statements below, go back and review the material in this chapter before you go on.

- An embedded language interpreter is just a template processor with more complex templates and logic to process the template data.
- Nested pattern matching is the ideal way to handle different contexts in your input data.
- At each level of nested pattern matching, choose whichever scanning action is most appropriate for processing the nested context.
- It is the job of the parent process to find the start of a new context. It is the job of the child process to find the end of that context.

Exercises
1. Add more functions to Perpetual Motion.
2. Experiment with a different syntax for Perpetual Motion markup.

3. Rewrite one of the earlier programs in this book as a Perpetual Motion application. You will need to implement the appropriate perpetual motion commands. Try to keep the commands you implement generic so that they could be used for other projects. When you are done, ask yourself which approach — straight coding or perpetual motion — is most appropriate for the program you have chosen.

12: Converting complex ASCII tables

Here's a variant of the ASCII table problem we looked at earlier. In the previous version, each table cell was a single line high and therefore the cell data was contiguous in the ASCII data stream. The following table includes cells that are more than one line high. As a result, the cell data is not contiguous in the ASCII data stream and the data must be rearranged in order to create an HTML table. We have to pick up the separate pieces of the contents of each cell and put them together inside the appropriate HTML markup:

```
+------+-----------+-----------+-----------+-----------+
|      |Jan        |Feb        |Mar        |Apr        |
+------+-----------+-----------+-----------+-----------+
|North |aaaa aaaa  | bbbbb bbb | cc ccc ccc | ddddd dd d |
|      |aaaa aaaa  | bbbbb bbb | cc ccc ccc | ddddd dd d |
|      |aaaa aaaa  | bbbbb bbb | cc ccc ccc | ddddd dd d |
|      |aaaa aaaa  | bbbbb bbb | cc ccc ccc | ddddd dd d |
+------+-----------+-----------+-----------+-----------+
|South |e eeee eee | ffff f fff | g gggggggg | hhh hhh hh |
|      |e eeee eee | ffff f fff | g gggggggg | hhh hhh hh |
|      |e eeee eee | ffff f fff | g gggggggg | hhh hhh hh |
+------+-----------+-----------+-----------+-----------+
|East  |iiiiiiiii i | jj jj jj j | kk kkkk kk | 1 1 1 11 1 |
|      |iiiiiiiii i | jj jj jj j | kk kkkk kk | 1 1 1 11 1 |
|      |iiiiiiiii i | jj jj jj j | kk kkkk kk | 1 1 1 11 1 |
|      |iiiiiiiii i | jj jj jj j | kk kkkk kk | 1 1 1 11 1 |
+------+-----------+-----------+-----------+-----------+
|West  |mm mmmmmmm | nnn n nn n | ooo o oooo | p pp ppp p |
|      |mm mmmmmmm | nnn n nn n | ooo o oooo | p pp ppp p |
+------+-----------+-----------+-----------+-----------+
```

There are a number of ways to approach this problem. I will examine three different solutions, each of which has something important to teach about streaming programming.

First solution: Referents

Here is one possible solution to this problem:

```
;asciitable3.xom
global integer column initial {1}
global integer row initial {1}
global stream current-cell

define function output-to-referent
 value stream referent-name
 as
    output-to #main-output
    reopen current-cell as referent referent-name
    output-to current-cell

process
    output "<HTML>%n<BODY>%n"
    submit file "complextable.txt"
```

```
    output "</BODY>%n</HTML>%n%n"

find "|%n+" ("-"+ "+")+ "%n" lookahead not "|"   ;table end
    output-to #main-output
    output "</tr>%n</table>%n"

find "-"+ "+"   ;column header
    output-to #main-output
    output "<TD>"
        || referent "%d(row)-%d(column)"
        || "</TD>%n"
    increment column

find "|"? "%n|" ;start of line in a row
    set column to 1
    output-to-referent "%d(row)-%d(column)"

find "|%n+" ;start of row
    increment row
    set column to 1
    output-to #main-output
    output "</TR>%n<TR>%n"
    output-to-referent "%d(row)-%d(column)"

find "|" ;column boundary
    increment column
    output-to-referent "%d(row)-%d(column)"

find line-start "+" ;beginning of table
    output "<TABLE BORDER=%"1%">%n<TR>"
```

Technique

This code introduces two new pieces of syntax, output-to and referent.
The keyword output-to is fairly simple. It changes the destination of the current
output scope. You will recall that using output as creates a new output scope.
output-to does not. It changes the destination of the current output scope.

You won't need to use output-to very often. You should use using output as
to control the destination of output whenever you can. Here, however, I need to
change the destination of the current output scope so that the unmatched data from
each cell streams through into the right place. Since stream-through happens outside

of individual find rules, an output scope created in a find rule would be out of scope by the time the stream-through happened. Stream-through happens in the output scope in which the submit occurred. I need to be able to change the destination of that output scope, rather then create a new one. The keyword output-to changes the destination of the current output scope. I use output-to in the find rules to change the destination of the output scope in which the submit occurred.

Why do I need to keep changing destinations? My strategy for reassembling cells is to set up a bucket for each cell and keep switching buckets so that the proper bucket is always in place when the next bit of cell data falls through. Each of those buckets is a different output destination. I use output-to to change buckets.

The problem with this bucket strategy is that I need to wrap the contents of each bucket in HTML "<TD></TD>" tags. One solution to this problem, the one I would probably have to use in any other language, is to set up an array of strings with each cell in the array serving as one of my buckets. Once I finished the table, I would then loop over the array and create the entire table. I could certainly implement that strategy in OmniMark as well (try it, if you feel the need to consolidate your knowledge of shelves). But in a streaming language like OmniMark you try as far as possible to keep the data flowing. To do so, I use referents as my buckets.

A *referent* is simply a variable that you can output first and assign a value to later. In this program, I output the HTML table cell markup as soon as I detect a new cell. Between the "<TD>" and the "</TD>" I output a referent, which is the bucket I will use to accumulate the text of that cell as I encounter it:

```
output "<TD>"
       || referent "%d(row)-%d(column)"
       || "</TD>%n"
```

The referent is output now. The value of that referent will be set later when I have the data.

The simplest way to set the value of a referent (when you do eventually have the data) is to use set:

```
set referent "foo" to bar
```

But in this program, the material going into the referents is the unmatched data falling through the find rules. In order to get that data into a referent, I need to make the referent a destination of the current output stream. We do this using a global stream current-cell and attaching it to the referent we want to use with the reopen statement:

```
reopen current-cell as referent referent-name
```

I then make `current-cell` the destination of the current output scope using `output-to`:

```
output-to current-cell
```

I encapsulate the change of referent buckets in a function. This is because you cannot change the attachment of a stream while it is in the current output scope. In order to attach a new referent to `current-cell`, I have to remove `current-cell` from the current output scope. I do this by using `output-to` to change the destination of the current output scope to `#main-output`. (It doesn't matter that it's `#main-output`, `#suppress` would do just as well.) Then I can reopen `current-cell` as a new referent and then use `output-to` to place it in the current output scope again:

```
define function output-to-referent
        value stream referent-name
        as
     output-to #main-output
     reopen current-cell as referent referent-name
     output-to current-cell
```

Faking multidimensional arrays

The collection of referent buckets forms a multidimensional array representing the rows and columns of the table. However, OmniMark does not support conventional multidimensional arrays with multiple array indexes. Instead of a multidimensional array, I use shelf keys to create multidimensional addressing on a simple shelf – in this case, the referent shelf. (The set of referents in a program are simply items on a built-in shelf of referents. Referent names are simply keys for the referent shelf. The syntax is different from regular shelves, but the structure is the same.)

Each cell is defined by row and column position. We build referent names dynamically using the current row and column positions:

```
output-to-referent "%d(row)-%d(column)"
```

Supposing that the current value of row was 3 and column was 4, this would produce a referent name of "3-4". This is the multidimensional key value (in the form of a referent name). I access the value of this item using exactly the same logic to build the referent name:

```
output "<TD>"
        || referent "%d(row)-%d(column)"
        || "</TD>%n"
```

By the way, one big advantage of using multidimensional addressing through keys, rather than conventional multidimensional arrays, is that you get sparse arrays for free. Conventional multidimensional arrays allocate all the items of the array when they are declared. Using multidimensional key names, you only create a new item in the array when you assign it a value. No storage is allocated for empty cells.

Second solution: Nested pattern matching

Here is a slightly different solution that uses the nested pattern matching technique we discussed in the last chapter. Nested pattern matching is a technique for managing different contexts in your input data. An ASCII table is a special context that may occur in the middle of a document that may have quite different properties from the table and may require quite different processing. Just to process the ASCII table alone, I had to put together a fairly sophisticated set of find rules and I had to be careful of the order in which they occurred in the program. If you try to write a program to process a complex source with many different structures using a single set of find rules, it will become much more difficult to keep things straight.

In fact, it may become impossible to handle a variety of different structures in the same document if those structures share common features. The pattern "|", for instance, may well occur elsewhere in the document and have a quite different meaning from the meaning it has in an ASCII table. Outputting "</TD><TD>" may not be the appropriate thing to do in another context.

This is an important truth about pattern matching and about data processing in general: Patterns have meaning in context. The same pattern may mean two different things in two different contexts. To successfully process complex data, you must be able to manage the context in which data appears and treat each pattern appropriately for its context.

Nested pattern matching is one technique you can use in OmniMark to manage context.

Here is the program using nested pattern matching. The nested scanning process is initiated by the repeat scan #current-input in the body of the find rule:

```
;asciitable4.xom
global integer column initial {1}
global integer row initial {1}

process
    output "<HTML><BODY>%n"
```

```
    submit file "complextable.txt"
    output "</BODY></HTML>%n%n"

find line-start "+" ;beginning of table
    output "<TABLE BORDER=%"1%">%n<TR>"
    using nested-referents
    repeat scan #current-input
        ;table end
        match "|%n+" ("-"+ "+")+ "%n" lookahead not "|"
            output "%n</tr>%n</table>%n"
            exit

        ;column header
        match "-"+ "+"
            output "<TD>"
                || referent "%d(row)-%d(column)"
                || "</TD>%n"
            increment column

        ;start of line in a row
        match "|"? "%n|"
            set column to 1

        ;start of row
        match "|%n+"
            increment row
            set column to 1
            output "%n</TR>%n<TR>"

        ;column boundary
        match "|"
            increment column

        ;cell data
        match [\ "|"]+ => cell-data
            local stream current-cell
            reopen current-cell
             as referent "%d(row)-%d(column)"
            put current-cell cell-data

    again
```

The special structure this program is looking for is an ASCII table. The job of the single find rule in the program is to find the start of a table. Inside the body of a find rule it uses `repeat scan #current-input` to initiate a new scanning process on the current input. The job of that `repeat scan` is to find and process the rest of the table. If you extended the program to handle other features of the document that contained the ASCII table, you would add other find rules to handle the other features of the document.

Since there is no stream-through in a repeat scan, the program must explicitly match the cell data using a bucket match. Since the other match alternatives exhaustively match every part of the ASCII table markup, the bucket match can work more efficiently by matching any number of characters as long as they are not part of the markup. A quick glance at the data shows that the only markup character that ever ends a sequence of data is the vertical bar "|". Once we are in a row of data, therefore, I can match any character except "|" and be confident that I am matching data. Thus I can write the bucket match with a user defined character class [any except "|"]+ to grab an entire line of data from a cell. any++ "|" would work just as well.

Because it is explicitly matching the data portions of the table, this program can do all the manipulation of referents in the bucket match. Appropriately, it uses the bucket match to change buckets. As a consequence, the coding of the other match alternatives is much simpler.

Output with put

The bucket match uses the keyword `put` to assign the value to the referent. `put` is simply a shortcut for `using output as` followed by a single `output` statement. It creates a new output scope, outputs the data, and restores the original scope. It is a useful shortcut when you have to output only a single value to a new destination.

I have delayed introducing `put` until this far into the book because it looks a little too like the familiar print-like statements found in many other languages. `put` does not work like these statements and you should not use it the way you would use "print" in other languages. The correct and normal form in OmniMark is to keep the issue of where output goes separate from the issue of actually generating output. `put` is just a shortcut way of combining the two actions. It is appropriate only in situations like the one in this program, where only a single value is written to a destination.

Just to remind you of the power and generality of `output`, consider the trio of find rules used in many of the programs in this book to escape markup-start characters when creating an HTML or XML document:

```
find "<"
    output "&lt;"

find ">"
    output "&gt;"

find "&"
    output "&amp;"
```

These rules could be invoked many times in the course of a program. Perhaps the output being generated is going to a different destination each time they are invoked. It does not matter to the rules. They use **output** to send output to the current output scope. It is the responsibility of the routine that submits data to these rules to create the appropriate output scope with the appropriate destination.

There is no effective way to write rules like this using **put**.

Another problem with **put** is inefficiency. Consider the following piece of code:

```
open foo as buffer
put foo "1"
put foo "2"
put foo "3"
put foo "4"
close foo
```

This code creates a new output scope for every invocation of **put**. It tears down that output scope after the put. So the code above creates a new output scope and tears it down four times. By contrast, the following code creates and destroys an output scope only once:

```
open foo as buffer
using output as foo
 do
    output "1"
    output "2"
    output "3"
    output "4"
 done
close foo
```

There are times when it is appropriate to use **put** in OmniMark. It is appropriate when only a single value needs to be written to a particular destination and where **set** is not an appropriate choice.

It is generally more efficient to use put to append a value to a stream rather than using set like this:

```
set foo to foo || "bar"
```

That said, put is appropriate only when you have just a single value to output to a particular destination. If you will be outputting to the same destination more than once consecutively, you should use using output as and output. Whenever you find yourself typing put in an OmniMark program, take a second to ask yourself if you shouldn't be using output. The number one secret to becoming a successful OmniMark programmer is to learn to think in terms of streaming data and the separation of the issues of where output goes from the issues of creating output.

Third solution: Using measurement

Here is a third version that makes even greater use of nested pattern matching. This version counts the sizes of the cells in the first row of the table and then does the rest of the matching based on those measured sizes.

```
;asciitable5.xom
process
    output "<HTML><BODY>%n"
    submit file "complextable.txt"
    output "</BODY></HTML>%n%n"

find line-start "+" ;beginning of table
    local integer cell-size variable
    local integer row initial {1}
    local integer col initial {1}

    output "<TABLE BORDER=%"1%">%n"

    repeat scan #current-input
       match "-"+ => cell-head "+" "%n"?
          set new cell-size to length of cell-head
    again

    using nested-referents
    repeat scan #current-input
       match line-start "|"
          local stream current-cell
          set col to 1
          repeat over cell-size
             do scan #current-input
```

```
            match any{cell-size} => cell-data "|" "%n"?
                reopen current-cell
                  as referent "%d(row)-%d(col)"
                put current-cell cell-data
        done
        increment col
    again

  match line-start "+"
      set col to 1
      output "<TR>%n"

  match ("-"+) "+"
      output "<TD>"
        || referent "%d(row)-%d(col)"
        || "</TD>%n"
      increment col

  match "%n"
      output "</TR>%n"
      increment row

again

output "</TABLE>%n"
```

The strategy in this version of the program is to measure the width of table cells using the top border of the table. As the program scans the border, it grabs each sequence of "-" characters, takes the length of the sequence, and adds that value to the cell-size shelf. This leaves the shelf cell-size with one item for each cell in the table and each item containing the width of the cell.

With this information in hand, it does a **repeat scan #current-input** to process the rest of the table. When it matches the beginning of a data row (that is, line-start "|"), it uses the measurements in cell-size to grab the data from the cells one at a time. It does this by repeating over cell-size, to get the cell sizes in order, and using **do scan #current-input** with a single match alternative to grab exactly one cell's width of data:

```
match any{cell-size} => cell-data "|" "%n"?
```

Here I use a dynamically defined occurrence indicator {cell-size} to grab one cell's worth of data. The ability to define occurrence indicators dynamically is an important part of OmniMark pattern matching.

I also match the cell boundary character, to get it out of the way, and I optionally match "%n" so that the program consumes the linefeed character after the last cell. I don't have to worry about knowing when to quit matching one line and go on to the next. The whole operation is based strictly on measurement, and when the program has finished repeating over cell-size then it will pop back out to the repeat scan.

Notice that there are now three levels of nested pattern matching, and, in the case of the do scan inside the repeat over, there are several sequential scans of #current-input to process the data. The nesting mirrors the real nesting of structures in the data. The data has a table, which contains rows, which contain cells. The program uses a find rule to find the table, a repeat scan to find the row, and a do scan to grab the cell.

The other matches in the repeat scan take care of counting rows and cells and outputting the appropriate referents.

An interesting feature of this program is that there is no need to search explicitly for the end of table as in the other programs. The program will simply drop out of the repeat scan when it encounters a line that does not start with "|" or "+". The end of table markup is output at the end of the find rule so that it will be output when the program falls out of the table context.

Another interesting feature of this program is that the referents are output after their values are set. It would be easy to eliminate the use of referents and replace them with a conventional array, but there is no need to do so. All you would accomplish is to write more code to buffer data yourself, when you can use referents and have OmniMark do it for you.

Referents free you of concerns about the order of your input and the order of your output. They remove the need for two-step approaches to programming where you first analyze the input into a complex data structure and then create output from that structure. In OmniMark, you can avoid the complex structure, and the second step, by using referents to reorder your data.

Syntax

These are the new syntax items introduced in this chapter.

output referent

The `output referent` statement outputs a referent with the name given to the current output. The name of a referent is a string value. (You may think of referents as a kind of built-in shelf with the referent names being the keys of that shelf.) To output a referent, you use code like the following:

```
output referent "Fred"
```

The referent may or may not have been given a value at the time it is output. This makes no difference, since the value assigned to the referent may be changed later. The value of the referent is not actually merged into the output stream until the referent is resolved. Referents are resolved when the referent scope in which they are created is destroyed. A referent scope is established by the `using nested-referents` statement. Referents created outside of a scope that was created by using nested referents are not resolved until the program ends.

Don't make the common mistake of assuming that referents written to a file are resolved once you close the file. They are not, for two reasons:

1. You can't close a file in OmniMark. You can only close the stream attached to the file. Usually this results in the file being closed but, if there are unresolved referents in the data output to that file, it won't be closed until the referents are resolved.
2. Just because you have reached the point in your program where it is appropriate to close a stream, it doesn't mean that you have reached the point in the program where you know what the values of the referents are supposed to be.

set referent

You can assign a value to a referent using the `set referent` statement. You can assign values to referents in all the usual ways you can output to a data destination as well, but because referent values are usually short, `set referent` is the most commonly used form. You can also attach a referent as the destination of a stream and stream data to it.

You can set the value of the same referent as often as you like. Only the last assigned value will be used when the referent is resolved. Don't make the common mistake of treating the value of a referent like the value of a common variable whose value you can change and output at different times, resulting in a different value being output each time. Thus, the following code will output "CCC", not "ABC":

```
using nested-referents
do
    set referent "Fred" to "A"
    output referent "Fred"
    set referent "Fred" to "B"
    output referent "Fred"
    set referent "Fred" to "C"
    output referent "Fred"
done
```

using nested-referents

You can establish a referent scope with the statement `using nested-referents`. Establishing a new referent scope gives you a new referent shelf that will be resolved when the referent scope ends.

put

The keyword `put` is a shortcut that you can use when you need to establish a new output scope just long enough to output a single value. The code:

```
put current-cell cell-data
```

is equivalent to:

```
using output as current-cell
  output cell-data
```

Notice that `put` does not simply output data to the specified destination. Output in OmniMark always goes to the current output scope. `put` changes the current output scope to the specified destination, outputs the data, and restores the previous output scope. For this reason, you should never use multiple cases of `put` to output multiple values to the same destination. It is always preferable to establish a new output scope with `using output as` and then output the data with `output`.

Note the differences between `put` and `set`. `put` requires that a stream be open, and it always appends any `put` data to data already in the stream. `put` does not close the stream it writes to after it is done. `set` requires a closed stream, replaces the entire contents of the stream, and closes the stream when it is done.

Review

The following are the main points covered in this chapter. If you don't understand any of the statements below, go back and review the material in this chapter before you go on.

- There is more than one way to approach a pattern matching problem.
- The keyword output-to changes the destination of the current output scope. It does not create a new output scope.
- A referent is a variable you can output before setting its value.
- You can create a multidimensional array in OmniMark by using the key of a shelf to implement a multidimensional addressing scheme. This technique also lets you implement sparse arrays efficiently and with no coding overhead.
- A format item is a shortcut that allows you to format a variable, or perform other stream-related functions, as an escape sequence within a string.
- Nested pattern matching is a useful method of processing a data source that has several distinct features requiring different treatment.
- If you want to output the unmatched material from a repeat scan, you must write a bucket match to explicitly capture and output the material. Not only is there no fall-through in a repeat scan, the repeat scan will terminate if it encounters data it can't match.
- If you need a new current output scope for a single output action, you can use put to create the output scope and output to it in a single statement.

Exercises

1. In Chapter 4, I commented that the link-finding program presented there had a problem in that it would not find a link if the anchor tag had an attribute other than "href". Now you should be able to rewrite that program to fix this problem.
2. You now have enough OmniMark knowledge to tackle a wide variety of data translation problems, so pick a piece of data that is important to you and write a program to convert it to HTML, or to any other format that is important to you.

13: Mailing a web form

The programs we have looked at up to now have all done simple output to a single destination. In this chapter, we will look at programs that do output to more than one destination. You will also see how you can output to network destinations such as email servers.

The project for this chapter is a program that will mail the contents of a web form to a specified mailing address. It works with any form. The output is formatted in XML, which will make it easy to process the results. In a later chapter, we'll look at a program that retrieves these messages from a mailbox, parses the XML, and puts the data into a database.

```
#!omnimark.exe -sb
;formmail1.xom

declare #main-input has unbuffered

include "omcgi.xin"
include "omtcp.xin"
include "omnetutl.xin"

define function smtp-send
  value stream message
  subject value stream subject
```

```
from value stream sender-email
to value stream recipient-email
via value stream smtp-server
port value integer smtp-port optional initial{25}
elsewhere

global stream sender-name
 initial {"webserver"}
global stream sender-email
 initial {"webserver@yourcompany.com"}
global stream recipient-email
 initial {"formfiler@yourcompany.com"}
global stream smtp-server
 initial {"mail"}


declare catch smtp-communication-error
 message value stream error-message

process
   local stream form-data variable
   local stream email-message

   cgiGetQuery into form-data

   open email-message as buffer
   using output as email-message
    do
      output "<?xml version=%"1.0%"?>"
         || "<form>%n"
      repeat over form-data
         output "<field name=%""
            || key of form-data
            || "%">"
         submit form-data
         output "</field>%n"
      again
      output "</form>"
   done
   close email-message

   smtp-send email-message
    subject "Form data"
    from sender-email
```

```
    to recipient-email
    via smtp-server

    output "Content-type: text/html"
        || crlf
        || crlf
        || "<HTML><BODY>Your form has been mailed."
        || "</BODY></HTML>"

find "<"
    output "&lt;"

find ">"
    output "&gt;"

find "&"
    output "&amp;"


;============================
; smtp-send function
;
define function smtp-send
 value stream message
 subject value stream subject
 from value stream sender-email
 to value stream recipient-email
 via value stream smtp-server
 port value integer smtp-port optional initial{25}
 as

    local tcpConnection connection
    local stream commands
    local stream response initial {""}

    set connection
     to tcpConnectionOpen
     on smtp-server
     at smtp-port

    TCPConnectionSetBuffering connection enabled false
    open commands as tcpConnectionGetOutput connection
    using output as commands
     do
```

```
       repeat
          exit unless
          TCPConnectionHasCharactersToRead connection
          timeout 500
          set response
          to response
          || tcpConnectionGetCharacters connection
again
throw smtp-communication-error message response
 unless response matches "220"

output "HELO " || NETGetHostName || crlf
set response to tcpConnectionGetLine connection
throw smtp-communication-error message response
 unless response matches "250"

output "MAIL FROM:" || sender-email || crlf
set response to tcpConnectionGetLine connection
throw smtp-communication-error message response
 unless response matches "250"

output "RCPT TO:" || recipient-email || crlf
set response to tcpConnectionGetLine connection
throw smtp-communication-error message response
 unless response matches "250"

output "DATA" || crlf
set response to tcpConnectionGetLine connection
throw smtp-communication-error message response
 unless response matches "354"

output "Subject: " || subject || crlf || crlf
repeat scan message
   match (any** lookahead
   (line-start "." | value-end)) => stuff
      output stuff
   match line-start "."
      output ".."
again

output crlf || "." || crlf
set response to tcpConnectionGetLine connection
throw smtp-communication-error message response
 unless response matches "250"
```

```
    output "QUIT"  || crlf
    set response to tcpConnectionGetLine connection

    catch smtp-communication-error
        output "QUIT" || crlf
        rethrow
done
```

To see this program in action:

1. Place the program in your scripts directory.
2. Substitute your name and email address as the initial values of the global streams sender-name and sender-email.
3. Substitute your email address as the initial value of the global stream recipient-email.
4. Create an HTML form using this program as the "ACTION" attribute of the FORM tag.
5. Bring up the form in your browser.
6. Fill in the form and press the submit button.
7. Check your email for an XML-encoded version of the form data.

Technique

OmniMark abstracts data sources and destinations. External data sources and destinations are accessed using OMX (OmniMark Extension) components that manage the specifics of each type of source and destination and present the OmniMark program with a standard OmniMark source and destination. In this program I open a stream to an SMTP server and send it commands and data. I derive OmniMark sources from the server and use them to retrieve data. I do this using the OMX components in the TCP/IP library.

Subscribers to the OmniMark Developer's Network (OMDN) can use the OmniMark mail library to provide simpler (and more robust) access to e-mail systems that I do here. The function smtp-send in this program is a very bare bones piece of code and certainly not a full implementation of all a mail library should be. However, it does let us explore network communication in OmniMark, and it illustrates that holding basic conversation with many kinds of network server can be very easy and straightforward in OmniMark.

OMX components

All data destinations are alike in OmniMark and network servers are no exception. To talk to a network server using TCP/IP, you simply open a stream with an attachment to a TCP/IP connection and stream the data to it. Here is the code that creates the stream, creates the connection, and forms the attachment between them:

```
local tcpConnection connection
  local stream commands
  local stream response

  set connection
   to tcpConnectionOpen
  on smtp-server
  at smtp-port

...

open commands as tcpConnectionGetOutput connection
```

The first thing to notice here is what looks like a new data type, tcpConnection. tcpConnection is an OMX variable. It is used to contain a reference to an OMX component that will be created by the omtcp library. All connections to external data sources and destinations (other than files) are handled by OMX components.

The line beginning set connection to tcpConnectionOpen invokes the tcpConnectionOpen function that actually instantiates a tcpConnection OMX. It is the task of the OMX to manage the connection to the specified port on the remote machine. All you have to do is tell the OMX the machine to connect to and the port to use. This is done with the function parameters on and at. OMX components take all the hard work out of using network data sources.

Now that the tcpConnection OMX component is set up, all that is needed is a way of sending data to it. This is done by opening an ordinary OmniMark stream with an attachment provided by the function tcpConnectionGetOutput. tcpConnectionGetOutput is a *stream function*. A stream function is used to attach an OmniMark stream to an OMX component. Data output to the stream then flows to the OMX component, which deals with it appropriately for the final destination it is managing. Now that the stream is attached to the mailbox, you can forget about where the data is going and just generate output in the ordinary way.

Holding a conversation with an SMTP server

Sending a piece of mail to an SMTP server involves engaging in a conversation
with the server. First, both parties must introduce themselves, then the client (this
program) must tell the server that it wants to send mail, who it is from, and who it is
to. If the server is satisfied with this information, the client then sends the data. This
whole conversation takes place over a single TCP/IP connection. In OmniMark
terms, the connection is both a source and a destination. To hold a conversation
over the connection, the program must alternately read data from the source and
write to the attached stream. The biggest problem in holding a conversation of this
type is figuring out when it's your turn to talk, and when it is time to listen.

When two people talk on a telephone, they can merrily interrupt each other and both
talk at once if they wish, but that kind of confusion would not work well for
computers. In two-way radio communication, where the users have to toggle
between receive and send modes, it becomes important to signal when you have
finished talking so that the other person knows to switch to send mode while you
switch to receive mode. The convention for doing this is to say "over" when you
have finished what you have to say so that the other person knows it is their turn to
talk. This use of "over" is a communication protocol that is required for successful
communication. In a client-server conversation, you also need a protocol, a way for
both the client and the server to say "over" when they have finished what they have
to say.

Actually, such protocols exist in all forms of computer communication. They exist
when a program requests a file from the operating system, for instance. When an
OmniMark program is scanning data from a file, it relies on the OS saying "over"
at the end of a file. When it gets the "over" — the signal that there is no more data
coming — it fails all the patterns that are incompletely matched and ends the
scanning operation. Without the end-of-data signal, the scanning operation would
hang, waiting for more data that would never arrive.

You don't have to worry about the end-of-data signal from the file system, because
each file system does it in a consistent way and everything is taken care of for you by
OmniMark and the VOS. In a network communication, however, there is no one
single way of signaling the end of data, of saying "over" at the right time in the
conversation. Instead, there are a wide variety of protocols used. You have to
explicitly select and implement the protocol you are going to use for your server
application. All clients that use your server will need to know and use the protocol
you select.

The word "protocol", by the way, simply means an agreement, and there are many things that clients and servers need to agree on in network communication. The word "protocol" is used to describe several different sorts of agreements needed to make network communication succeed, so at any given moment in a network application you will be using several different protocols doing different jobs. Most of these you can safely ignore, but there are two you need to be concerned about. The first is the one we have been discussing, the problem of signaling the end of a piece of data, and the second is the question of what the data means. The rest of your program is dedicated to figuring out what the data means (and doing something about it). Here we will focus on finding where it ends.

I won't go into all the details of communication protocols here. Fortunately, the TCP/IP library and the I/O Protocol library provides support for all the common types of protocols used for signaling the end of data. You only need enough information to know which one to pick. Here are the basic approaches:

One approach is to use an end-of-data marker. This is the "over" strategy — put something at the end of the message that says "this is the end of the message". However, you have to be careful that the end-of-data marker is unique. In a radio conversation, a human listener won't be confused if you say "I'm having a hard time getting over you. Over." but a computer might have a harder time working out which "over" was which.

A common end-of-data marker for text data is the Ctrl-Z character, ASCII 26. For short messages, you can use line feeds as end-of-data markers. Or you can break the message up into sections (that is, lines) with line feeds and end the message with two line feeds in a row. This is how the HTTP protocol works.

Another approach is to drop the connection. This is the equivalent to hanging up a telephone. It makes it clear that the message is over, but it gives no opportunity for a response to be sent. The server may use this approach in replying to a client, but the client can't use it if it wants to get a response to the request it is making.

The most robust and most widely applicable approach is to use packets. We will look at packets in the next chapter.

Handling buffering

There is one other thing I must do to ensure a successful conversation with the server. I must disable buffering of data on the TCP/IP connection using the line:

```
TCPConnectionSetBuffering connection enabled false
```

If buffering remained enabled (the default), the program would not get to see data from the port until the buffer was full. If the program is waiting for the response from the server before sending more commands, buffering the response would bring the whole conversation to a grinding halt.

Reading data from the TCP/IP connection

Sending data to the TCP/IP connection proceeds exactly as you would expect. I attach a stream to the connection and wrap the whole conversation in a `using output as` block:

```
open commands as tcpConnectionGetOutput connection
using output as commands
  do
    ...
  done
```

All output within that block goes straight to the connection:

```
output "HELO " || NETGetHostName || crlf
```

Why not treat input the same way and use `using input as` to establish the connection as the current input for the conversation and then scan `#current-input` for the data? You can certainly write it that way, but then you are going to have to deal with all the end-of-data protocols yourself. This can lead to trouble if your processing patterns accidentally consume your end-of-data patterns, and in any case, why do the work yourself when the TCP/IP and IOProtocol libraries can do it for you.

Normally, the SMPT server indicates that it has finished talking by sending a CRLF. The function `TCPConnectionGetLine` is designed to read data delimited by a CRLF, so I use it to get the responses to my commands:

```
output "HELO " || NETGetHostName || crlf
set response to tcpConnectionGetLine connection
throw smtp-communication-error unless response matches "250"
```

The tcpConnectionGetLine function takes a single parameter, which is the OMX variable representing the connection to read from. It returns the line it reads. I check each response line for the response code I am expecting from the server. If I don't get the code I am expecting, I abandon the attempt to send the message with a throw to `smtp-communication-error`.

There is one special case. At the beginning of the conversation, the SMTP server reponds to my connection with a response line. It may also send additional information that I don't care about. I just read characters until it stops talking:

```
repeat
   exit unless
    TCPConnectionHasCharactersToRead connection
    timeout 500
   set response
    to response
    || tcpConnectionGetCharacters connection
again
throw smtp-communication-error message response
 unless response matches "220"
```

Sending a mail message to an SMTP server

Most of the time, the STMP server is expecting messages from the client to be delimited in the same way as its own messages: with a CRLF. All I have to do to send messages according to this protocol is use the CRLF macro instead of "%n" to end the lines I send.

Because a mail message contains multiple lines, however, the STMP server uses a different protocol for receiving the message itself. The message is delimited by the sequence CRLF, period, CRLF. So when I send the message I follow it with:

```
output crlf || "." || crlf
```

The only problem with this protocol is that the delimiting sequence can occur in an e-mail message. To handle this, we have to replace a period at the beginning of a line with two periods. The mail client that receives the message will then need to turn two periods at the beginning of a line back into one.

To keep the function self contained, I use **repeat scan** rather than **find** rules to do the escaping:

```
repeat scan message
   match (any** lookahead (line-start "." | value-end)) => stuff
      output stuff
   match line-start "."
      output ".."
again
```

Talking to many network servers is pretty much as easy as this. You mainly need to know what commands the accept and how they respond, and most of that information is easy to find on the web. In Chapter 17, I will show you how to talk to a POP3 server to retrieve mail.

Output to two different destinations

This program generates output to two different destinations. First it formats the form data in XML and sends it to the mail server. Then it sends a confirmation message to the user via the normal CGI mechanism (that is, output to standard output).

The form data is sent to the mail server, using using output as email-message and a do block. Once the do block is complete, the original output destination (standard output) is restored and the HTML of the response page is sent in the normal way.

Generating XML

Generating XML markup is no different from generating HTML markup. The program repeats over the form-data shelf and outputs the tags and the data just they way cgiinfo.xom did with the CGI information program in Chapter 5. As in that program, submit and a trio of find rules is used to escape any "<", ">", and "&" characters in the data.

Adding robustness

Because it deals with an external system (the mail server) this program could fail if there is a problem with that external system. To help detect such problems and prevent data loss, you can add logging to the program. If you log each transaction, as well as any errors that occur in talking to the mail server, you can tell if you missed any forms.

At the same time, introducing logging into the program creates an interaction with another outside system, the log file. It is important to make sure that a failure to create the log entry does not prevent the program from carrying out its primary purpose of mailing the form data.

This version adds logging and error recovery to the program:

```
#!omnimark.exe -sb
;formmail2.xom

declare #main-input has unbuffered

include "omcgi.xin"
include "omtcp.xin"
```

```
include "omnetutl.xin"

define function smtp-send
 value stream message
 subject value stream subject
 from value stream sender-email
 to value stream recipient-email
 via value stream smtp-server
 port value integer smtp-port optional initial{25}
 elsewhere

declare catch smtp-communication-error
 message value stream error-message

global stream sender-name
 initial {"webserver"}
global stream sender-email
 initial {"webserver@yourcompany.com"}
global stream recipient-email
 initial {"formfiler@yourcompany.com"}
global stream log-file-name
 initial {"mailform.log"}
global stream smtp-server
 initial {"mail"}

process
   local stream cgi-data variable
   local stream form-data variable
   local stream email-message
   local stream log-file

   cgiGetEnv into cgi-data
   cgiGetQuery into form-data

   output "Content-type: text/html"
       || crlf
       || crlf

   do
       reopen log-file as file log-file-name
       using output as log-file
        output date "=xY-=M-=D =h:=m:=s "
            || "Received form from "
            || cgi-data{"REMOTE_HOST"}
```

```
        || "%n"
    catch #program-error
done

open email-message as buffer
using output as email-message
 do
    output "<?xml version=%"1.0%"?>"
        || "<form>"
    repeat over form-data
        output "<field name=%""
            || key of form-data
            || "%">"
        submit form-data
        output "</field>%n"
    again
    output "</form>"
 done
close email-message

smtp-send email-message
 subject "Form data"
 from sender-email
 to recipient-email
 via smtp-server

output "<HTML><BODY>"
    || "Your form has been mailed."
    || "</BODY></HTML>"

catch smtp-communication-error
 message error-message
    do when log-file is open
        using output as log-file
            output date "=xY-=M-=D =h:=m:=s "
                || error-message
    catch #program-error
    done

    output "<HTML><BODY>"
        || "<P>There was an error."
        || "<P>Your form has not been mailed."
        || "<P>Please try again later."
        || "</BODY></HTML>"
```

```
find "<"
   output "&lt;"

find ">"
   output "&gt;"

find "&"
   output "&amp;"

;===========================
; smtp-send function
;
define function smtp-send
 value stream message
 subject value stream subject
 from value stream sender-email
 to value stream recipient-email
 via value stream smtp-server
 port value integer smtp-port optional initial{25}
 as

   local tcpConnection connection
   local stream commands
   local stream response initial {""}

   set connection
    to tcpConnectionOpen
    on smtp-server
    at smtp-port

   TCPConnectionSetBuffering connection enabled false
   open commands as tcpConnectionGetOutput connection
   using output as commands
    do
       repeat
          exit unless
           TCPConnectionHasCharactersToRead connection
           timeout 500
          set response
           to response
           || tcpConnectionGetCharacters connection
       again
       throw smtp-communication-error message response
```

```
   unless response matches "220"

output "HELO " || NETGetHostName || crlf
set response to tcpConnectionGetLine connection
throw smtp-communication-error message response
 unless response matches "250"

output "MAIL FROM:" || sender-email || crlf
set response to tcpConnectionGetLine connection
throw smtp-communication-error message response
 unless response matches "250"

output "RCPT TO:" || recipient-email || crlf
set response to tcpConnectionGetLine connection
throw smtp-communication-error message response
 unless response matches "250"

output "DATA" || crlf
set response to tcpConnectionGetLine connection
throw smtp-communication-error message response
 unless response matches "354"

output "Subject: " || subject || crlf || crlf
repeat scan message
   match (any** lookahead
    (line-start "." | value-end)) => stuff
      output stuff
   match line-start "."
      output ".."
again

output crlf || "." || crlf
set response to tcpConnectionGetLine connection
throw smtp-communication-error message response
 unless response matches "250"

output "QUIT" || crlf
set response to tcpConnectionGetLine connection

catch smtp-communication-error
   output "QUIT" || crlf
   rethrow
done
```

Because you want to append to a log file, rather than replace its contents each time you add an entry, this program uses the keyword **reopen** instead of **open** to open the log-file stream. When you use **open** to open a stream to a file, the data in the file is overwritten. When you use **reopen**, the material you output is appended to the existing data in the file.

Generating the log file entry is straightforward enough:

```
output date "=xY-=M-=D =h:=m:=s "
    || "Received form from "
    || cgi-data{"REMOTE_HOST"}
    || "%n"
```

This code use the CGI environment variable "REMOTE_HOST" to record the IP address of the computer the form came from, and it uses the OmniMark date function to insert the time the form was received.

What is interesting about this code is that it is wrapped in a do ... done block and ends with the statement **catch #program-error**:

```
do
    reopen log-file as file log-file-name
    using output as log-file
     output date "=xY-=M-=D =h:=m:=s "
        || "Received form from "
        || cgi-data{"REMOTE_HOST"}
        || "%n"
    catch #program-error
done
```

The purpose of the **catch #program-error** line is to catch any errors that may occur in opening and writing to the log file. If an error occurs, OmniMark will generate an exception which will result in a throw to **#program-error** in the nearest program scope. The purpose of the **do** block is to establish the appropriate scope. The failure to write to the log is contained and the main business of mailing the form can continue.

The next step is to open the mail outbox as before. This time, however, the program provides a catch for the throw **smtp-communication-error** which can be thrown by **smtp-send** function in the event of an error communicating with the SMTP server. The **message** parameter of the throw provides the error message received from the server, which will now be written to the log file.

The program first checks to make sure that the log file is open. If it isn't, that means there was an error opening it earlier and the program won't try any further to log this transaction. If the log file is open, the program outputs the error message to the log file. catch #program-error is used again to protect the rest of the program from terminating if any errors occur while writing to the log file.

Next the program sends the message to the user informing them that their form data has not been mailed. The rest of the program is the same as it was in the previous version.

Passing an error down the line

The smtp-send function can throw the exception smtp-communication-error. It also uses that same exception internally. Internally, it throws smtp-communication-error if it receives a response it does not expect. It then catches that exception in order to send a QUIT message to the server. But if the function catches the exception, how does the main program also get to catch the exception and log the error message?

The keyword rethrow allows you to re-throw any throw you have caught. Notice that while the catch in the function does not bother to retrieve the error message parameter of the throw, that parameter is still available to the catch in the main program. The rethrow statement re-throws the entire original throw, not just the part you have caught.

Syntax

These are the new syntax items introduced in this chapter.

TCPConnectionOpen

You can use the TCPConnectionOpen function to open a connection to a server. The TCPConnectionOpen function returns a TCPConnection variable representing the OMX component that handles the connection.

You use TCPConnectionOpen in a client program to establish a connection to a listening server. There is no difference between the connection OMXs returned by TCPConnectionOpen and TCPServiceAcceptConnection. The client and server operate as peers once the connection is established, and the TCPConnection components that manage each end of the connection operate identically. The communication differences between a client and a server lie in the different roles they play in establishing a connection. Once the connection is established, they communicate in exactly the same way using the same OMX components and library functions.

This is the syntax of the TCPConnectionOpen function:

```
set <TCP connection> to TCPConnectionOpen on <Server name> at <Port
Number>
```

where <TCP Connection> is a variable of type TCPConnection, and <Server name> is a string expression representing the name or IP address of the server the client is trying to connect to.

Example:

```
set connection to TCPConnectionOpen on server at port
```

TCPConnectionGetOutput

A TCP/IP connection is a two-way communication channel. In OmniMark terms, it is both a data source and an output destination. You can use the TCPConnectionGetOutput function to attach a stream to a TCP/IP connection. Once the stream is attached to the connection, you can write to the connection by placing the stream in the current output scope and using output as normal.

An example of TCPConnectionGetOutput is:

```
open reply as TCPConnectionGetOutput connection
 protocol IOProtocolMultiPacket

using output as reply
 do
    output ...
 done
```

This example uses the IOProtocolMultiPacket protocol handler implemented by the I/O Protocol library. (The I/O Protocol library is used by the TCP/IP library, and is included automatically when you include the TCP/IP library.) The job of the protocol handler is to deal with the end-of-data problem described above. If you do not specify a protocol, you will need to deal with the end-of-data problem yourself. (But I don't recommend that you try.)

You can also use it with set to send a single value to the connection:

```
set TCPConnectionGetOutput connection
    protocol IOProtocolMultiPacket
    to poison-pill
```

tcpConnectionGetLine

The tcpConnectionGetLine function retrieves a single line from a TCP/IP connection. It will accept either CRLF or LF alone as an end of line.

tcpConnectionGetCharacters

The tcpConnectionGetCharacters retrieves all the characters that have been received from the TCP/IP connection.

tcpConnectionHasCharactersToRead

You can use the function tcpConnectionHasCharactersToRead to determine if there are any characters waiting to be read from a TCP/IP connection.

is open

is open is one of a large collection of tests you can perform on a stream to determine its current status. You can use is open to determine if a stream is open before closing it or writing to it:

```
open log-file unless log-file is open
```

date

The date statement returns a string representing the current date and time. The string is formatted according to the date format string you supply. This example specifies a four digit year, a two digit month, and a two digit day, all separated by hyphens, and hours, minutes, and seconds separated by colons:

```
date "=xY=M=D =h:=m:=s"
```

rethrow

You can use the keyword rethrow in any catch block to cause the throw to be thrown again from the current point. All data associated with the original throw is included in the rethrown throw (even those parameters not received by the initial catch). You can use rethrow to select which throws you will handle in a particular scope and which you will handle in a later scope:

```
catch #external-exception identity error-code
   do when error-code = "OMDB501"
      output "An ODBC error occurred%n"
   else
```

```
    rethrow
done
```

Review

The following are the main points covered in this chapter. If you don't understand any of the statements below, go back and review the material in this chapter before you go on.

- OmniMark Extension (OMX) components provide connectivity to external data sources. OMX components manage the connection to the external data source and provide attachments to conventional OmniMark sources and streams. Once you are connected to the external data source, your OmniMark program works like any other.
- You can hold a conversation with a network server over a TCP/IP connection.
- When conducting a conversation with a server you must know and use the protocols it sues to determine whose turn it is to talk.
- Generating XML data is no different from generating HTML data. As with HTML, you must escape markup characters when generating XML.
- You can protect your program from the failure of a particular routine by wrapping the routine in a do...done block and ending the block with catch #program-error.
- If an error occurs in an OmniMark program, OmniMark generates a throw to #program-error. A throw can only be caught in the current execution scope (that is, any scope on the current call stack).
- An error in dealing with the outside world results in a throw to #external-exception.
- Some OmniMark libraries are not catch and throw enabled. You need to explicitly check for errors when using these libraries.
- You can guard any OmniMark statement with when or unless.
- You can test the state of a stream with tests such as is open.

Exercises

1. Dig into the OmniMark documentation for information on the FTP library and rewrite the program to send the form data to an FTP site instead of a mailbox.

14: XML Middleware

Middleware is any piece of software that works as an intermediary between two processes. You can use middleware to hide the complexity of external processes or data sources from your frontline web programs. This can make it easier to write your frontline applications and provide a level of abstraction between the applications and the data they use, so that you can change the structure and location of the source data without changing the applications themselves.

As an example of a middleware server, I will adapt the database-to-XML program from Chapter 8. Rather than simply dumping the structure of the table, however, I will generate data according to a specific XML language. This architecture hides the original format of the data from the program that uses it. If the database structure changes, or if the data is moved from a relational to an object database, all that would have to be done is to rewrite the middleware application and the programs that use it will still receive data in the form they expect.

In this case, I will build a server that retrieves customer information from a database and sends it to a client program as XML. I will also build a partial client program to illustrate how to access the services of the middleware application.

In this chapter I will also introduce another important OmniMark feature: dynamic initialization. Several of the programs we have studied have initialized variables to static values. In the program in this chapter, you will see variables initialized to dynamic expressions.

The customer data is located in a database with the following fields:

```
CustomerID
FirstName
LastName
Title
Address
City
State
Country
Code
Phone
Fax
Pager
```

A typical XML document returned by this application might look like this:

```
<customer status="ok">
<id>123ABC</id>
<name first="John &quot;Jack&quot;" last="Smith" title="Mr."/>
<address><mail street="123 Main Street" city="Anytown"
state="Elation" country="Vespugia" code="K12 16P"/>
<phone>555-6789</phone>
<fax>555-8765</fax>
<pager>555-1234</pager>
</address>
</customer>
```

Because the XML document is the only means of communication between the application and its clients, there must be some way of reporting errors via the XML document. I do using a status attribute in the root element, "customer".

There are three possible values for this attribute: "ok", meaning that the request succeeded and a valid customer record has been returned; "notfound", meaning that the requested customer was not found in the database; and "error", meaning that an error occurred in handling the request.

I use attributes, rather than elements, for the client's name and mailing address. The reason is ease of processing. When you process a sequence of elements, you only have access to each in turn. When you process a single element with multiple attributes, you have access to all the attributes at the same time. Since it seems reasonable that people will want to access names and mailing addresses as a whole, using attributes makes it easier for programmers using the services of the middleware application to get at the data.

Here is the middleware program

```
;customerserver.xom
include "omdb.xin"
include "omtcp.xin"
global integer port-number initial {5432}
global stream dsn initial {"customer"}
global stream poison-pill initial {"_die_"}
declare catch shut-down
declare catch customer-not-found
declare catch reset-server

process
   local dbDatabase db initial {dbOpenODBC dsn}
   local tcpService service
    initial {tcpServiceOpen at port-number}

   throw shut-down when tcpServiceIsInError service

   ;connection loop
   repeat
      local tcpConnection connection
       initial {TCPServiceAcceptConnection service}
      local stream request
       initial {tcpConnectionGetSource connection
       protocol IOProtocolMultiPacket}
      local stream query initial
      {   "SELECT * FROM Customer WHERE "
       || "CustomerID='%g(request)'"
      }
      local stream reply
      local dbField current-record variable

      throw shut-down when request = poison-pill

      open reply as TCPConnectionGetOutput connection
       protocol IOProtocolMultiPacket

      using output as reply
       do
         dbQuery db sql query record current-record
```

```
throw customer-not-found
 unless dbRecordExists current-record

output '<customer status="ok">%n<id>'
submit dbFieldValue current-record{"CustomerID"}
output '</id>%n<name first="'
submit dbFieldValue current-record{"FirstName"}
output '" last="'
submit dbFieldValue current-record{"LastName"}
output '" title="'
submit dbFieldValue current-record{"Title"}
output '"/>%n<address><mail street="'
submit dbFieldValue current-record{"Address"}
output '" city="'
submit dbFieldValue current-record{"City"}
output '" state="'
submit dbFieldValue current-record{"State"}
output '" country="'
submit dbFieldValue current-record{"Country"}
output '" code="'
submit dbFieldValue current-record{"Code"}
output '"/>%n<phone>'
submit dbFieldValue current-record{"Phone"}
output '</phone>%n<fax>'
submit dbFieldValue current-record{"Fax"}
output '</fax>%n<pager>'
submit dbFieldValue current-record{"Pager"}
output '</pager>%n</address>%n</customer>'

catch customer-not-found
   output '<customer status="notfound"/>'

catch #program-error
   output '<client status="error"/>'
    when reply is open

catch #external-exception
   output '<client status="error"/>'
    when reply is open
done
again

catch shut-down
```

```
catch #external-exception
 identity id
 message msg
 location loc
   output "Error:%n"
       || "ID: %g(id)%n"
       || "Msg: %g(msg)%n"
       || "Loc: %g(loc)%n"

find "<"
   output "&lt;"

find ">"
   output "&gt;"

find "&"
   output "&amp;"

find '"'
    output "&quot;"
```

Here is the stub client. It simply requests customer information, receives the XML document, and dumps it to output. A bare bones client like this is very useful in client-server development. When communication errors occur it is sometimes difficult to tell if the client or the server is at fault. A bare bones client, which simply dumps the data it receives, allows you to debug the server first and deal with clients later when you are sure the server is operating correctly.

```
;stub.xom
; a stub client to communicate with our middleware server
include "omtcp.xin"
declare catch connection-error
process
   local TCPConnection connection
    initial {TCPConnectionOpen on "localhost" at 5432}
   throw connection-error
    when TCPConnectionIsInError connection

   set TCPConnectionGetOutput connection
    protocol IOProtocolMultiPacket
    to #args[1]

   output TCPConnectionGetSource connection
```

```
protocol IOProtocolMultiPacket

catch connection-error
  output "Connection error%n"
```

To use this stub client, provide a customer ID on the command line:

```
omnimark -s stub.xom ABC123
```

Technique

A server program runs constantly and waits for a client program to connect and request a service. It is like a telephone that sits and waits for a call. When a call comes it, it is answered. Once the call is complete, the telephone goes back to waiting until the next call comes in.

A server program has three basic parts:

1. the startup routine, in which the service is established
2. the request service loop, in which requests are received and answered
3. the shutdown routine, in which the service is torn down and resources are freed

In most OmniMark server programs, all three parts will exist in the body of a single process rule. The request service loop will consist of a repeat...again loop. The startup code will precede the loop, and the shutdown code will follow it.

Startup

The first thing you must do when setting up a server is to put it into service so that clients can connect to it. Like a telephone, a server has a unique number that clients call to make a connection. The number consists of the network address of the machine the server is running on and the TCP/IP port that the server is using on that machine.

In order for your server to operate, it must be run on a machine that has a TCP/IP stack installed. A TCP/IP stack is the basic software used to communicate over a TCP/IP network and any computer connected to the Internet must have one running. Apart from making sure you have one, you don't need to know anything about the TCP/IP stack. (How do you know if you have one? If you can browse the Web, you have one.)

Communication between your OmniMark program and the TCP/IP stack is handled by the TCPService OMX component supplied by the TCP/IP library. Individual connections between your server and its clients are handled by the TCPConnection OMX.

To establish a service, you simply choose a port number and call the TCPServiceOpen function of the TCP library:

```
local tcpService service initial {tcpServiceOpen at port-number}
```

How do you choose a port number?

Port numbers are in the range 0 to 65535. Certain port numbers are well-known and should only be used for the service they are known for. Others belong to the system. Choosing port numbers higher than 1024 keeps you safe from any conflicts with well-known or system ports. After that, your only concern is to make sure that the port you want to use is not already in use on the machine your server will run on. My choice of 5432 as a port number in these examples has no significance other than its being easy to type and remember.

If your server program may be deployed on more than one machine, and needs a consistent port wherever it is used, you may need to do some research to determine what ports are available across all the servers in the environment you are deploying in.

The attempt to open the service may fail for a number of reasons. The most likely is that there is already a service on your machine using the port you have chosen. The TCP/IP library is not catch and throw enabled, so it won't throw to #external-exception if something goes wrong. Instead, the TCPServer OMX will be set to an error state if the service is not successfully established. You need to check for any errors before continuing and shut down the program if the service has not been successfully established. You do this with a call to the TCPServiceIsInError function:

```
throw shut-down when TCPServiceIsInError service
```

In the startup part of the program, you also need to establish any resources that will be persistent across all requests to the server. In the case of this program, there is just one such resource, the connection to the database. The database connection is established in the ordinary way:

```
local dbDatabase db initial {dbOpenODBC dsn}
```

Because the database library is catch and throw enabled, you do not have to check that this operation is successful. Any error in opening the database connection will result in a throw to #external-exception. This throw would be caught by the catch of #external-exception following the end of the request service loop. (The one inside the loop is not in scope at this point in the program and so won't be used.)

Packets

We looked a variaous network communication protocols in the last chapter. Here we use another kind of protocol: packets. A packet is a fixed-size chunk of data. To communicate using packets, you first tell the receiver how many bytes are in a packet and then you send that many bytes. If you send the whole message in one packet, you are using a single-packet protocol. If you send it as several small packets, you are using a multi-packet protocol. Multi-packet protocols can be more efficient for sending large sets of data, as you do not have to buffer the whole message while sending or receiving it.

The greatest advantage of packet-based protocols is that they work equally well for any kind of data. You do not have to worry about a false end-of-data marker in your data, because the protocol never looks at the data, it just counts bytes.

The TCP/IP protocol that transports your messages across the network also uses a multi-packet protocol. But this is not an electronic version of "pass the parcel" with your application-level packets having to fit nicely inside the communication-level packets created by the TCP/IP stack. The application-level protocol simply describes the structure of the stream of bytes that flows to the TCP/IP stack. The TCP/IP stack does not care about that structure. Its only job is to get that stream of bytes to its proper destination in the proper order. It will happily slice and dice your application-level packets to create its communication-level packets, and reliably put them together at the other end as if nothing had happened. You would have grounds for concern if the post office tried this approach with your Christmas parcels, but on the Net it is the right way to do things. You can go about your business, and let the TCP/IP stack go about its business, without worrying about it at all.

Choosing a protocol

Generally speaking, you should choose a protocol that is appropriate to the data you are sending. One implication of this is that the protocol used for the client to send data to the server need not be the same as the protocol used for the server to send data to the client. After all, the data that the client sends to the server may be very different from the data that the server sends to the client.

If you are communicating with an existing client or server, you will have to discover what protocol it uses and use that protocol yourself. If you are communicating with a server that uses a well-known higher-level protocol such as HTTP, FTP, or SMTP/POP3, you can use the appropriate OmniMark libraries for these protocols (available as part of the OmniMark Developers Network package) and leave all the details to them.

One benefit to using a line-based protocol (one that delimits a message with a line-end) is that it lets you use Telnet as a test client. This can greatly simplify development and debugging.

When in doubt, choose a multi-packet protocol. It may be overkill in some circumstances, but it will always work and it will always deal efficiently with large data sets.

Whatever protocol you choose, remember that the server and the client have to agree. Client and server must both use the same protocol for upstream communication and the same protocol for downstream communication, though the upstream and downstream protocols can be different.

Whatever protocol you choose, you will find support for it in the TCP/IP library. The TCP/IP library uses the I/O Protocol library to implement the various protocols for the appropriate functions of the TCP/IP library.

Implementing the multi-packet protocol

Our middleware application uses the multi-packet protocol for both upstream and downstream communications. Here is the code for receiving data using the multi-packet protocol:

```
local tcpConnection connection
 initial {TCPServiceAcceptConnection service}
local stream request
 initial {tcpConnectionGetSource connection
 protocol IOProtocolMultiPacket}
```

First you accept a connection from a client. (The program will stop at this line until a client connects.) When a client does connect, the TCPServiceAcceptConnection function returns a TCPConnection OMX variable that will manage this particular connection. A TCP/IP connection is a two-way communication channel. In order to get information from that channel, you need to derive an OmniMark source from the connection. You do this with the TCPConnectionGetSource function, specifying the protocol IOProtocolMultiPacket. This is all that is required to receive data using the multi-packet protocol. From this point on you have a regular OmniMark source for the data and you can treat it as such.

Choosing the multi-packet protocol for client-to-server transmission is a little bit of overkill. The reason for not choosing the simpler line-based protocol is a trivial one: the `TCPConnectionGetLine` function appends a line feed to the end of the line it returns. It would have to be stripped out before the value was used. The multi-packet protocol gives us the value without the extraneous line feed.

Once the source is derived from the connection, the data received from this source is assigned to the variable `request`. First the program checks if the request is the poison-pill (an instruction to shut down the server, discussed below):

```
throw shut-down when request = poison-pill
```

Next it attaches a regular OmniMark stream, named `reply`, to the output side of the TCP connection using the `TCPConnectionGetOutput` function. Since the program is using the multi-packet protocol for downstream communications, the protocol is again specified as `IOProtocolMultiPacket`:

```
open reply as TCPConnectionGetOutput connection
 protocol IOProtocolMultiPacket
```

At this point, communications are all hooked up and everything else is standard OmniMark programming. Just as you would with any attached output stream, the program now makes it the current output scope:

```
using output as reply
```

Now the program queries the database and builds a response in the normal way. As always when creating an XML document, the data is submitted to find rules that escape any markup characters. Since some of the data is going into attributes, the quotation mark character must also be escaped because it is used to delimit attribute values.

Robustness

A middleware program is a server. This means it is expected to keep running and serve the needs of many clients over many days, weeks, and months without crashing or getting confused. If you experience an error you can't fix in a CGI program, you can just let the program die. The worst that will happen is that one user will not get their reply. With a server, you have to keep the program running no matter what happens.

The other key requirement of a server is that it must be in exactly the same state every time it receives a request. If the server is not in the same state each time it receives a request, it may behave inconsistently. This is not acceptable behavior for a middleware application, or any other kind of server.

Robustness refers to the ability of a server to stay running and return to a stable state when an error occurs. When you program a server, you must program for robustness. Some languages make it very difficult to program for robustness, either because they are not robust themselves or because they do not directly support features for programming robustly. Fortunately, OmniMark is ideally suited for robust server programming.

The minimum requirement of robustness is that the server must stay up and running despite an error in the execution of any one request. This is accomplished very simply by including the line

```
catch #program-error
```

at the end of the request service loop. Any error that occurs in an iteration of the request service loop (that is, in the handing of a request), and if not handled within the loop, will result in a throw to this catch. That throw will result in all of the resources local to the request loop being cleaned up, followed by a return to the top of the loop, ready for the next request.

Return to initial state

Returning to the top of the request loop ensures that the server stays running, but this is not enough if the server is not in its normal initial state. The server could start to behave erratically if you have left variables with values different from their defaults or other resources not in their default states. And this applies just as much after successful requests as after ones that had errors. No matter how the handling of one request ends – with success or failure – the server must return to the same initial state before each new request is received.

Any resources created within a loop in OmniMark will be destroyed and cleaned up after each iteration of the loop. You do not need to do any explicit cleanup. OmniMark will see to it that all internal and external resources are properly cleaned up. The resources will then be created fresh at the beginning of the next loop.

Ensuring that your server always returns to a stable state between requests, therefore, can be accomplished simply by ensuring that all the resources used to service a request are local to the request service loop. That way you will be sure that all your resources start fresh for each request.

Your watchword in developing a robust server, therefore, is to keep every resource, every variable, as local as possible, and in particular to keep everything local to the request service loop. To check your program for vulnerabilities, simply check the list of global variables and the list of variables declared local at the process rule level. Here is the complete list for customerserver.xom:

```
global integer port-number initial {5432}
global stream dsn initial {"customer"}
global stream poison-pill initial {"_die_"}
local dbDatabase db initial {dbOpenODBC dsn}
local tcpService service
  initial {tcpServiceOpen at port-number}
```

Do any of these represent a threat to the stability of our server?

port-number, dsn, and poison-pill are global constants used to establish the port to use, the database to connect to, and the poison-pill string to recognize. They are declared as global variables simply so that you can change their values in an argument file. There is no reason that any of these values should be changed during the execution of our code, so there is no threat here.

service is the OMX variable for our TCPService OMX which establishes the server and listens for requests. Obviously it cannot be local to the request loop, or there would be nothing to receive the requests.

db is the OMX variable for our database OMX which establishes our connection to an ODBC data source. db does not have to be declared at this level. It could be in the request loop. But moving it into the request loop would mean the connection to the database would have to be made fresh each time through the loop. Re-establishing the connection to the ODBC data source for every request would slow things down considerably. Here I have made a compromise of robustness for the sake of performance.

To compensate, you could provide additional error checking. Since the database library is catch and throw enabled, if you lose the database connection, any attempt to use the database will result in an #external-exception being thrown. If you can catch this exception, you can try to reconnect to the database. To do this, you place the connection to the database inside a repeat loop and place the catch at the end of the loop. Once the error is caught, the loop will repeat and the program will try again to establish the connection to the database.

The only problem in this strategy is identifying errors that indicate that the database connection is down, as opposed to other error conditions. The error code for the exception will be "OMDB501", which is the code for an error reported by the ODBC driver. The problem is that the ODBC driver can report many different types of error, and the messages are system dependent. You can scan the error message text to discover which errors to treat as database connection errors, but it will take some research into your own system to determine which messages to react to. In the code sample that follows, I look for the codes "[S1000]" and "[IM002]", which are the codes the Microsoft ODBC driver on Windows reports when it cannot find an Access database file or when the specified DSN is not found.

```
;dbrestore.xom
include "omdb.xin"
include "omutil.xin"
global stream dsn initial {"customer"}
global integer connection-failure-count
global integer max-connection-failures initial {60}
global integer connection-failure-wait-time initial {60}
process
    local dbDatabase db
    local dbField current-record variable
    local stream query

    repeat ;database connection loop
        output "Trying to connect to database%n"
        set db to dbOpenODBC dsn
        set connection-failure-count to 0
        output "Connected successfully%n"
        repeat ;request service loop

            ;receive request and service it
            ;database access code

            catch #external-exception
             identity error-code
             message error-message
               do when error-code = "OMDB501"
                and error-message
                matches any** ("[S1000]" | "[IM002]")
                  rethrow
               else
                  ;handle it here or rethrow
               done
        again
```

```
      catch #external-exception
        identity error-code
        message error-message
          do when error-code = "OMDB501"
           and error-message
           matches any** ("[S1000]" | "[IM002]")
             increment connection-failure-count
             do when connection-failure-count
              < max-connection-failures
                output "Unable to connect to database.%n"
                    || "Error message:%n"
                    || error-message
                    || "%nFailure count = "
                    || "d" % connection-failure-count
                do when connection-failure-count > 1
                    output "%nWill try again in "
                        || "d" % connection-failure-wait-time
                        || " seconds%n"
                done
             else
                output "Unable to connect to database. "
                    || "Failure count = "
                    || "d" % connection-failure-count
                    || "%nGiving up in disgust!%n"
                halt
             done
             UTIL_Sleep(connection-failure-wait-time)
              when connection-failure-count > 1
          else
             rethrow
          done
      again
```

When an #external-exception is thrown inside the request service loop, it is
caught by the catch #external-exception at the end of the loop. I check the
error code and the contents of the error message to see if it is a database connection
error. If it is, I use the keyword rethrow to pass the message on to the next catch
#external-exception. I will also rethrow it if it is an error I am unwilling or
unable to handle at this point in the program.

The next catch #external-exception occurs in the database connection loop.

(Remember that "next" here does not mean next in the lexical order of the file, but next in the current execution stack of the program.) I again check to make sure this is an error I want to handle here and `rethrow` it if it is not.

Then I increment an integer, `connection-failure-count`, to count the number of failures. If this is the first consecutive failure, I print out a message and allow the loop to repeat, thus reconnecting to the database. If the number of consecutive failures is greater than one, the program waits 60 seconds before allowing the loop to repeat, to give time for the database to come back online. After 60 attempts it gives up and halts.

Note that, by itself, this recovery strategy does not save the client's request for data. Successfully reconnecting to the database will come too late to save the client session. You could handle this by using `catch` inside the client service loop to send a try-again message to the client, or you could code the database recovery mechanism into the client service loop itself so as to recover the database connection without losing the client session.

Handling startup errors

There is one other time when a server can fail. The server program may never get to the point where it can create the service at all. This can occur if the TCP/IP service cannot be established (perhaps because the port is already in use), or if global resources, such as the connection to the database, cannot be created.

If a server fails to start, it should report the reason for its failure on the command line. This program does some of this by adding a `catch #program-error` to the end of the process rule and outputting the error message that accompanies the throw.

```
catch #external-exception
  identity id
  message msg
  location loc
    output "Error:%n"
        || "ID: %g(id)%n"
        || "Msg: %g(msg)%n"
        || "Loc: %g(loc)%n"
```

This will take care of reporting errors for any resources that are catch and throw enabled. Since the TCP/IP library is not catch and throw enabled, a different system will be needed to handle a failure to start the service. Half the job is done by the catch of `shut-down`, however, this does no reporting. I leave it as an exercise for you to add the appropriate reporting code. To test your reporting code, start one copy of the server, and then start up another copy on the same machine. The second copy will fail to start because the first is using the port. You should see the appropriate error message.

Poison pill

Server programs run remotely, and it is useful to have a way to shut them down by remote control. This becomes particularly important if you use OmniMark Technologies' SureSpeed™ load manager to dynamically load and run multiple copies of servers as needed. SureSpeed makes clones of servers as required to meet demand. When demand declines, it shuts down unneeded clones so that it can use the processing resources for a service in higher demand. SureSpeed needs a way to tell a server to shut down.

The solution is a poison pill. A poison pill is a special request, sent by a client, that the server program interprets as an instruction to shut itself down. In the application, the default value of the poison pill is the string "_die_". I use a global stream to hold the poison pill so that you can change it in an arguments file.

I test for the poison pill in the following line:

```
throw shut-down when request = poison-pill
```

To shut down the server, all I have to do is exit the connection loop. I do this with a throw to a catch named **shut-down** which is outside the connection loop. This initiates an orderly shutdown of the connection. Once outside the loop, the program runs to its natural end, cleanly terminating the server.

In this case, since I am only exiting a single repeat loop, I could simply have used the line:

```
exit when request = poison-pill
```

But using throw and catch is preferable for two reasons:

First, it is more general and will work even from within several levels of nested loops. This is important for scalability. As your program grows and adds levels of nesting, your catch-and-throw-based control mechanisms will continue to work correctly and without modification.

Second, it is more explicit and thus easier to read. The ability to produce highly readable programs is one of the key reasons to use OmniMark, and using catch and throw to make program flow more explicit is an important part of writing readable OmniMark programs.

Building a client

A client is simpler to build than a server. Like a server, it must be able to establish a TCP/IP connection, but a client does not have to establish a service, process multiple requests, or return to a stable state.

To initiate a conversation with a server, the client attempts to open a connection:

```
set connection to TCPConnectionOpen on "localhost" at 5432
```

Because the TCP/IP library is not catch and throw enabled, I have to check to make sure the connection succeeded:

```
throw connection-error when TCPConnectionIsInError connection
```

Once I know that I have a good connection, I attach a stream to the connection, specifying that the IOProtocolMultiPacket protocol be used for transmission. Then I send it the request, which is the customer ID for the customer data I want. Since I am sending only a single value, I can do it all with a single set statement:

```
set TCPConnectionGetOutput connection
  protocol IOProtocolMultiPacket
  to #args[1]
```

Having sent the request, I derive a source from the connection so that I can receive the reply. Since all I want to do in this stub client is make sure I am getting back the data I expected, I can do it all in a single output statement:

```
output TCPConnectionGetSource connection
  protocol IOProtocolMultiPacket
```

Client programming in OmniMark is that simple. You establish a TCP/IP connection. You attach a stream to the sending side of the connection, derive a source from the receiving side, and program as usual.

A poison pill client

Here is a special client designed for sending poison pill messages. All the key variables can be set from the command line or an argument file, so you can use this client as a general tool for shutting down servers that use poison pills and communicate using the multi-packet protocol.

```
;killmp.xom
;Kills a server using the multi-packet protocol
include "omtcp.xin"
declare catch connection-error
global stream server initial {"localhost"}
global stream port initial {"5432"}
global stream poison-pill initial {"_die_"}

process
   local TCPConnection connection
   local stream s

   set connection to TCPConnectionOpen on server at port
   throw connection-error
    when TCPConnectionIsInError connection

   set TCPConnectionGetOutput connection
    protocol IOProtocolMultiPacket
    to poison-pill

   catch connection-error
      output "error"
```

Dynamic initialization

This program takes advantage of OmniMark's dynamic initialization capability.
Dynamic initialization provides a shortcut for those situations in which you first
declare a variable and then immediately give it a value in a set statement that
takes a dynamic expression as its argument:

```
local tcpConnection connection
set connection to TCPServiceAcceptConnection service
```

You can consolidate this into a single statement by using dynamic initialization:

```
local tcpConnection connection
 initial {TCPServiceAcceptConnection service}
```

You can use one dynamically initialized variable in another dynamic initializer.
Naturally, you must follow the order of operations as you would for a set operation.
A variable must be initialized before it is used:

```
local tcpConnection connection
 initial {TCPServiceAcceptConnection service}
```

```
local stream request
 initial {tcpConnectionGetSource connection
 protocol IOProtocolMultiPacket}
local stream query initial
 {"SELECT * FROM Customer WHERE CustomerID='%g(request)'"}
```

Syntax

These are the new syntax items introduced in this chapter.

TCPServiceOpen

You can use the TCPServiceOpen function to create a TCP/IP service. Establishing a service opens a port, allowing your program to receive connections. You need to establish a service in order to receive connection requests, but not in order to send them. In other words, a server needs to establish a service, but a client does not.

The TCPServiceOpen function returns an OMX variable of type TCPService that represents the service that has been created. You use this variable to refer to the service in other functions of the TCP/IP library.

The syntax is:

```
set <TCP Service> to TCPServiceOpen at <Port Number>
```

where <TCP service> is a variable of type TCP service and <Port Number> is an integer expression representing the chosen port.

Example:

```
set service to TCPServiceOpen at 5600
```

TCPServiceAcceptConnection

You can use the TCPServiceAcceptConnection function to listen for and accept TCP/IP connections in a server loop.

The TCPServiceAcceptConnection function takes a TCPService variable as an argument and returns a TCPConnection variable representing the OMX component that handles the connection.

The TCPServiceAcceptConnection function is used in a server to listen on the port opened by TCPServiceOpen. It is not used in a client program.

The syntax is:

```
set <TCP connection> to TCPServiceAcceptConnection <TCP Service>
```

where <TCP connection> is a variable of type TCPConnection and <TCP Service> is a variable of type <TCP Service>.

Example:

```
set connection to TCPServiceAcceptConnection service
```

TCPConnectionGetSource

You can use the function TCPConnectionGetSource to make a TCP connection the current input source. Possible uses include:

```
using input as TCPConnectionGetSource connection
 protocol IOProtocolMultiPacket
 do
   ...
 done

submit TCPConnectionGetSource connection
 protocol IOProtocolMultiPacket

do XML parse document
 scan TCPConnectionGetSource connection
 protocol IOProtocolMultiPacket
   ...
done

output TCPConnectionGetSource connection
     protocol IOProtocolMultiPacket
```

Review

The following are the main points covered in this chapter. If you don't understand any of the statements below, go back and review the material in this chapter before you go on.

- A server program has three basic parts: the startup routine, the request service loop, and the shutdown routine.
- A server must be placed into service on a particular port on a particular machine. The server then waits for clients to connect.

- OmniMark manages client-server communications using two OMX components — TCPService and TCPConnection.
- The TCP/IP library is not catch and throw enabled, so you must check for errors when establishing a service or a connection.
- A protocol is an agreement between a client and a server about how the two will communicate. There are multiple layers of protocols involved in any client-server connection.
- The protocol you choose should be appropriate to the data you are sending. For this reason, you may choose a different protocol for upstream and downstream communications.
- A server must be robust. Errors in processing a request must not bring down the server. Placing a catch of #program-error at the bottom of the request service loop gives you this kind of robustness, though it does nothing to salvage the request that experienced the error.
- A server must return to the same initial state after each request, whether or not an error occurs. To achieve this, keep as many variables as possible local to the request loop.
- You can use a poison pill to shut down a server remotely.
- It is often preferable to use catch and throw for flow control even in situations where a simple loop exit will work. Later edits may introduce new levels of nesting that will cause the loop exit to not work anymore. The catch and throw mechanism will continue to work correctly even if many more layers of nesting are added.
- A client program does not need to establish a TCP service. It just makes a connection to an established server.

Exercises

1. Adapt the killmp.xom program to accept a command-line parameter specifying the protocol to use and use that parameter to select the protocol to use. This will give you a truly general kill program. Write test servers using the various available protocols in order to test the kill program.
2. Add logging to the server application so that errors are recorded. If you are really ambitious, have the server mail an error report to the administrator when an error occurs.

15: A client for the middleware application

Now that the middleware server is working, it is time to build a client to communicate with it. This client doesn't do anything fancy with the data. It just processes the XML and creates HTML output. There are, of course, many different applications that would want to access customer data. All those that use the customer.xom to retrieve that information will have one thing in common: they will need to process the XML they receive. This client lets us explore XML processing with OmniMark.

```
;customerclient.xom
include "omtcp.xin"
declare catch connection-error
declare catch abort-parse

process
   local TCPConnection connection
    initial {TCPConnectionOpen on "localhost" at 5432}
   throw connection-error
    when TCPConnectionIsInError connection

   set TCPConnectionGetOutput connection
    protocol IOProtocolMultiPacket
    to #args[1]
```

```
do xml-parse
 scan TCPConnectionGetSource connection
 protocol IOProtocolMultiPacket
   output "<HTML><HEAD></HEAD><BODY>%c"
   always
      output "</BODY></HTML>"
done

catch abort-parse
catch connection-error
   output "Unable to connect.%n"

element "customer"
   do scan attribute "status"
      match "ok" =|
         output "%c"
      match "error" =|
         output "Sorry, customer information "
            || "is not available at this time."
            || " Please check back later.%n"
         throw abort-parse
      match "notfound" =|
         output "Sorry, there is no "
            || "record of that customer.%n"
         throw abort-parse
      else
         output "Sorry, an error has occurred. "
            || "Please try again later.%n"
         throw abort-parse
   done

element "name"
   output "<H2>Name</H2>%v(title) %v(first) %v(last)%n%c"

element "address"
   output "<H2>Contact information</H2>%c"

element ("phone" | "fax" | "pager")
   output "<H3>"
      || name of element
      || "</H3>%c"

element "mail"
```

```
    output "<H3>mail</H3>"
        || "%v(street)<BR>%n%v(city)<BR>%n%v(state)<BR>%n"
        || "%v(country)<BR>%n%v(code)<BR>%n%c"

element "id"
    suppress

markup-error
    output "Sorry, an error has occurred. "
        || "Please try again later.%n"
        || "Error: " || #message
    throw abort-parse
```

Technique

We have looked at several programs that generate XML data, but this client is the
first program that processes XML to create another form of output.

XML processing

I should begin the discussion of XML processing by making a firm distinction
between XML parsing and XML processing. XML parsing is the process of
recognizing the syntax of an XML document and breaking down that document into
its constituent parts. XML processing is doing something with the data exposed by
the parser.

Stand-alone parsers need to provide an interface that a programming language can
use to access the data. The two most common are the DOM (Document Object
Model) and SAX (Simple API for XML). The DOM specifies the object model of a
data structure that the parser will build and the program will subsequently access.
SAX specifies an event-based API, which various languages can use to receive
reports of parser events as they occur.

OmniMark's XML parser is integrated into the language and does not require either
of these interfaces. Instead, the OmniMark XML parser integrates with the rule-
based structure of the OmniMark language. OmniMark has a number of specialized
rule types designed for XML (and SGML) parsing. The most important of these rule
types is the element rule.

XML processing is initiated by the following code block:

```
do xml-parse
 scan TCPConnectionGetSource connection
 protocol IOProtocolMultiPacket
    output "<HTML><HEAD></HEAD><BODY>%c"
    always
        output "</BODY></HTML>"
done
```

The xml-parse keyword initiates parsing of the XML document. The xml-parse keyword is always used in the body of a do block. In fact, do xml-parse constitutes a special kind of do block structure. Within the body of the do xml-parse block, many pieces of information about the XML document being parsed are available, though I don't need any of this information in this program.

The scan keyword introduces the XML document to be parsed. In this program I take that document directly from the TCP/IP connection.

The do xml-parse structure warms up the parser, but does not actually start it parsing. Actually kicking the parsing process into gear is the job of the *parse continuation operator*, which takes the form of a text escape "%c". You must call "%c" once (and only once) in the body of the do xml-parse block to actually commence parsing. It follows that any actions before "%c" occur before the document is parsed, and any actions after it occur after the document is parsed.

This makes it very easy to output the beginning and ending tags of an HTML document with a statement like this:

```
output "<HTML><HEAD></HEAD><BODY>%c</BODY></HTML>"
```

This statement will cause the string "<HTML><HEAD></HEAD><BODY>" to be output. When "%c" occurs, execution of the output statement is suspended and the entire document is parsed, which will cause other output to be generated. Once the parse is complete, execution of this statement resumes and the string "</BODY></HTML>" is output, wrapping the output of the XML processing in the required HTML tagging.

This program is almost this simple, but because I have to handle error conditions and put out the error messages as valid HTML, I put the output of the closing tags into an always statement:

```
output "<HTML><HEAD></HEAD><BODY>%c"
always
    output "</BODY></HTML>"
```

This ensures that even if the parse is aborted because of an error, the ending tags will still be output.

Element rules

Once the parsing of the document commences, element rules are fired as the parser identifies the relevant elements. Once an element rule (or any other kind of markup rule) fires, the parser pauses and you have to kick it into gear again with a call to "%c". You must call "%c" once and only once in the course of processing each markup rule.

The first rule to fire will be the rule for the root element, "customer". The principal thing I am interested in from the customer element is the value of the status attribute. It will determine how to handle the rest of the file. I access that value with the attribute operator.

```
do scan attribute "status"
```

The attribute operator returns the value of the named attribute. Thus the code above returns the value of the attribute "status" of the current element. I then use do scan to select the appropriate action to take based on that value.

If the value is "ok" I kick the parser back to life with output "%c". output "%c" by itself does not, in this case, create any output. I am simply using an output statement here as a carrier for "%c". "%c" takes the form of a text escape because it is almost always used in the context of generating output data. There are times, though, when you simply want to restart the parser, and in these cases you just use output "%c" by itself.

In an element with data content, such as "fax", output "%c" does create output, but it results in the data content of the element being output. This does not happen because "%c" actually returns the data content, but because the parser outputs data content to the current output scope, which is always the output scope in which the current "%c" occurs.

In the case of the other two status values, I output an appropriate message and, since I am not interested in the rest of the document, I abort the parse. I don't need any special language to abort a parse. Simply throwing to a catch outside the do xml-parse block that initiated the parse will do it. Shutting down the parser is a part of the normal cleanup that OmniMark does in executing this throw. (Note, by the way, that any throw from a markup rule will abort the parse and can only be caught outside the do xml-parse block. Parsing is an inherently linear process, and you cannot use catch and throw to jump about from one markup rule to another. You can, however, use catch and throw within the body of a single markup rule or code called from it.)

Note that I do not call "%c" in these two match alternatives. Since I am aborting the parse, there is no point in trying to continue it.

The next rule that will fire is the "id" element rule. I am not interested in the ID, so I use the **suppress** keyword in place of **output "%c"**. (Alternatively, you could compare it to the value sent in the request, as a form of error checking.)

The next rule that will fire is the "name" element rule. Here you can see why using attributes for the component parts of a name makes for easier processing. You can simply pull all the attributes together and output them at once:

```
output "<H2>Name</H2>%v(title) %v(first) %v(last)%n%c"
```

This line uses the "%v" format item, which is an inline shortcut for the **attribute** operator. "%v" is followed by the name of the attribute in parentheses. Using "%v" lets us write the single output line above rather than having to write:

```
output "<H2>"
    || attribute "title"
    || " "
    || attribute "first"
    || " "
    || attribute "last"
    || "%n</H2>%c"
```

The other rules are fired as the elements occur. Unlike find rules, the order in which element rules occur in the program does not matter at all. The parser alone determines the order in which they are called, driven entirely by the input data. At any time during the parse there must be one and only one element rule that can fire for the current element.

Note that element rules for nested elements are themselves nested in the execution of the program. When the "mail" element rule fires, it is as a consequence of the parse continued from the "address" element, which is in a state of suspended execution at the point at which "%c" occurs. This is true all the way back to the "%c" in the do xml-parse block. This nested execution occurs dynamically, driven by the order of elements in the data. It is easier to see this than to say it, so step through the program in the IDE until you are comfortable with how XML processing works.

It is possible to write a rule that covers more than one element:

```
element  ("phone" | "fax" | "pager")
    output "<H3>"
        || name of element
        || "</H3>%c"
```

The name of the current element is one of the many pieces of information available from the parser as a document is being parsed. Here I use it to output headings for the various pieces of information covered by the rule.

The "%q" format item also returns the name of the current element, so I could rewrite the above rule like this:

```
element ("phone" | "fax" | "pager")
    output "<H3>%q</H3>%c"
```

But in this case the gain in brevity probably isn't worth the loss in clarity.

Handling XML errors

It is always possible that the XML data the program receives may be invalid in some way. Detecting and recovering from invalid data is the parser's business. You just have to decide what to do if the parser reports a markup error. You can do this with a markup-error rule.

```
markup-error
    output "Sorry, an error has occurred. "
        || "Please try again later.%n"
    throw abort-parse
```

Note two things about this rule:

First, a markup error does not cause the parser to abort the parse. The parser will always recover from a markup error and continue parsing. You have to make the decision whether or not the error is fatal and whether or not you want to try to repair it. In most cases you will simply reject the document if it is not valid. I do this here with the throw to abort-parse.

Second, a markup error does not create a throw, either to #program-error or anywhere else. An error in the markup of an XML document is not an error in your program. It is simply an event that the parser reports to you by firing an OmniMark rule.

Syntax

These are the new syntax items introduced in this chapter.

do xml-parse

You can use do xml-parse to initiate parsing of an XML document.

There are a number of parts to the do xml-parse block, and you should refer to the OmniMark documentation for the full story. Here I will break down a typical call to do xml-parse that will cover your needs in most cases. Consider the following snippet of code:

```
do xml-parse
    scan file "foo.xml"
    output "<HTML>%c</HTML>"
done
```

The keyword **scan** introduces the source of the XML data. It can be any OmniMark source. Note that this does not initiate an OmniMark scanning operation. Rather, it is an instruction to the parser to scan this source. You now leave it to the parser to recognize patterns in the data, according to the rules of XML, and report the structure of the XML document to you by firing markup rules.

At this point, I have set up the source to be parsed, but I have not actually started parsing. To actually start the parse I must output the parse continuation operator "%c". This begins the recursive process of processing the element structure of a hierarchical document. I will use "%c" again in each element rule to kick the parser back to life.

After the "%c" I can perform any actions that I want to perform after the parsing is complete, such as outputting closing wrapper markup like "</HTML>".

element

The keyword **element** introduces an element rule. The parser fires an element rule whenever it encounters an element of the appropriate name. Thus when the parser encounters an element named "product" it will fire the element rule:

```
element "product"
```

Within an element rule you can do anything you can do in a find rule, but at some point in the rule you must kick the parser back to life again by outputting "%c".

Any actions you place before the "%c" take place before the element is processed. Any actions you place after the "%c" take place after the content of the element is parsed.

%c

The keyword "%c" is the parse continuation operator. The parser pauses each time it fires a markup rule, giving you the opportunity to process the element. You must restart the parser by outputting "%c". Since the parser outputs the data content of an element to current output scope, thus placing it where "%c" occurs in an output string, you can think of "%c" as in some sense representing the content of the element. However, you cannot use "%c" twice in a markup rule in an attempt to access the content of the element again. The first instance of "%c" causes the content of the current element to be parsed. The second instance would occur after the content had been parsed and it could not parse it again.

suppress

The suppress keyword is an alternative to "%c". It causes the parser to continue, but suppresses all output. This includes both output generated by the parser and output generated by code in any child elements.

suppress creates a new output scope with the #suppress stream as its destination. You can use using output as or output-to to create a new output scope or to attach a different destination to the current one, just as you would with any other output scope.

attribute

You can access any attribute of the current element using the keyword attribute. Thus to access an attribute named "number" from the element "product", you would write:

```
element "product"
   local stream id-number
   set id-number to attribute "number"
```

%v

Since you often want to output the content of an attribute in a text string, you can use the format item "%v" as a shortcut for the attribute keyword:

```
element "product"
   output "Product %c has id %v(number)"
```

| (or)

You can use the "or" operator | to join the names of multiple elements where you want one element rule to handle more than one element:

```
element  ("phone" | "fax" | "pager")
```

Review

The following are the main points covered in this chapter. If you don't understand any of the statements below, go back and review the material in this chapter before you go on.

- XML parsing is the process of recognizing XML markup. XML processing is the manipulation of the structure of an XML document (as exposed by the parser). Parsing is the responsibility of OmniMark's XML parser. Processing is your responsibility.
- OmniMark's parser is integrated into the language, so a parser API such as DOM or SAX is not needed.
- The parser reports the structure of the document it is parsing by firing markup rules, mostly element rules. You process the XML data by writing the appropriate code in the markup rules.
- XML processing is recursive. A hierarchy of rules are fired following the hierarchy of elements in the document being processed. Each rule is suspended at the point where "%c" occurs until processing of its child elements is completed.
- A throw from an element rule that is not caught in the same rule aborts the entire parse.
- The parser outputs all data content to the current output scope.
- You can retrieve the value of an attribute using the attribute keyword.
- An error in an XML document is not an error in your program and does not cause a throw. Instead, an error in your XML document is a markup event which triggers a markup-error rule, if you provide one.

Exercises

1. Build your own exercise. Go out and find some XML on the Web or create some yourself. Write an OmniMark program to translate that XML file into HTML or another format of your choosing.

2. Experiment with using XML for inter-process communication. Instead of sending a document, write a client and server that communicate with each other by sending requests and replies as XML.
3. This program outputs HTML, but it is not an interactive application. Rewrite this program as a forms based CGI program so that the user can enter a customer code and get back the information in their browser.

16: Database update via the Web

In this chapter, I will demonstrate a simple update utility that will let someone add customers to the customer database used in the last two chapters. I will use an HTML form to gather the data. The principal language feature introduced in this chapter is buffers. Memory buffers in OmniMark are, as you will see, just another data source and destination which you can create and process using streaming techniques.

The home page of the application presents a list of the customer names and customer IDs. From the home page, you can click on any customer ID to get to the customer detail screen. You can also click the [NEW] button to add a new customer.

The customer detail page shows all the information for a particular customer and gives you the option to edit or delete this customer or to add a new customer.

The customer edit page is a form with the existing values filled in. You can submit changes or cancel the edit.

The customer edit page.

The new page presents the same form, only blank.

Adding or editing a record returns you to the detail page for that record.

Deleting a record returns you to the home page. There is no confirmation of a delete. You can add that yourself.

The program is structured like the other CGI programs in this book. It uses extra path information to select the operation to perform and uses a function to implement each function. This program makes use of additional HTTP headers such as Date, Expires, and Location to ensure that pages are not cached and that updates don't happen twice. For this reason, the HTTP header, which has been output in the process rule in previous programs, is not output separately in each function, allowing each function to output an appropriate header.

The functions that actually update the database do not return a page. If they did so, a user could accidentally perform the same update again simply by refreshing the page. Instead of displaying a page, they use the "303 See other" HTTP response and a Location header to redirect the browser to one of the display functions. Doing a refresh of the page displayed by the display function simply results in a refresh of the displayed page.

You will find the program in Appendix 3.

Technique

Database update

You update a database by sending the appropriate SQL statement using the dbExecute function of the database library:

```
dbExecute db sql query
```

You can use **dbExecute** to send any SQL statement that does not return data. (For statements that return data, you use the **dbQuery** function.) You should consult the documentation for your database system to determine the exact SQL syntax it expects. However, you will find the SQL statements used here to update a record and to add a new record will work in most cases. Sending these SQL statements to the database is not the interesting part of this program. The interesting part is gathering the data and constructing the SQL statements.

Buffers

In this program, I need to build up complex SQL statements using data drawn from several form fields and processed using find rules. However, I cannot simply stream the data to its final destination as I have done in previous programs. The SQL statement I am building must be passed as a parameter to a function in the OmniMark database library. You cannot stream data to a function argument. And if I tried to build up the statement by progressive string concatenation, I would have a lot of bulky code and some additional logic in the find rules to figure out which string I was building at any given moment.

To solve this problem, we turn to buffers. An OmniMark buffer is, as you would expect, simply an area of computer memory. However, in OmniMark you can treat a buffer just like any other data destination: you can attach a stream to it, make that stream the current output scope, and stream data to the buffer. This is what I do in the lines:

```
open query as buffer
using output as query
```

OmniMark buffers are never named. They can only be created by opening a stream with a buffer as its attachment. The buffer exists as long as the stream is attached to it. To manipulate them, you use the attached stream. To read the data from a buffer, you close the stream and then use the stream name as if it were a source name:

```
close query
set db to dbOpenODBC dsn
dbExecute db sql query
```

Actually, we have been using buffers for a while. Whenever a program has used a stream variable to hold a string value, it has in fact been using a stream attached to a buffer. The first time you use set on an unattached stream variable, OmniMark attaches a buffer to the stream and streams the data to the buffer. So the statement:

```
set query to "SELECT * FROM Customer WHERE CustomerID='"
          || cgi-data {"QUERY_STRING"}
          || "'"
```

is creating and using a buffer just like the open ... using ... output ... close sequence explained above. Since you have already seen that you can use set to write the complete contents of a file, the equivalence of these two methods should not come as a great surprise. OmniMark streams are the great equalizers.

Escaping characters for different encodings

Previous programs have used submit and a set of find rules to escape characters that would be mistaken for markup when creating HTML pages from data in a database. This program creates data in three different languages, HTML, SQL, and URL encoding. When creating data in any of these languages, you have to make sure that any characters that require special coding are appropriately marked up. This program does this the same way as before, by submitting the data to find rules that do the required encoding. But now there are three different encoding schemes to deal with. How do we separate the find rules used for each of the encodings?

Rules in an OmniMark program can be combined into groups. By default, all the rules in a program are in a single group called #implied. You can create other groups with the group keyword followed by a group name:

```
group html-escaping
```

All rules following this group declaration belong to the group named in the declaration. To use the rules in a particular group, you use a using group statement:

```
using group html-escaping
  do
    ...
  done
```

Like the other using keywords, using group creates a scope in which the named group is the current set of rules. That set of rules will be used by any submit statements that occur, as long as that rule scope is in force. Remember that using statements are prefixes to other statements. You can apply more than one using statement to a statement or block:

```
using output as query
using group sql-escaping
  do
    ...
  done
```

This creates a do block with an output scope that is the stream query and a group scope that is the group sql-escaping. All output generated within that output scope (including, of course, in find rules fired as the result of a submit in that output scope) go to query. All the submits called in that rule scope use the find rules in the sql-escaping group.

Syntax

These are the new syntax items introduced in this chapter.

group

You can use the group declaration to divide the rules that make up your program into different groups. You can then make a particular group active with the using group statement or the next group is statement (see the OmniMark documentation for this one.)

By default, all rules are in the group #implied. Any rule that appears before a group statement is in the group #implied. You can also place rules in group #implied explicitly with the statement:

group #implied

When your program starts, group #implied is active and all other groups are inactive. It follows that you must have a process rule in group #implied in order to activate any other groups.

using group

You can use using group to create an execution scope in which a certain group of rules is active. Remember that the #implied group of rules is always active. It is not disabled when you activate another group.

dbExecute

You can use the dbExecute function from the OMDB library to send an SQL statement to a database. Use dbExecute for SQL statements that do not return data (for example, statements that add records or edit existing records). Use dbQuery for statements that return data.

dbExecute db sql query

Review

The following are the main points covered in this chapter. If you don't understand any of the statements below, go back and review the material in this chapter before you go on.

- You can update a database by building an update statement in SQL and sending that statement to the database using the dbExecute function.
- When you use an OmniMark stream variable as a string variable, you are in fact creating a buffer. You can output data to a buffer, just as you would any other data destination. You can process the data in a buffer just as you would any other data source.
- You can use groups to turn sets of rules on and off as needed.

Exercises

1. While the display program accesses the data in this database through a middleware application, the update utility talks to the database directly. Create a middleware application to handle the database updating and adapt the client in this chapter to communicate with that middleware application using XML.

17: A mailbot

In Chapter 13, I showed a CGI script that took form data and sent it to an email address using XML. In this chapter, I will build a mailbot that will regularly check a mail box, download the messages, find the XML portion of the message, process the XML and update a database.

While our form mail script is generic, this mailbot needs to be specific to a particular database and form. I will use the same customer database we used in Chapter 16. Here is the HTML page you can use with the form mailer to create the emails:

```
<HTML><BODY>
<H1>Customer Database</H1>
<H2>New customer</H2>
<FORM METHOD="POST" ACTION="/scripts/formmail1.xom">
<TABLE>
 <TR>
  <TD>CustomerID</TD>
  <TD><INPUT TYPE="text" NAME="CustomerID"></TD>
 </TR>
 <TR>
  <TD>Title</TD>
  <TD><INPUT TYPE="text" NAME="Title"></TD>
 </TR>
 <TR>
```

```
  <TD>First name</TD>
  <TD><INPUT TYPE="text" NAME="FirstName"></TD>
 </TR>
 <TR>
  <TD>Last name</TD>
  <TD><INPUT TYPE="text" NAME="LastName"></TD>
 </TR>
 <TR>
  <TD>Address</TD>
  <TD><INPUT TYPE="text" NAME="Address"></TD>
 </TR>
 <TR>
  <TD>City</TD>
  <TD><INPUT TYPE="text" NAME="City"></TD>
 </TR>
 <TR>
  <TD>State</TD>
  <TD><INPUT TYPE="text" NAME="State"></TD>
 </TR>
 <TR>
  <TD>Country</TD>
  <TD><INPUT TYPE="text" NAME="Country"></TD>
 </TR>
 <TR>
  <TD>Code</TD>
  <TD><INPUT TYPE="text" NAME="Code"></TD>
 </TR>
 <TR>
  <TD>Phone:</TD>
  <TD><INPUT TYPE="text" NAME="Phone"></TD>
 </TR>
 <TR>
  <TD>Fax</TD>
  <TD><INPUT TYPE="text" NAME="Fax"></TD>
 </TR>
 <TR>
  <TD>Pager</TD>
  <TD><INPUT TYPE="text" NAME="Pager"></TD>
 </TR>
</TABLE>
<INPUT TYPE="submit" NAME="Submit" VALUE="Submit">
<INPUT TYPE="reset" VALUE="Reset">
</FORM>
```

Use this form along with the form mailer from Chapter 13 to generate mail for the mailbot to check.

You will find the code for the mailbot itself in Appendix 3.

The operation of the program is straightforward. It then enters a loop that has a time delay built in (defined, in seconds, by the global variable sleep-time). Each time through the loop it checks the mail box, using the function MailInBoxGetNumberOfMessages from the ommail library to determine how many messages are waiting.

The program then enters another loop and downloads each waiting message in turn. It scans each message to find the XML content and then parses the XML and updates the database. I have taken a little bit of a shortcut by assuming that the names of the fields on the HTML form match the names of the fields in the database. This simplifies the program. Of course, you won't always be able to make this assumption.

Because of this shortcut, the program is mostly generic. Only the query is specific to the database. You can adapt this program to a different database simply by replacing the to portion of the set statement with a query for another database.

Of course, you will probably want to implement more specific business logic and validity checking than I do here. This program does no validity checking itself, though it relies on the database to check that the data meets it standards.

The program takes a very conservative approach to emails that cannot be processed successfully. It waits until the database update has succeeded before marking a message for deletion. This means that it will keep trying to process those messages repeatedly until someone removes them from the mail server by hand. This ensures that no data is lost. You may wish to take a more aggressive approach with unprocessable data.

Technique

The mailbot program is a cross between a client and a server. Like a server program it runs continually, has a loop at its heart, and needs to be robust so that it stays up and returns to the same ready state between circuits of the loop. Unlike a server, it does not establish a TCP/IP service or accept connections from clients. Instead it acts as a client of two other services, the mail server and the database, and periodically transfers data from one to the other.

The "repeat for" loop

This program introduces another looping structure, the repeat for loop. This is the structure that is called a "for loop" in many other languages, but in OmniMark, all loops start with repeat and end with again, so the "for" loop is repeat for. In this program, the repeat for loop is used to download each message in a mailbox in turn:

```
repeat for integer message-number
 from 1 to message-count
   output "RETR " || "d" % message-number || crlf
   ...
again
```

The for clause declares a control variable of type integer named message-number. The from clause specifies its value for the first iteration of the loop. The to clause specifies its value for the last iteration of the loop (the variable message-count). The value of message-number will be incremented by one on each repetition of the loop. The loop will exit when the value of message-number exceeds the value of message-count.

Using referents in a persistent program

In any persistent program such as a server or this mailbot, any referents used must be inside a nested referent scope. Referents are not resolved until the referent scope they are created in ends. Since the default referent scope is the program as a whole, referents outside the referent scope defined by a using nested referents are not resolved until the program terminates. Since a server or the mailbot hopefully will not terminate for weeks or months, the program can't wait that long. Therefore, if you use referents in any kind of persistent program, make sure you establish a nested referents scope.

In this case I am using referents to fill in values in the SQL update query. This takes place inside a repeat loop that is moving through the messages in the mailbox. Since I need referents resolved before I send each update query, I need to establish the nested referent scope inside the repeat loop.

```
repeat for integer message-number
 from 1 to message-count
   output "RETR " || "d" % message-number || crlf
   using nested-referents
   do
     set query
      with referents-allowed
```

```
      defaulting {""}
      to "INSERT INTO Customer ("
      || "CustomerID, "
      || "Title, "
      || "FirstName, "
      || "LastName, "
      || "Address, "
      || "City, "
      || "State, "
      || "Country, "
      || "Code, "
      || "Phone, "
      || "Fax, "
      || "Pager) VALUES ('"
      || referent "CustomerID" || "', '"
      || referent "Title" || "', '"
      || referent "FirstName" || "', '"
      || referent "LastName" || "', '"
      || referent "Address" || "', '"
      || referent "City" || "', '"
      || referent "State" || "', '"
      || referent "Country" || "', '"
      || referent "Code" || "', '"
      || referent "Phone" || "', '"
      || referent "Fax" || "', '"
      || referent "Pager" || "')"

    do xml-parse
      scan input get-mail-message connection
        suppress
      done
    done
  dbExecute db sql query

  output "DELE " || "d" % message-number  || crlf
  set response to tcpConnectionGetLine connection
  put #error response
again
```

Combining scanning and parsing

The message retrieved from the mail server is an email message containing an XML document. In addition, it contains the double-period encoding of any periods at the end of lines. (This encoding is used to protect the end of data maker, CRLF ".."

CRLF, described in Chapter 13. In order to use the XML document I need to remove this encoding from the message and strip away the headers before submitting the XML to the parser.

I do this using an input function to feed the parser. The input keyword in a do xml-parse statement lets you designate a function whose output will become the input of the parser:

```
do xml-parse
 scan input get-mail-message connection
   suppress
 done
```

The function get-mail-message and the parser will then run as co-routines. The function will run for a while, then the parser will run and consume the data produced by the function. Then the function will start up again to create more data. The parser and the input function run in turn until all the data is consumed and processed.

This allows me to stream the original message through a scanning process and a parser in a single stream, without having to buffer the output of the scanning before feeding it to the parser.

The input function itself is just an ordinary function:

```
define function get-mail-message
 value tcpconnection connection
 as
    do scan tcpConnectionGetSource connection
     protocol ioprotocolEndDelimited (crlf || '.' || crlf)
      match any** lookahead ul "<?xml "
         submit #current-input
    done
```

Notice that it is not a value-returning function. The effect of the keyword input is to create an output scope that is bound to the input of the parser and then to call the function in that input scope. Therefore, any output generated by the function, or any code called as a result of actions in the function, such as submit, go to the parser.

The function itself just uses a do scan to strip off everything before the XML declaration that begins the XML document. It then submits #current-input to a find rule that removes the double-period encoding. The output — the XML document — streams to the parser. (Technically speaking, I should do double-period decoding on the entire message — you should decode data in the reverse order of its encoding — but I don't care about the headers, so why bother decoding them?)

Syntax

These are the new syntax items introduced in this chapter.

input

You can use the input keyword in a do xml-parse action to instruct the parser to take its input from the output of a function. You can use the function to initiate a scanning process, so that the output of the scanning process becomes the input of the parser. This has many uses. For instance, if you write a program that generates an XML document, you can use the parser to check that the document you create is well formed. The input function would look like this:

```
define function generate-xml as
   using output as #current-output & output-file
      submit file #args[1]
```

The XML is generated by the find rules that process the submitted document. The using output as statement direct the output of the find rules simultaneous to the parser and the output file. (#current-output represents the current output scope, which will be the parser when the function is called as an input function.

The corresponding do xml-parse statement will look like this:

```
do xml-parse
 scan input generate-xml
 suppress
done
```

And the program will contain a single element rule:

```
element #implied
   suppress
```

And a markup-error rule:

```
markup-error
   throw you-made-bad-xml
```

All output from the parser is suppressed, because we want the original output of the find rules to go to the file. In effect, the parser is receiving a copy of that document and will throw you-made-bad-xml if it finds a markup error in the document.

An input function and the parser run as co-routines, which means that the data is not buffered between the scanning process and the parsing process. This allows you to process very large input files without using a lot of resources in the processing.

It also means that the scanning process will be aborted as soon an error is found by the scanning process, rather than running the scanning process to the end.

repeat for

You can use a repeat for loop to repeat an action a specific number of times. There are four parts to a **repeat for** loop statement:

- **for** specifies the name and type of a control variable
- **from** specifies the initial value of the control variable
- **to** specifies the upper limit of the control variable
- **by** specifies the value to increment the control variable by each time through the loop

The following program will print the odd numbers from 1 to 9:

```
process
   repeat for integer i from 1 to 9 by 2
      output "d" % i || "%n"
   again
```

You can implement a **repeat for** loop that counts down instead of up:

```
process
   repeat for integer i from 9 to 1 by -2
      output "d" % i || "%n"
   again
```

Review

The following are the main points covered in this chapter. If you don't understand any of the statements below, go back and review the material in this chapter before you go on.

- If you use referents in a persistent program, you must place them inside a nested referent scope, or they will not be resolved until the application terminates.
- If you need to scan a piece of data to create or retrieve an XML document, and then parse that document, you can use an input function to make the parser the output destination of the scanning process. The effectively performs both the scanning and the parsing operation on a single stream of data.
- When you are dealing with an XML instance embedded in a network data stream, such as an email message, you can switch from scanning to parsing using **drop** to return the XML portion of the message.

Exercises

1. Write a spam-bot, that is, an application that periodically checks a mailbox and deletes any messages that look like spam. How you define "looks like spam" is up to you.

18: Fixing URLs

I have said several times that OmniMark abstracts all data sources and data destinations so that, for example, you never actually open or close a file. OmniMark opens and closes files automatically when it needs to. Sometimes, however, you need to exercise some direct control over the file system. In this case, you can turn to the file system library. The file system library provides platform independent access to the important features of the file system on all platforms that OmniMark runs on. When using the library, you need to be aware that there are some differences between file systems that cannot be abstracted away and you may have to write platform specific code to handle these differences. Fortunately, there are no such platform dependencies in the code in this chapter.

Problems often arise when HTML pages are prepared on a Windows system and deployed on a UNIX web server. Windows preserves case on file names, but recognizes them insensitively, so the file names "INDEX.HTM" and "index.htm" refer to the same file. On UNIX systems, however, file names are case sensitive, so the file names "INDEX.HTM" and "index.htm" refer to different files.

This can mean the web pages that linked successfully when developed and tested under Windows can fail when deployed under UNIX.

This program allows you to fix this problem for a directory tree of HTML files by forcing all file and directory names to lowercase and all relative URLs to lowercase.

(Note that this is not foolproof, since someone could use an absolute URL to refer to a file on their own site.)

```
;fixurls.xom
;Fixes pathname sensitivity problems by
;1. forcing all file names to lower case
;2. forcing all directory names to lower case
;3. forcing all relative urls to lower case

include "omfsys.xin"

macro parameter-name is
  (letter [letter | digit | ".-"]*)
macro-end
macro parameter-value is
  (( '"' any** '"')|( "'" any** "'")|([\ white-space]+))
macro-end
macro parameter is
  (
   parameter-name
   white-space* "=" white-space*
   parameter-value
   white-space*
  )
macro-end

;Function iterates over a directory tree and submits
;all the files in the tree for processing.
define function process-tree
    value stream old-path
    into value stream new-path
    as

    local stream list variable
    local stream stat
    do when file old-path is directory
       FS_ListDirectory old-path into list status stat
       FS_MakeDirectory ("lg" format new-path)
        with "00007" status stat
       repeat over list
          process-tree (old-path || "\" || list)
            into ("lg" % new-path || "\" || list)
       again
    else
       local stream out-file
```

```
        open out-file as file ("lg" % new-path)
        using output as out-file
          submit file old-path
      done

process
    do unless number of #args = 2
        output "Usage: omnimark -s fixurls.xom "
            || "<source-dir> <dest-dir>%n"
        halt
    done

    do when file #args[1] isnt directory
        output "Source directory does not exist.%n"
        halt
    done

    do when file #args[2] exists
        output "Destination directory already exists.%n"
        halt
    done

    process-tree #args[1]
      into #args[2]

find
  (ul "<a" white-space) => anchor-start
  parameter+ => parameters
  (white-space* ">") => anchor-end

    output anchor-start
    repeat scan parameters
      match
        word-start
        (ul ("href" or "name")
        white-space*
        "=" white-space*) => p-name
        parameter-value => url
        white-space* => padding

          output p-name
          do when url matches any** ul "http://"
            output url
          else
```

```
            repeat scan url
               match uc => upper-letter
                  output "lg" % upper-letter
               match any++ => stuff
                lookahead (uc | value-end)
                  output stuff
            again
            output padding
        done
    match any
again
output anchor-end
```

This program iterates over the directory tree passed as the first command line argument. The iteration is done with a recursive function that submits each file in a directory for processing and calls itself to process each directory in a directory. It creates a directory tree starting at the root given as the second command line argument. In creating the new directory tree, it forces all names to lowercase.

When processing files it looks at every anchor tag and finds the "href" or "name" attributes and forces them to lowercase. It does not change the case of absolute URLs since they are presumably external to the site.

Technique

Recursive function calls

This program traverses a directory tree using recursive function calls.

The first call to the function **process-tree** uses the path passed on the command line as a starting point. The function tests to see if the path is a directory, and if it is, it uses the file system library function FS_ListDirectory to get a list of all the files in the directory. It then calls itself for each item in this list.

If any item is not a directory (and is therefore a file), it submits the item to the find rules for processing.

At the same time, the function creates new directories and files in the output file structure, using the second path passed on the command line as a root.

Lowercasing

The job of the program is to lowercase file and directory names, both in the file structure it creates and in the files it processes. To lowercase strings, it uses the format operator (%) with the format string "lg". The "g" is the format command used for formatting strings. The "l" is the format modifier specifying that the output be in lowercase.

Positional patterns

This program introduces the positional pattern word-start. It is used to ensure that the attribute names "href" and "name" are matched only as whole words. This avoids the possibility of accidentally matching attribute names "petname" or "xhref".

Positional patterns are a test. They do not consume any input. They simply test to see if a certain condition is true. In this case, the test is to make sure that the position immediately before the names is a word-start position. That is, it ensures that these words are not matched in the middle of other words.

You don't always need word-start and its counterpart, word-end, because you can often rely on other delimiters, such as white-space, to ensure that you are matching whole words. Sometimes, however, the words you are looking for may occur at the beginning or end of a value or may be surrounded by punctuation characters. In this case, it is easiest to use the word-start and word-end tests.

Syntax

These are the new syntax items introduced in this chapter.

is directory

You can use the is directory test to test if a file system path corresponds to a directory.

```
do when file old-path is directory
```

FS_ListDirectory

You can use the FS_ListDirectory function of the file system library to list the files in a directory. You pass the function a variable stream shelf (heralded by into) and it populates the shelf with one item for each file name in the directory. The status parameter returns status information. See the OmniMark documentation for details.

```
FS_ListDirectory old-path into list status stat
```

The file system library implements a subset of the POSIX file system interface. See the OmniMark documentation for details.

FS_MakeDirectory

You can use the `FS_MakeDirectory` function to create a directory on the file system. The `with` parameter sets file system permissions according to the POSIX codes for directory permissions. "00700" means give the file owner read, write, and execute permissions. See the OmniMark documentation for full details.

```
FS_MakeDirectory ("1g" % new-path)  with "00007" status stat
```

"g" format command

The "g" format command is use to apply formatting to strings. It can be used alone in a format item to include the value of a stream variable in a string:

```
process
    local stream planet initial {"Earth"}
    output "Hello %g(planet)%n"
```

You don't need "g" to output the content of a stream as is. You can output the value of a stream variable directly. In other words, you can rewrite the above program like this:

```
process
    local stream planet initial {"Earth"}
    output "Hello " || planet || "%n"
```

If you want to modify the format of the value of the stream, however, you can use the "g" format command with the appropriate format modifiers. For instance, to format the value of the string in all caps you can write:

```
process
    local stream planet initial {"Earth"}
    output "Hello %ug(planet)%n"
```

This will output "Hello EARTH".

word-start

The keyword word-start is one of the family of positional patterns, which includes:

- line-start (the beginning of a line)
- line-end (the end of a line)

- word-start (the beginning of a word)
- word-end (the end of a word)
- value-start or |= (the beginning of the scanned source)
- value-end or =| (the end of the scanned source)

For purposes of word-start and word-end, a word is defined as a sequence of letters or digits. To see where any positional pattern falls in a piece of data, you can write a simple program that inserts an asterisk where the positional pattern occurs:

```
process
    submit "abc 234 a2b a-b a:7 2:4 8hn"

find word-start
    output "*"
```

The thing to remember about positional patterns is that they do not represent any data in the source. line-end, for example, does not match or consume a line feed character. Positional patterns are tests. You use them to restrict a search so that a pattern is only matched in a particular position. For instance, the rule:

```
find "term"
```

will match the string "term" in the words "term", "terminate", and "indeterminate"; the rule:

```
find word-start "term"
```

will match the string "term" in the words "term" and "terminate" but not "indeterminate"; and the rule:

```
find "term" word-end
```

will match the string "term" in the words "term" but not "terminate" or "indeterminate".

Review

The following are the main points covered in this chapter. If you don't understand any of the statements below, go back and review the material in this chapter before you go on.

- You can make recursive function calls in OmniMark.
- Positional patterns allow you to match a pattern only at a specific place in the data.
- You can use the file system library to deal with the file system in sophisticated ways.

- You can do a submit from within a function. Any find rules that fire do so within the context of the function, and therefore within any output scopes (or other scopes) established within the function.

Exercises

1. This program uses a capture and rescan approach to finding links and URLs. This is simple to program, but it involves some loss of efficiency. Rewrite the program to use the nested pattern matching technique discussed in Chapter 11.

19: Link checker

A link checker is a basic part of every webmaster's toolbox. It is also an example of a useful class of tools: web crawlers. The link checker presented here can be adapted to perform a wide variety of tasks that involve traversing a website.

As a streaming language, OmniMark is designed to reduce the necessity of building data structures. However, you will still sometimes need to build data structures, especially for process control purposes. The link check program needs to maintain multiple queues to keep track of what has been checked and what is scheduled for checking. I will use shelves to create the queues.

The URL-fixing program in the previous chapter used recursive function calls to perform a depth-first traversal of a directory tree. Doing a depth first traversal of a web, which would involve nested scans of lined pages to an arbitrary depth, is not likely to be efficient. For this program, therefore, I take a queue-based approach. The program starts at the page fed to it on the command line. It adds that page to the queue, then scans it to find links. Each link it finds is added to the queue (unless it is already in the queue). The program then works through the queue, checking to see if each page exists, and if it does, scanning it for more links and adding them to the queue.

I restrict the main queue to the domain of the initial page. Any URLs for pages outside the domain go into a separate queue. When I have finished the main queue,

I check the existence of pages in the external pages queue, but I don't download and scan them.

This means that the program checks for the validity of all the links on all the pages of a particular domain that can be found by following links from the initial URL specified on the command line. Note that this is not a guarantee that all pages in a particular domain have been checked, since it is perfectly possible to have two or more entirely separate "webs" of pages in a single domain, and it is also possible for a web of pages to be constructed tree-fashion with links in only one direction, so that you can climb up but you can't climb back down again. If the initial URL points into the middle of such a tree, the crawler has no way of finding its way down to the lower levels.

This is the basic structure of the program:

1. Analyze the initial URL to find the domain. Save the domain name so that it can be used to restrict the search to the current domain.
2. Add the initial domain to the main queue. Pages are added to the queue by adding their URLs as keys to a shelf named **pages**.
3. Process the queue, starting at the first item.
4. Get the path and resource names for the current item in the queue.
   They will be used to normalize relative URLs found on the current page.
5. Get the page and check the response code. Report the response code.
6. If the page is retrieved successfully, scan it for links.
7. Normalize the URLs of the links found.
8. Add http URLs in the local domain to the main queue. When a URL is added to the main queue, the URL itself is used as the key and the URL of the current page is added to the value portion of the shelf item. It the page is already in the queue, it is not added again, but the URL of the current page is added to its item value. In this way, each page in the queue accumulates a list of the pages that link to it. This information is useful for reporting.
9. Add external http URLs to the external pages queue.
10. Add all other URLs to the list of ignored URLs.
11. When the main queue is exhausted, process the external-pages queue. Check that the external pages exist, but don't download them or scan them for more links.
12. When the external-pages queue is exhausted, list the ignored pages.
13. Report all the broken links and the pages on which they occur.

The program reports its progress to #error and outputs its final report to #main-output. You can capture the report to a file by naming that file on the command line with the "-of" option:

```
omnimark -s linkcheck.xom www.foobar.com -of report.txt
```

The program is in Appendix 3.

Technique

There is one minor piece of pattern matching technique introduced in this chapter, sequential pattern matching, but the majority of what is new and interesting here has to do with process and flow control.

Using shelves as queues

A queue is a data structure that works on the principle first-in, first-out (FIFO). In other words, the first one in line is first to get on the bus. This means that newly arriving items are added to the end of the queue, while items to be processed are taken from the front of the queue.

When you do a new on a shelf, the new item is added to the end of the shelf. All that is required to add an item to a queue, therefore, is to do a set new:

```
set new pages{url}
 to key of pages[current-page] || "%n"
```

The usual way to read an item from a queue is to read the value of the first item and then remove the item:

```
set page to pages[1]
remove pages[1]
```

Since new shelf items are added to the end by default, reading and removing the first item on a shelf gives you the FIFO behavior you want in a queue. (To implement a stack, you simply read and remove items without an item qualifier. This removes items from the end of the shelf, giving you LIFO (last-in, first-out) behavior.)

In this application, however, I need to keep some items in the queue for later reporting purposes. So I use an integer variable, current-page, to track the read position in the queue. Rather than specify

```
pages[current-page]
```

every time I want to refer to this item in the queue, I use using to establish item current-page as the current item. Within the scope of the using, the specified item, rather then the lastmost item, is the default item of the shelf. This allows us to write code like this:

```
using pages[current-page]
do
    output pages
done
```

Sequential pattern matching

We have looked at many examples of nested pattern matching in this book. As we have seen, #current-input plays a vital role in implementing a nested pattern matching strategy. But in the function normalize-url I have used it to implement a sequential pattern matching structure.

A URL consists of a several pieces of information joined end to end. The challenge in normalizing a URL is to detect each of those sequentially joined pieces. We do this with a series of do scan structures. Each do scan scans #current-input, but they are arranged sequentially, rather than nested as in previous examples.

The current input for this structure is provided by an old friend we haven't seen since Chapter 2: using input as. using input as establishes a current input scope but does not initiate scanning. Usually you take the shortcut of naming the scanning source directly in the scanning action. Here, where I need a common scanning source for multiple scanning operations in succession, using input as allows me to establish the scanning source outside of any one of the do scan operations that will process it:

```
using output as normalized-url
 using input as url
 do
```

Creating data structures

OmniMark does not have user-defined data types. However, using shelves, markup processing, and catch and throw, you can easily solve most of the problems that you would solve with a user-defined type or object in another language. "linkchk.xom" illustrates some of the most useful methods of doing this, specifically:

- using markup to represent data structures
- using catch and throw to provide extended function return types
- using parallel shelf indexing to relate values
- using shelves as pseudo objects

Using markup to represent data structures

A URL is a perfect example of a complex piece of data coded as a single string value using markup.

One of the things any kind of web crawler needs to do is to normalize URLs. A URL has four basic parts:

1. the domain name (for example: www.omnimark.com)
2. the path (for example: /develop/om5/doc/concept/)
3. the resource name (for example: alpha.htm)
4. optional extra information such as query strings and internal references

The URLs found in web pages fall into three categories:

1. Absolute URLs that describe the complete path to a resource, including domain name, path, and resource name.
2. Relative URLs that describe the path to a resource in relationship to the current page. They may contain a partial path or just a resource name.
3. Relative URLs that give the complete path within the current domain.

Since the program has to request each page by its absolute URL (domain, path, and resource), it has to maintain information about the domain and path of the current page so that it can use them to transform the relative URLs it finds into absolute URLs. (This is the same job the web browser has to do when you click a link.)

The program normalizes each URL as it finds it, using information about the domain and path of the page it is scanning. It then adds each new URL to the queue. When it comes time to check that URL, it scans the URL to get the domain and path parts and stores them in global variables. In another language, I might have created a data structure for the URL with separate fields for domain, path, and resource name. In OmniMark, I use the scanning power of the language to break out those parts when I need them:

```
do scan key of pages
    match ul ([any except "/"]* => domain-part
              ([any except "/"]* "/")* => path-part
              any* => resource-part
             ) => whole-url
    set domain to domain-part
    set current-path to path-part
    set current-path to "/" when current-path = ""
    set current-resource to resource-part
done
```

Since linkchk.xom is designed to confine its operations to a single domain, I don't bother to reset the domain as I work through the queue. Each new page is scanned with the following code to get the current path and resource names:

```
do scan key of pages
```

```
    match ([any except "/"]*
            ([any except "/"]* "/")* => path-part
            any* => resource-part
           ) => whole-url
    set current-path to path-part
    set current-path to "/" when current-path = ""
    set current-resource to resource-part
done
```

With a small data item like a URL, there is no appreciable inefficiency involved in scanning to get the individual data units we need. With large data items, of course, it would be better to use another method such as parallel indexed shelves (a method I also use in this program and will discuss later in this chapter).

In some cases, using this technique, you would need to add markup to shelf items to delineate them clearly. In this case, I don't have to invent any markup of my own; I simply take advantage of the markup inherent in the data object given to me and break out the data elements I need by scanning.

Using catch and throw to provide extended function returns

Two functions in this program use catch and throw to provide extended function return information.

The function normalize-url does two jobs. First, it transforms the URL found by the find rule into an absolute URL that can be used to retrieve a page. Second, it determines whether the URL represents an HTML page that should be checked for more links, another kind of file that should be checked to see if it exists but should not be downloaded and scanned, or a link that should be ignored altogether, such as a mailto link. It needs to return two pieces of information: the normalized URL, and the kind of check to perform on that URL.

I could do this by passing two modifiable parameters to the function and reading their values when the function returns. The function definition would change from this:

```
define function normalize-url
  value stream url
  elsewhere
```

to this:

```
define function normalize-url
```

```
modifiable stream url
check modifiable stream check-type
elsewhere
```

And the function call would change from this:

```
normalize-url url-c
...

catch ignore-this-url url url
    do when ignored-pages hasnt key url
        new ignored-pages{url}
    done
catch check-existence-only url url
    do when external-pages hasnt key url
        set new external-pages{url}
         to key of pages[current-page] || "%n"
    done
catch check-and-scan url url
    do when pages hasnt key url
        set new pages{url}
         to key of pages[current-page] || "%n"
    else
        set pages[url]
         to pages[url]
         || key of pages[current-page] || "%n"
    done
```

to this:

```
set url to url-c
...
normalize-url url check check-type

do scan check-type
    match "ignore"
        do when ignored-pages hasnt key url
            new ignored-pages{url}
        done
    match "existence"
        do when external-pages hasnt key url
            set new external-pages{url}
             to key of pages[current-page] || "%n"
        done
    match "scan"
        do when pages hasnt key url
```

```
          set new pages{url}
            to key of pages[current-page] || "%n"
      else
          set pages key url
            to pages{url}
            || key of pages[current-page] || "%n"
      done
done
```

There is nothing wrong with this approach. I simply choose to use the catch and throw approach in this program. Doing so does give one small advantage. The advantage, though small, is worth looking at, because it could be a big advantage in another program.

Because of the three different quoting styles used for attribute names in HTML, I use three different patterns, and three different pattern variables to pick out the URL:

```
match ul "href"  white-space*
           "=" white-space*
           (
           ('"'  [\ '"']* => url-a '"')
           or
           ("'"  [\ "'"]* => url-b "'")
           or
           [any except white-space or ">" ]+ => url-c
           )
           do when url-a is specified
              normalize-url url-a
           else when url-b is specified
              normalize-url url-b
           else
              normalize-url url-c
           done
```

Because the => operator declares a pattern variable as well as assigning data to it, I cannot use the same pattern variable name more than once in a pattern (otherwise I would be declaring it more than once, which is not allowed). So I need three different variants of the url pattern variable, url-a, url-b, and url-c. I then use the is specified test to see which one was actually used and then call the normalize-url function with that URL.

Because I have three different function call points, I need to either triplicate the logic that evaluates the function return or move it outside the scope in which the function calls occur (as I have done in the code above). This creates distance between the function call and the evaluation of its return value, which is dangerous because that value could be changed accidentally in that distance. The greater the distance, the greater the chance of accidental modification, and accidental modification of variables is an enormous source of program errors.

You might argue that the distance between the function call and the evaluation of its return value is just as great in the catch and throw example, but that is only true in lexical terms. This distance is just as great in lines of code, but the distance is zero in terms of execution. There is no possibility of the return value being changed by any intervening code, because the appropriate catch occurs immediately as a result of the throw in the function. And I have saved myself a variable. Not only is there no distance in which the value could be corrupted, there is no modifiable variable that can be corrupted.

Using catch and throw to provide extended function returns, therefore, is a safe technique. It allows us to have several different function calls which all return to a single point, or even to different points depending on the outcome of the function, since different catches could be in different scopes.

The get-page function illustrates another advantage of using catch and throw for extended function returns. The get-page function needs to return a variety of different information depending on what happens when it tries to retrieve a page. It may successfully retrieve a web page, which it must pass back to the caller to be scanned. It may encounter an HTTP error or receive a response from the web server that indicates that the page cannot be found. It needs to report this. Finally, it may be called in a way that requires it to check the existence of a page but not retrieve its contents. This too requires different reporting.

Functions that need to return different data depending on their result occur frequently. The usual approach in other languages is to create a data structure that is the union of all the data types they might need to return, and have every call return that data structure. This can lead to several problems. In the first place, you have to maintain the data structure. Any change to any of the return types of the function requires an update to the data structure. Secondly, each call to the function receives the same data structure. Some of the fields of that data structure contain relevant data, and some do not. There is always the risk of a programmer accidentally using data that is not relevant to the type of return value produced by the function.

Rather than constructing a complex data structure for the function to return, and then implementing elaborate logic to check the result after the call, you use catch and throw to provide a variety of function return types. Since each throw can include a different set of parameters, you can have, in effect, many different return types for a single function. And because each throw is caught by a corresponding catch, our calling routine does not have to do any analysis of the returned values to determine what happened. Instead, the function itself analyzes its result and returns to a different place in the calling routine depending on that result. The function is now doing more of the work and centralizing analysis code that would otherwise have to be repeated at each function call.

Notice that most of the logic of the get-page function is actually devoted to analyzing the result of the function and generating the appropriate throw:

```
do when HTTPObjectIsInError request
   HttpObjectGetStatusReport request into request-report
   set error-message to " HTTP ERROR%n"
   repeat over request-report
      set error-message to error-message || request-report
   again
   throw page-not-found reason error-message
done
do scan response key "status-code"
   match "2"
      do when existence-only
         throw page-exists
      else
         throw page-found contents response{"entity-body"}
      done
   match "3"
      do scan HTTPObjectGetHeader response for "location"
      match ul "http://" ? any+ => url
         throw page-is-redirected url
      done
   else
      throw page-not-found
      reason (response{"status-code"}
         || " " || response{"reason-phrase"} )
done
```

This technique also solves the problem of proper error handling for functions. Traditionally, function error reporting has been achieved either by returning error values in the function return, or by raising an exception that then required separate return handling logic from successful invocations. With catch and throw, you can integrate the error handling for your functions fully with the successful returns. **get-page** does this by throwing page-not-found in case of an HTTP error. Since the consequences of getting an HTTP error and getting an error response from the web server are the same for our link checker, they are nicely brought together by using the same throw in both situations.

Using parallel shelf indexing to relate values

After the link checker is run, I want to create a report showing each broken link encountered, the HTTP response code received for that link, and a list of the pages that reference the broken link. I use the key of the **pages** and **external-pages** shelves to record all the URLs checked. I use the shelf item to build up a list of the pages that reference this URL. That leaves nowhere to record the HTTP response code.

To handle this, I create another shelf called **broken-links**. Every time the program finds a broken link, it creates a new item on the **broken-links** shelf with the URL as the key and the HTTP response as the item value.

When it is time to create the report on broken links the program repeats over the **broken-links** shelf, which contains a complete set of broken links, both internal and external. (In fact, it is the only way to know which links were broken, since the **pages** and **external-pages** shelves contain no information on the state of the link.) It then compares the keys of the **broken-links** shelf with the keys of the **pages** and **external-pages** shelves to find the list of pages where the broken links are referenced:

```
repeat over broken-links
    output "%nA link to "
        || key of broken-links
        || "%nreturning the response: "
        || broken-links
        || "%noccurs on the following pages:%n"
    do when pages has key key of broken-links
        output pages{key of broken-links}
    else
        output external-pages{key of broken-links}
    done
again
```

Using shelves as pseudo objects

linkchk.xom does not use this technique directly, but it uses the OmniMark HTTP library, which makes extensive use of this technique. The technique is simple. You create a pseudo object by creating a shelf with a key for each data point in your object. You then pass that shelf to a function that reads the object data and may create and return another object.

You can see this technique at work in the following lines:

```
local stream request variable
...
HttpRequestSetFromUrl request from url
...
HttpRequestSend request into response timeout timeout
do when HTTPObjectIsInError request
   HttpObjectGetStatusReport request into request-report
```

The pseudo-object is the variable-sized shelf `request`. It will be used as an HTTP request object to be passed back and forth between several functions which will be used to create, send, and receive a response from this request.

The request stream is the first parameter passed to the functions `HttpRequestSetFromUrl`, `HttpRequestSend`, `HTTPObjectIsInError`, and `HttpObjectGetStatusReport`.

These functions declare this parameter as either modifiable or read-only, depending on whether or not they need to modify it. `HttpRequestSetFromUrl` declares it modifiable, since it modifies it to include the basic items needed to create an HTTP request.

Notice that the actual shelf used as the pseudo object is created in the main program and passed into the functions of the library that uses it. OmniMark functions cannot return entire shelves, only single values. A shelf must be passed as a modifiable argument.

Syntax

These are the new syntax items introduced in this chapter.

optional arguments

When defining a function, you can choose to make certain arguments optional. This simplifies the use of the function when the optional parameters are not needed. To declare a function argument optional, simply use the keyword `optional` after the definition of the argument:

```
timeout value integer timeout optional
```

In many cases, you will want to supply a default value for an optional argument. You do this with the keyword initial, followed by the initial value in curly braces:

```
timeout value integer timeout optional initial {60000}
```

If you do not supply a default value and the function call does not supply the optional argument, the argument will not be instantiated. If you do not supply a default value, therefore, you should check to see if a value has been supplied by using the is specified test.

is specified

You can use the is specified test to determine if a variable was ever instantiated. The need to do so arises in two places: in patterns, and in functions with optional arguments. In the case of a pattern it can occur when an optional sub-pattern is never matched. Failure to match an optional sub-pattern does not prevent a pattern as a whole from matching, but it does prevent any pattern variables in that sub-pattern from being instantiated.

In the following code, the use of the keyword or means that only one of the three sub-patterns can be matched:

```
match ul "href"  white-space*
  "=" white-space*
  (
   ('"'  [\ '"']* => url-a '"')
   or
   ("'"  [\ "'"]* => url-b "'")
   or
   [\ white-space or ">" ]+ => url-c
  )
```

Only one of url-a, url-b, or url-c can possibly be instantiated. You can use the is specified test to find out which one it is:

```
do when url-a is specified
   normalize-url url-a
else when url-b is specified
   normalize-url url-b
else
   normalize-url url-c
done
```

Note that there is a difference between a pattern variable that is not specified and one that has simply received no data. Given the input:

ac

this pattern:

```
find "a" "b"? => letter-b "c"
```

will match and will leave the pattern variable letter-b specified but containing an empty string, while this pattern:

```
find "a" ("b" => letter-b)? "c"
```

will leave the pattern variable letter-b unspecified.

To test your understanding of this concept, ask yourself whether or not letter-b would be specified in the following pattern:

```
find "a" ("b"? => letter-b) "c"
```

If you are in any doubt about the answer, write a program to find out.

Also, ask yourself if the following code is legal:

```
find "a" ("b" => letter-b)+ "c"
```

Remember, => both declares a pattern variable and assigns data to it.

The other place you will need is specified is in a function with optional arguments for which default values have not been specified.

using <shelf item>

By default, any reference to a shelf by name refers to the last item on that shelf. The last item is considered the current item on the shelf. If you need to make frequent reference to another item on a shelf, you can change the current item with a using scope:

```
using pages item current-page
do
    <actions on this shelf item>
done
```

The specified item is the current item on the shelf for the duration of the using scope, allowing you to refer to this item alone without an item qualifier or key. The following code will output the third item on the pages shelf:

```
using pages[3]
do
    output pages
done
```

Review

The following are the main points covered in this chapter. If you don't understand any of the statements below, go back and review the material in this chapter before you go on.

- You can use shelves to implement queues and stacks.
- You can use markup to represent complex data structures within your program logic.
- You can use catch and throw to implement extended function returns.
- You can use parallel shelf indexes to relate values from different shelves.
- You can use using input as to define a current input source for a series of scanning operations that process sequential patterns.

Exercises

1. I said that a web page is not the root of a tree, but a node in a web. Nonetheless, each page exists in a directory tree and each URL uses directory notation. You can rewrite the program to check only the pages that are further up the same directory tree than the initial page. (Note that this does not guarantee that a whole branch is searched, since there could be pages on the same branch that do not reference each other.)
2. As written, this link checker does not check for the existence of images. Adapt the program to include image checking.
3. As written, the program does not handle frames. It will only search the frame set document, but will not load and check the frames themselves. Adapt the program so that it works with frames.

20: Catalog with shopping cart

You have now learned all the basic features of OmniMark (though there is a great deal more advanced functionality for you to explore.) In this chapter I will try to bring together many of the techniques we have studied to build a business-to-customer e-commerce web site. Actually, I will build about half the application. The rest I will leave to you.

Like most e-commerce applications, this will not be a single monolithic program. Instead, it will be a system of small interacting applications that will communicate with each other by sending XML data over TCP/IP. I will use two separate databases: one to hold the customer information, and one to house the catalog data. For each database, I will build a middleware server to handle requests for that data. These applications will use XML to transport the data they deliver. Finally, I will build the catalog CGI program itself.

I will not give you all the code for this application. Most of what is presented here is simply an application of techniques already presented in earlier chapters. I will just give you enough code to get the shopping cart working and show you how to use BCD numbers for financial calculation. The rest you can adapt from earlier chapters or write from scratch using what you have learned.

Since this is a fairly complex application, let's start with a brief functional specification. By the way, this spec should not be taken as an example of good UI design. It follows the model of one function = one page. This makes for simple programming, which is appropriate to an introductory book, but not necessarily for a good user experience.

goldilocksonline.com functional specification

goldilocksonline.com will be the Internet site for the Goldilocks Products Company. (goldilocks.com was taken – I looked it up.) The site will feature an online catalog listing the full range of merchandise from the Goldilocks Products Company. Shoppers will be able to browse the site by product line (the Papa, Mama, and Baby Bear lines) or by product type (Chairs, Porridge Bowls, and Beds). Shoppers will be able to add items to a shopping cart and purchase those items online.

The Goldilocks product catalog is a relational database with the following tables:

- Product
- ProductLine
- ProductType

The table "Product" has the following fields:

- ProductID
- ProductName
- ProductLineID
- ProductTypeID
- ProductDescription
- ProductPrice

The field ProductDescription is a memo field that contains an XML document looking like this:

```
<description>
<p>The Papa Bear Bowl is a big bowl with great insulating
properties. It will keep your porridge hot much longer than our
<prodref id="5">Mama Bear Bowl</prodref>.</p>
<p>If you like lots of hot parridge, this is the bowl for you.</p>
</description>
```

The "prodref" field allows us to highlight the names of products within the product description field and to create links to the descriptions of those other products. The is a good example of how XML markup can be used to enhance database data.

The table "ProductLine" has the following fields:

- ProductLineName
- ProductLineDescription

The table "ProductType" has the following fields:

- ProductTypeName
- ProductTypeDescription

The application will maintain the shopping cart using a cookie that will be an XML document looking like this:

```
<cart>
 <item id="5" quantity="2">
 <item id="7" quantity="4">
</cart>
```

When the shopper decides to purchase the items in their shopping cart, they will be asked for their user name (Customer ID). If the Customer ID is not found, we ask them to register. Then we generate an order in the form of an XML document looking like this:

```
<order customerid="5436234578">
 <item id="5" quantity="2">
 <item id="7" quantity="4">
</order>
```

This order will be emailed to the shipping department.

Navigation of the site is as follows:

The home page will give the user the opportunity to browse by product type or by product line. It will list the available product types and the product lines, with links to the line and type pages.

Clicking a product type or a product line links the user to a list of products in that product line or type. The user can purchase a product from the list, or can go to a product detail page for a particular product. Within the description of a product, you can jump to the product detail page for any other product that is mentioned in the description.

Adding an item to the shopping cart takes the user to the shopping cart page. From the shopping cart page they can:

- delete an item from their shopping cart
- change the quantity of an item in their shopping cart
- return to the home page
- check out

If they change their order, they are returned to the shopping cart page.

The first stage of the checkout process is to enter a Customer ID. New customers must choose a username and enter their name and contact information. An error returns the user to the customer ID page, with the errors marked in red.

Once the customer is properly identified, display the order confirmation page. If the user confirms the order, send the "order accepted" page.

All pages contain a link to the home page and the shopping cart page.

goldilocksonline.com programs

The goldilocksonline website is run by a number of CGI programs, templates, and middleware applications. Here is the list. You will find the code in Appendix 3. Those items marked with an asterisk are not provided. It is up to you to write them yourself using what you have learned:

- customer.xom, the middleware application developed in Chapter 14
- prodsrv.xom, a middleware application for accessing the product database
- gold-home.xom, the CGI program that generates the home page
- gold-line.xom, the CGI program that generates the product line listing page
- *gold-type.xom, the CGI program that generates the product type listing page
- *gold-product.xom, the CGI program that generates the product detail page
- gold-cart.xom, the CGI program that displays the shopping cart
- *gold-customer.xom, the CGI program that displays the customer identification page
- *gold-confirm.xom, the GGI program that displays the order confirmation page
- *gold-accept.xom, the CGI program that displays the order accepted page
- gold-home.txt, the template for the home page
- gold-line.txt, the template for the product line listing page
- *gold-type.txt, the template for the product type listing page
- gold-product.txt, the template for the product detail page
- *gold-cart.txt, the template for the shopping cart
- *gold-customer.txt, the template for the customer identification page
- *gold-confirm.txt, the template for the order confirmation page
- *gold-accept.txt, the template for the order accepted page

Technique

This application is a complex system of interacting pieces. To get it working you have to make sure all the pieces are in place and running.

1. Set up a DSN for the customer database.
2. Set up a DSN for the product database.
3. Start the customer server.
4. Start the product server.
5. Load the scripts and the templates into the appropriate directories.
6. Point your browser at the home page and start shopping.

To start the part of the system that I have provided, before you add your parts of the system, you can skip steps 1 and 3 above.

BCD numbers

This project introduces OmniMark's BCD library. BCD (Binary Coded Decimal) numbers are the ideal data type for dealing with financial data such as currencies and taxation rates. In fact, they are the best choice for most numerical calculations involving fractional quantities.

Programmers have become used to floating point numbers as the common means of dealing with non-whole numbers in computer languages. Most programming languages support floating point (as does OmniMark, through its omfloat library). But the ubiquity of floating point has more to do with the ubiquity of hardware support for floating point calculation than it does with the appropriateness of floating point numbers for common programming tasks.

As the name implies, floating point numbers allow the decimal point to float, allowing you to trade whole number magnitude off against fractional precision to represent an extremely wide range of numbers, but with variable precision. This is invaluable for certain kinds of scientific calculation, but not the best for financial calculation, or for most other everyday applications.

OmniMark's BCD numbers, by contrast, provide a whole number of unlimited size and a fixed fractional precision of 16 decimal places.

The second disadvantage of floating point numbers is that they are base 2 numbers. This means that they cannot accurately represent fractions that are powers of 10 such as 1/10 or 1/100. Since these fractions are essential to accurately calculating dollars and cents, and most other currencies, this inaccuracy is a serious problem.

BCD numbers are implemented as true decimal numbers, so they handle decimal fractions accurately.

There are, of course, fractions that neither base 10 nor base 2 numbers handle accurately, such as 1/3. But there are no fractions that float handles accurately which BCD does not, so BCD is generally preferable for most types of calculation.

The "price" element rule from gold-cart.xom shows the use of BCD numbers for dealing with prices:

```
element "price"
   local bcd price initial {"%c"}
   local integer quantity
    initial order{current-product-id}
   set grand-total to grand-total + (price * quantity)
   output '<TD>'
       || "<$,NNZ.ZZ>" % price
       || '</TD>%n'
       || '<TD><FORM ACTION="gold-cart.xom" METHOD="POST">'
       || '<INPUT TYPE="TEXT" VALUE="%d(quantity)" '
       || 'NAME="Quantity" SIZE="3">'
       || '<INPUT TYPE="HIDDEN" NAME="id" '
       || 'VALUE="%g(current-product-id)">'
       || '<INPUT TYPE="SUBMIT" VALUE="Change" NAME="Change">'
       || '</FORM></TD>%n'
       || '<TD>'
       || "<$,NNZ.ZZ>" % (price * quantity)
       || '</TD>%n'
```

Notice that the variable price is declared to be of type BCD, and that it is set to the data content of the price element (which is streamed to it as a result of the call to "%c" in its initializer). This value is then formatted as a dollar amount using the template formatting language supported by the BCD library:

```
"<$,NNZ.ZZ>" % price
```

The template "<$,NNZ.ZZ>" specifies formatting with two places after the decimal point, one or more places before the decimal, grouping of digits in groups of three with comma separators, and a leading dollar sign. It is the most commonly used format for Canadian and American currency.

This same template is used again when we print out the total for the item (price times quantity):

```
"<$,NNZ.ZZ>" % (price * quantity)
```

Template processing with referents

In gold-cart.xom we see yet another approach to template processing. In this case, the program captures the placeholder name and uses it to create a referent. Later it supplies the value of the referent from the information pulled from the database or from the CGI environment.

One feature of this approach is that if a template has an unknown placeholder, the program will create a referent for that placeholder, but will never give a value to that referent. Normally, OmniMark raises an error if a referent has not been given a value by the time referents are resolved. This means you need to supply a value for those erroneous placeholders or else your program will fail.

The error handling approach I am using here is passive. If the program gets a placeholder it doesn't recognize, it will just ignore it. To accomplish this, I give all referents a default value of an empty string. I do this with the declaration:

```
declare #main-output has referents-allowed defaulting {""}
```

Because the use of referents results in OmniMark temporarily buffering output, you must explicitly permit the use of referents in a stream. #main-output is an exception. If you use referents anywhere in your program, they are automatically allowed in #main-output. Here I explicitly state that they are allowed in #main-output because the defaulting keyword is part of the referents-allowed statement.

Using XML based cookies

Gold-line.xom sets cookies to preserve shopping cart information. I have written the code to send and receive cookies directly into the program rather than using any cookie library. OmniMark handles text data of this sort so elegantly that handling cookies is a very minor chore. If you do want support for creating cookies, you can use the HTTP library to build your HTTP header instead of doing it by hand as I do here. You cannot use the HTTP library function to receive and decode cookies, however, because a CGI program is not receiving an HTTP packet directly, but is receiving it though the CGI interface.

I have used XML to encode the cookie. It is generally useful to pack all the information you need into one cookie, rather than having to deal with many different cookies. Given this, you need some method of structuring that information, and XML is an obvious candidate.

Because gold-cart.xom is receiving information in XML from both the cookie and the product server, it uses rule groups to organize the markup rules used to process each type of information. Here is the code to read the cookie and build a shelf representing the order:

```
do when cgi-data has key "HTTP_COOKIE"
   using group process-cookie
   do xml-parse
   scan get-cookie-value "order"
      suppress
   done
done
...
group process-cookie

element "order"
   suppress

element "item"
   set new order{attribute "id"} to attribute "qty"
   suppress
```

Syntax

These are the new syntax items introduced in this chapter.

referents-allowed

Because a stream that may contain referents must be buffered internally by OmniMark, you must state explicitly that a stream is allowed to contain referents. If you try to write a referent to a stream that does not have referents allowed, you will get an error. To allow referents in a stream you create yourself, you must add the clause with referents-allowed to the open statement when you open the stream:

```
open out-file with referents-allowed
```

To allow referents in one of OmniMark's built-in streams such as #main-input, you must add a declaration to your program:

```
declare #main-output has referents-allowed
```

Actually, it isn't necessary to declare #main-output has referents-allowed unless you need to set the defaulting (see below). If the OmniMark compiler sees referents being used anywhere in your program it will automatically allow them in #main-output. If your program uses referents but does not ever write them to #main-output, you can speed things up a little by including the following declaration, which will prevent #main-output from being buffered for referents:

```
declare #main-output has referents-not-allowed
```

defaulting

By default all referents are unattached (that is, they have null values).
It is an error if any referent values are unattached when the referents are resolved.
If you expect that some of your referents may not have values assigned to them,

```
declare #main-output has referents-allowed defaulting {""}
```

BCD numbers

BCD number support is provided by the BCD library. To use BCD numbers,
you must include the file "ombcd.xin" in your program.

Once you have included the BCD library in your program, you can declare and
use BCD numbers just like any built-in type.

template formatting

You can use template-based formatting to output the values of BCD numbers.
A useful template for positive dollar values is `"<$,NNZ.ZZ>"`.

Here is what each character in this format template means:

- The "<" and ">" characters indicate that this is a template and not a format
  command string
- The "$" is a literal dollar sign.
- The "," is a group character. When the group character precedes the digit
  placeholders, it indicates that the template may be extended to the left as far as
  needed, with groups of the same size as the group following the "," (which in
  this case extends to the ".").
- The "N" is a digit placeholder. If the number being formatted does not contain
  a digit to replace the placeholder, it is omitted.
- The "Z" is a digit placeholder. If the number being formatted does not contain a
  digit to replace the placeholder, it is replaced by a zero ("0").
- The "." is the decimal point. The decimal point is printed if there are characters
  printed to the left of it, otherwise it is suppressed. (In this case the use of the
  "Z" to the left of the "." ensures that there are always characters to the left of
  the decimal, so the decimal itself is always printed.)

The template language is available for BCD numbers only; however, you can use it
with integers simply by casting the integer into a BCD before formatting it:

```
include "ombcd.xin"
```

```
process
   local integer foo initial {"200"}
   output "<$,NNZ.ZZ>" % bcd foo
```

Review

The following are the main points covered in this chapter. If you don't understand any of the statements below, go back and review the material in this chapter before you go on.

- BCD variables are base 10, infinitely large, fixed precision numbers. Floating point variables are base 2, finitely large, variable precision numbers. Use BCD for all numbers with fraction components unless you have a specific reason to choose floating point instead.

- Referents give us yet another way of processing templates. Because referents are named dynamically at run time, you can set their names from data.

- XML is a handy way to handle small packets of information across a network.

- You can build a web application as a collection of interacting pieces. This allows you to build a complex application out of simple pieces. It also allows you to distribute the load of an application over different machines.

Exercises

1. Complete the Goldilocks Online application by writing the templates and CGI programs not provided here. While you're at it, spruce up the look and feel a little.

21: From CGI to server

If you build a successful site, it will soon get busy. Running CGI programs on your web server can really slow things down. CGI programs present two problems. First, they share the CPU with the web server (not to mention all the other CGI programs on your site). Second, they have to be started up every time they are used. A new process has to be created to run them. Connections to servers and databases have to be established. It all takes time and ultimately slows down your site. On a busy site, you can do two things to ensure fast responses:

1. Convert your CGI programs to servers so they run all the time and don't have to start up and establish network connections every time.
2. Get your CGI programs right off your web server and onto another machine.

In this chapter, I will show you how to do both these things using the OmniMark web relay and the OmniMark Application Server Framework.

The OmniMark web server relay, omcgir.exe, is a CGI program written in C. Its job is to package up all the information produced by the CGI environment (the information returned by the CGI library functions CGIGetEnv and CGIGetQuery) into a message that can be sent over a TCP/IP connection to a server program. The server program can be running on the same machine or another machine.

The OmniMark Application Server Framework is an OmniMark program template and include file that creates a server to receive messages from the web server relay.

The framework takes care of the network stuff and decoding the CGI data. All you have to do is adapt your CGI program to fit into the framework.

The program is in Appendix 3.

Setting up the web server relay

Before you can use this version of the hangman program, you need to set up and configure the web server relay. Here's what you do:

1. Move the file omcgir.exe to the scripts directory (for example, "scripts", "cgi-bin", or "cgi") of your web server.
2. Edit the file omcgir.ini to point the relay at the hangman server. Here's what it looks like on my machine:
3.

```
#------------------------------------------------------------------
#  OmniMark          Load Manager     Load Manager
# Service Name       Host Name/IP     Port Number
#--------------      ------------     ------------
    hangman          localhost            5800
#------------------------------------------------------------------
```

The lines starting with # are comments. The uncommented line consists of the name of the service, the name of the machine it is on, and the port number of that machine, separated by spaces.

3. Add a system level environment variable WSPLUGIN_INI_FILE, and make its value the path and filename of the omcgir.ini file.
4. If you have a static HTML page that links to the hangman program, change the URL to look like this:

```
<domain>/<script directory>/omcgir.exe/hangman
```

You will notice that the program itself has been changed to create paths in this way. Our previous version of hangman used extra path information to determine which program function to perform. The web server relay uses extra path information to determine which server to call. It matches the extra path information from the URL against the service name in the omcgir.ini file. This means that you cannot use extra path for function selection, so you have to use the query string instead. Another approach is to create a separate server for each function.

5. Create an argument file for the server to set the values of the variables ListenPort, PoisonPill, and ServiceName. These are global variables defined in omasf.xin. They must be given values appropriate to the server you are writing.

Here is the argument file for the hangman server:

```
;hangman.xar
-s hangman.xom
-c ListenPort 5800
-d PoisonPill "POISON PILL"
-d ServiceName "hangman"
```

6. Start the server.
7. Point your browser at the URL from step 4.

Technique

The OmniMark Application Server Framework is very straightforward. The omasf.xin library file includes all the code to receive and process the information from the web server relay. All you have to do is write three functions: ServiceInitialize, ServiceMain, and ServiceTerminate.

The process rule and the server loop are inside the omasf.xin file. The process rule calls ServiceInitialize before entering the server loop. It calls ServiceMain each time a request is received. It calls ServiceTerminate after the server loop exits. Thus, you put any initialization code into ServiceInitialize, the main processing into ServiceMain, and any shutdown code into ServiceTerminate.

The process rule passes two shelves to ServiceMain: requestHeader and requestBody. These shelves are identical to the shelves created by the CGI library functions CGIGetEnv and CGIGetQuery that have been used in all the CGI programs in this book. To convert that code, simply eliminate the calls to those two functions and substitute the variable names requestHeader and requestBody for the names used in your CGI program (cgi-data and form-data in the programs in this book).

Debugging

One of the advantages of writing an OMASF program instead of a conventional CGI program is ease of debugging. CGI programs are notoriously hard to debug because the way they are run by the web server makes it impossible to trace a running CGI program in an IDE.

An OMASF program, on the other hand, is a server. You can run your server in the OmniMark IDE, set a breakpoint at the start of ServiceMain, click the appropriate link on your browser, and step through your code.

Optimizing

Because it is running all the time, an OMASF server program is much more efficient than a CGI program, which must be started each time it is needed. But this is only the beginning of the optimizations available when you switch from CGI to OMASF.

A CGI program has to establish all its resources each time it is run. If it needs database access, it has to open a connection to a database. If it needs a network connection, it has to create it. If it needs a file, it has to open it and read it. The CGI version of the hangman program reads several files each time it is run. It reads the words file. It reads the templates file. All of this takes time and slows the program down.

In the server version, I can avoid all this file overhead by loading the word list when the server is first started. Since the word list changes, I write it back to disk when the server is shut down.

Two further optimizations are available. The OMCGIR web server relay does its job very efficiently, but it is still a CGI program. You can replace the CGI web server relay with ISAPI, NSAPI or Apache plug-ins that eliminate the CGI overhead. These relays are available to subscribers of the OmniMark Developers Network and as part of OmniMark Technologies' SureSpeed™ load manager.

The final optimization is to use SureSpeed, OmniMark Technologies' advanced load-management system for high-traffic websites. While using the OmniMark web server relay and the OMASF framework allows you to create a single server to server your active content requests, SureSpeed can clone your OMASF server programs, creating and managing multiple running copies on one machine or several machines. It can also clone CGI programs written in OmniMark or in other languages, using its SatelliteCGI™ technology.

SureSpeed optimizes your hardware resources by creating and destroying application clones for multiple servers as required to meet load. Its load management is application-based, meaning it does not wait for a machine to be overloaded before redirecting requests elsewhere. Instead it tracks the number of running applications on each machine, never letting any one machine exceed its capacity.

Running multiple OMASF servers

You can have more than one OMASF server program, just as you can have more than one CGI program. Each OMASF server requires a separate address, which means that for the second and third server you create on each machine, you must choose a different port number.

You can set the port number and name of the server using the arguments file:

```
;hangman.xar
-s hangman.xom
-integer ListenPort 5801
-define PoisonPill "POISON PILL"
-define ServiceName "monopoly"
```

You must have a line for each server in the omcgir.ini file:

```
#-------------------------------------------------------------------
#  OmniMark        Load Manager    Load Manager
# Service Name     Host Name/IP    Port Number
#--------------    ------------    ------------
    hangman          bigserver        5800
    monopoly         bigserver        5801
#-------------------------------------------------------------------
```

Shut down

OMASF uses a poison pill to shut down a running OMASF server. Note that if you do not shut down the server with a poison pill, the ServiceTerminate function will not be called. In the case of the hangman program, this would mean that the updated word file would not get written to disk.

Here is a poison pill client that you can use to shut down an OMASF server.

```
;poison.xom
;Sends a poison pill to an OMASF server
include "omtcp.xin"
declare catch connection-error
global stream server initial {"localhost"}
global stream port initial {"5800"}
global stream poison-pill initial {"POISON PILL"}

process
    local TCPConnection connection
    local stream s

    set connection to TCPConnectionOpen on server at port
    throw connection-error
     when TCPConnectionIsInError connection
```

```
set TCPConnectionGetOutput connection
 ;protocol IOProtocolMultiPacket
 to poison-pill

catch connection-error
    output "Connection error%n"
```

Syntax

This chapter does not introduce any new OmniMark syntax.

Review

The following are the main points covered in this chapter. If you don't understand any of the statements below, go back and review the material in this chapter before you go on.

- The OmniMark web server relay packages up a CGI request and sends it to an OMASF server for processing.
- As OMASF server give better performance than a conventional CGI program.
- OMASF programs are easier to debug than conventional CGI programs.

Exercises

1. Edit the hangman server program so that it pre-loads the template files as well as the word list.
2. Convert the Goldilocks Online CGI programs to a set of servers using OMASF and the OMCGIR relay.
3. Implement Perpetual Motion using OMASF.

Appendix 1: OmniMark patterns vs Perl regular expressions

If you are familiar with Perl, you will have noticed that OmniMark's pattern matching language uses a very different syntax from Perl's regular expressions. (Strictly speaking, OmniMark's language is a regular expression language too, but the term "regular expression" is commonly associated with the specific regular expression syntax used in Perl and the various UNIX utilities from which Perl's regular expressions were derived.)

While Perl was designed to bring together the power of a number of different utilities and languages, OmniMark was designed from the ground up to be a streaming programming language. The difference between the two approaches to pattern matching arises from these differences in origin. This appendix is designed for Perl programmers who want to learn how OmniMark does things. It only covers those issues that commonly cause confusion for Perl programmers coming to OmniMark. If you are not a Perl programmer, you can safely skip this appendix.

Verbosity

The most obvious difference is that OmniMark pattern matching is verbose, while Perl regular expressions are terse. The regular expression language originated with command-line utilities, in which the whole regular expression had to fit on a command line and had to meet command-line conventions to ensure it was unambiguous. OmniMark's pattern matching syntax, on the other hand, was designed for use in a programming language. It is deliberately verbose because complex patterns can be hard to read and understand. OmniMark aims to make it as easy as possible to read and understand complex patterns.

Greediness

Perl regular expressions and OmniMark patterns could both be described as greedy, but in different ways. Consider the following data:

abcd!efghi!jklmn!opqrs!tuvw!xyz

The following Perl regular expression:

/.+!/

will match:

abcd!efghi!jklmn!opqrs!tuvw!

This is Perl's "greediness". The string "abcd!" qualifies as one or more of any character followed by "!", but Perl is not satisfied with this and takes the longest possible match that satisfies the regular expression: "abcd!efghi!jklmn!opqrs!tuvw!".

Perl allows you to make the expression non-greedy:

/.+?!/

The equivalent non-greedy expressions in OmniMark are:

any++ "!"

and

[\ "!"]+ "!"

The OmniMark equivalent of the greedy Perl expression /.+!/ is formed simply by grouping either of the expressions above and adding a + (one or more) occurrence indicator:

(any++ "!")+

or

([\ "!"]+ "!")+

Programmers coming from Perl to OmniMark often expect the following expression to work:

any+ "!"

But this pattern will never match anything. The reason is that OmniMark's any+ is "greedier" than Perl's ".+". While Perl's ".+" defers to the claims of the next sub-pattern that follows, OmniMark's any+ just gobbles up characters without deference to the claims of any other sub-pattern. It follows that any+ will match any number of characters, and thus all the characters in any input data. By the time the sub-pattern any+ has finished matching, all the data has been matched. Therefore there is nothing left for the sub-pattern "!" to match and the pattern as a whole fails. This is OmniMark's greediness. The non-greedy form in OmniMark is any++, which is exactly equivalent to Perl's ".+".

Line ends

By default, Perl's . matches any character except a line end. This makes it equivalent to OmniMark's any-text character class. When the /s modifier is used in a Perl pattern, the . behaves like OmniMark's any.

Variables vs input streams

In Perl, you do pattern matching on variables. In OmniMark, you do pattern matching on the current input stream. You can make a variable the source of the current input stream, if you like, but you never apply pattern matching directly to the variable.

This means first that you don't have to copy source data into a variable before doing pattern matching. If you have a 20-gigabyte file, you can do pattern matching on it without any special provisions.

It also means that your text processing activity is not confined to a single line of code or the scope of a single variable. If one text processing operation finished without consuming all the data, another can pick up at the point in the data where the first one stopped.

Appendix 2: Configuring your web server to run OmniMark CGI programs

This appendix describes how to configure Microsoft IIS and Apache web servers to run OmniMark CGI programs.

The OmniMark command line

When configuring your web server to run OmniMark CGI programs, you will need to enter an OmniMark command line, either in a web server configuration file or in the hash-bang line of your OmniMark program. This section examines the command line you will need to enter.

Identifying the source

OmniMark C/VM is the OmniMark language interpreter. You use it to run OmniMark programs from OmniMark source files. You invoke OmniMark C/VM by typing omnimark at the command line and identifying the source code file to run.

Most language interpreters take the name of the source file as the first command-line parameter, and pass remaining command-line parameters on to the program itself.

OmniMark is different. With OmniMark, the source file name may appear anywhere on the command line and is heralded by the command-line option -s or -sb. (Using -sb suppresses the OmniMark banner, and is required for use with CGI programs.) Thus the command line to run the OmniMark program "foo.xom" is:

```
omnimark -sb foo.xom
```

Preventing source code snooping

You can use the "-expand" command-line option to make OmniMark C/VM write out a version of your program with all macros expanded in-line. This is a debugging tool for the OmniMark programmer, but it represents a potential security hole when running OmniMark CGIs. Anyone invoking an OmniMark CGI program with the -expand option could cause the entire program to be sent back to the browser, even if there are no macros in the program. To prevent this, you can add the -noexpand command-line option to the command line to prevent the use of -expand. Always configure your web server to invoke OmniMark with the -noexpand option.

Locating OmniMark's system libraries

OmniMark uses system environment variables to find its system libraries and include files. On Windows platforms, the installation procedure sets the environment variables.

On UNIX systems, you will need to ensure that the following environment variables are set (assuming the location of OmniMark is /usr/local/bin/omnimark):

```
OMNIMARK_INCLUDE /usr/local/bin/omnimark/xin/
OMNIMARK_XFLPATH /usr/local/bin/omnimark/lib/=L.so
```

Each UNIX system has its own procedure for setting environment variables.

Using OmniMark's argument and project files

The OmniMark C/VM supports several command-line options. Often, web servers only allow the substitution of a single option, the name of the program. You may want to associate more options, most important of which is a log file to capture compiler and interpreter errors. You can do this with an OmniMark "argument" file or a "project" file. The two files accomplish the same thing. The argument file uses command-line syntax. The project file uses XML syntax and is generated automatically by the IDE when you create a project.

OmniMark's argument file

By convention, an OmniMark argument file has the suffix ".xar". So the program "hello.xom" should have the argument file "hello.xar".

An argument file is a file containing the command-line arguments to be passed to an OmniMark program. It is passed to OmniMark using the "-f" option.

```
c:\omnimark\omnimark -f -noexpand hello.xar
```

Assuming "hello.xar" contains the lines

```
-sb hello.xom
-alog hello.log
```

this command line is equivalent to the command line:

```
c:\omnimark\omnimark -noexpand -sb hello.xom -alog hello.log
```

OmniMark reads the argument file, ignoring comments and extra white space, and treats its contents exactly like command-line options.

Hash-bang notation in argument files

UNIX systems do not have a file extension to key on for program invocation. They rely heavily on the hash-bang notation. The hash-bang line may be placed at the top of the argument file.

```
#!/usr/local/bin/omnimark -f
-sb hello.xom
-alog /www/root/log/hello.log
```

Note that on a UNIX system (including Apache on Windows), the .xar file must also be made executable.

Assuming the file "hello.xar" is in "/www/root/cgi-bin/" the URL

```
/localhost/cgi-bin/hello.xar
```

will invoke hello.xom and append any log messages to "hello.log".

OmniMark's project file

By convention, a project file has the suffix ".xop", so the OmniMark program "hello.xom" should have the project file "hello.xop".

A project file is an XML file that performs the same function as an argument file and is invoked in exactly the same way. It, too, can have a hash-bang line as the first line (although XML doesn't strictly provide for this).

The OmniMark IDE generates project files directly, and the capabilities of project files will expand over the next few years. In order for a project file to work correctly for a CGI program, you must modify Edit -> Project Options and add "-brief" under the "Extra" tab. If you don't do this, OmniMark will emit its banner information before your program can output its HTTP headers, the web server will become confused, and your CGI program will break.

Microsoft web servers

Personal Web Server (PWS) and Internet Information Server (IIS) on Windows NT

To configure Personal Web Server or Internet Information Server on Windows NT to run OmniMark programs as CGIs:

1. Log in to your machine with administrative privileges.
2. If you are running PWS, ensure that you have Internet Service Manager installed. If Internet Service Manager is not installed, reinstall PWS, select the subcomponents of PWS, and check Internet Service Manager.
3. Start the Microsoft Management Console (through the Start menu: Windows NT 4.0 Option Pack -> Microsoft Personal Web Server -> Internet Service Manager).
4. Ensure that you have a directory set up for running CGI scripts, with the appropriate permissions set. See the web server documentation for details on setting up a directory for CGI scripts.
5. Right-click on the CGI directory, and select Properties. A Properties dialog box will appear.
6. Click "Configuration" on the Virtual Directory tab. The Application Configuration dialog box will appear.
7. On the App Mappings tab, in the Application Mappings frame, click "Add". The "Add/Edit Application Extensions Mapping" dialog box will appear.
8. In "Executable", enter the command line to start the OmniMark C/VM, substituting "%s" for the file name of your script. Typically it will look like this:
   `c:\omnimark\omnimark.exe -noexpand -sb %s`
9. Enter ".xom" in the Extension field.
10. Under Method exclusions, enter PUT, DELETE.
11. Ensure that "Script engine" is checked, and click "OK".

12. Repeat steps 11 through 15 for the extension .xop using the command line:
    `c:\omnimark\omnimark.exe -noexpand -f %s`
13. Repeat steps 11 through 15 for the extension .xar using the command line:
    `c:\omnimark\omnimark.exe -noexpand -f %s`
14. Repeat steps 11 through 15 for the extension .pmo using the command line:
    `c:\omnimark\omnimark.exe -noexpand -s pmo.xom %s`
15. Click "OK" to accept the settings in the "Application Configuration" dialog box.
16. On the directory's Properties dialog box, ensure that the "Permissions" radio button is set to "Execute (including script)", and click "OK" to accept.

Personal Web Server (PWS) on Windows 95/98

To configure Personal Web Server on Windows 95/98 to run OmniMark programs as CGIs:

1. As a safety measure, back up your registry.
2. Under the Start -> Run menu enter regedit and select OK.
3. Select HKEY_LOCAL_MACHINE -> System -> CurrentControlSet -> Services -> w3svc -> parameters -> ScriptMap.
4. In the right window, you will see at least one string value icon (with a little "ab" on it).
5. Select Edit -> New -> String Value. This will create a new string value icon and allow you to set its name.
6. Type ".xom" as the name of the icon.
7. Double-click on the icon. The Edit string dialog box will appear.
8. In the "Value data" field, type the command line for running .xom files, typically: `c:\omnimark\omnimark.exe -noexpand -sb %s`
9. Click OK.
10. Repeat steps 5 to 9 for the extension .xop using the command line:
    `c:\omnimark\omnimark.exe -noexpand -f %s`
11. Repeat steps 5 to 9 for the extension .xar using the command line:
    `c:\omnimark\omnimark.exe -noexpand -f %s`
12. Repeat steps 5 to 9 for the extension .pmo using the command line:
    `c:\omnimark\omnimark.exe -noexpand -s pmo.xom %s`
13. Close the regedit window.
14. Ensure that you have a directory in your server configuration that is set up for running CGI programs. See the PWS documentation for information on setting up and configuring such a directory.

The Apache web server

The simplest way to make CGI scripts work in any version of Apache is to use the ScriptAlias directive in the web server's configuration file. This directive maps a virtual directory to a physical directory, and tells the web server that any files in this directory are to be run as CGI programs.

Notice that this directive just creates a virtual to physical directory mapping: it does not map file extensions to interpreters. Apache will use the hash-bang line at the top of each script to determine the appropriate command line to use.

Apache on Windows 9x/NT

Add the following line to Apache's configuration file (often called "httpd.conf" in the directory in which you installed Apache):

```
ScriptAlias /virtdir/ "c:/www/root/cgi-bin/"
```

where "virtdir" is the name of the virtual directory you want to create, and "c:/www/root/cgi-bin/" is the name of the physical directory your CGI scripts reside in. Note the forward slashes on the physical path.

All of our examples are going to assume that /virtdir/ is /cgi-bin/ so the command should be:

```
ScriptAlias /cgi-bin/ "c:/www/root/cgi-bin/"
```

Stop and restart the Apache server by selecting Start -> Settings -> Control Panel -> Services to force the server to reread its configuration file.

Now a request to the web server for http://hostname/cgi-bin/hello.xom will cause the server to run C:/www/root/cgi-bin/hello.xom.

Apache on UNIX/Linux

To configure Apache on UNIX or Linux machines to run OmniMark CGI programs:

Add the following line to Apache's configuration file (often called "httpd.conf" in the directory in which you installed Apache):

```
ScriptAlias /virtdir/ "/www/root/cgi-bin/"
```

where "virtdir" is the name of the virtual directory you want to create, and

"/www/root/cgi-bin/" is the name of the physical directory your CGI scripts reside in. Note the forward slashes on the physical path.

All of our examples are going to assume that /virtdir/ is /cgi-bin/ so the command should be:

```
ScriptAlias /cgi-bin/ "/www/root/cgi-bin/"
```

Stop and restart the Apache server by running

```
apachectl restart
```

to force the server to reread its configuration file.

Now a request to the web server for

```
http://hostname/cgi-bin/hello.xom
```

will cause the server to run

```
c:/www/root/cgi-bin/hello.xom
```

Appendix 3: Long programs

Some of the programs in the book are too long to be presented in-line.
They are collected here, organized by chapter number.

Chapter 9

hangman.xom

```
#!omnimark.exe -sb
; hangman.xom
declare #process-input has unbuffered
include "omutil.xin"
include "omcgi.xin"
declare catch unoriginal-new-word
declare catch game-over
declare catch you-win
macro num-chances is "10" macro-end

global stream cgi-data variable
global stream form-data variable

define function new-page elsewhere
define function guess-page elsewhere
define function login-page elsewhere
```

```
process
   cgiGetEnv into cgi-data
   cgiGetQuery into form-data

   output "Content-type: text/html"
       || crlf
       || crlf
       || "<HTML><BODY>"
       || "<H1>Hangman</H1>"

   ; get the extra path information
   ; used to tell us which mode to run in
   ; by dropping the script name
   ; from the path info
   do scan cgi-data{"PATH_INFO"}
    drop ~cgi-data {"SCRIPT_NAME"}
      match "/login" =|
         login-page
      match "/guess" =|
         guess-page
      else
         new-page
   done

   output "</BODY></HTML>"

   ;catch any unanticipated errors and report them
   catch #program-error
    code c
    message m
    location l
      output "<P>We're sorry, an error occurred.%n"
          || "<p>%d(c)%n<p>%g(m)%n<p>%g(l)"



;==============================
; function new-page
;
; displays the initial page for a new game

define function new-page as
```

```
    output '<P>In order to play you must provide a new word '
        || 'to add to the dictionary. Please keep it clean.'
        || '<FORM METHOD="POST" ACTION="'
        || cgi-data {"SCRIPT_NAME"}
        || '/login%">'
        || '<B>Your word:</B>'
        || '<INPUT TYPE="text" NAME="new_word" SIZE=16>'
        || '<INPUT TYPE="submit" VALUE="Submit Word">'
        || '</FORM>'

;=================================
; function login-page
;
; Accepts the login and displays guess page
; or asks for new login

define function login-page as
    local integer num-words
    local integer words-seen initial {0}
    local integer chosen-word-offset
    local stream chosen-word
    local stream words-file
    local integer rnd

    ; choose a word by offset into the existing list
    set num-words to file "numwords.txt"
    UTIL_Srand(UTIL_GetMilliSecondTimer)
    set rnd to UTIL_Rand
    set chosen-word-offset to (rnd modulo num-words) + 1

    ; Make sure the new word is original
    ; While we're looking at the word list,
    ; grab the chosen word
    repeat scan file "words.txt"
        match any-text+ => current-word
            throw unoriginal-new-word
            when form-data{"new_word"}
            matches ul current-word =|
            set chosen-word to current-word
            when words-seen = chosen-word-offset
            increment words-seen
        match "%n"
    again
```

```
; update the words file
reopen words-file as file "words.txt"
using output as words-file
 ; force the word to lowercase
 output "lg" % form-data{"new_word"} || "%n"
close words-file
set file "numwords.txt" to "d" % (1 + num-words)

; output the guess page
output '<p>' || "-" ||* length of chosen-word
    || '<P>ABCDEFGHIJKLMNOPQRSTUVWXYZ'
    || '<P>You have '
    || num-chances
    || ' wrong guesses before you die.'
    || '<P>Guess a letter'
    || '<FORM METHOD="POST" ACTION="'
    || cgi-data{"SCRIPT_NAME"}
    || '/guess">'
    || '<B>Your guess:</B>'
    || '<INPUT TYPE="hidden" NAME="word" VALUE="'
    || chosen-word || '">'
    || '<INPUT TYPE="hidden" NAME="wrong" VALUE="">'
    || '<INPUT TYPE="hidden" NAME="right" VALUE="">'
    || '<INPUT TYPE="text" NAME="guess" SIZE="1">'
    || '<INPUT TYPE="submit" VALUE="Submit guess">'
    || '</FORM>'

; if word is not original, ask for a new one
catch unoriginal-new-word
output '<P>Sorry, I already know "'
    || form-data{"new_word"}
    || '".'
    || '<P>In order to play you must provide a new word '
    || 'to add to the dictionary. Please keep it clean.'
    || '<FORM METHOD="POST" ACTION="'
    || cgi-data{"SCRIPT_NAME"}
    || '/login">'
    || '<B>Your word:</B>'
    || '<INPUT TYPE="text" NAME="new_word" SIZE=16>'
    || '<INPUT TYPE="submit" VALUE="Submit Word">'
    || '</FORM>'

;==============================
; function guess-page
```

```
;
; Shows what you have guessed so far and
; asks for your next guess

define function guess-page as
    local stream right-guesses
    local stream wrong-guesses
    local stream guess
    local stream word
    local stream word-letters initial {""}
    local integer chances
    local stream guesses

    set right-guesses to form-data{"right"}
    set wrong-guesses to form-data{"wrong"}
    set guess to "lg" format form-data{"guess"}
    set guesses to right-guesses || wrong-guesses || guess
    set word to form-data{"word"}
    set chances to num-chances - length of wrong-guesses

    ; list the letters in the word
    repeat scan word
      match any => the-letter
         do unless word-letters matches any** the-letter
            set word-letters to word-letters || the-letter
         done
    again

    do when word matches any** guess
      ; good guess
      set right-guesses to right-guesses || guess
      throw you-win
       when length of right-guesses = length of word-letters

      output "Right! There are one or more "
         || form-data{"guess"}
         || "'s in the word."
    else
      ; bad guess
      set wrong-guesses to wrong-guesses || guess
      output "Wrong! There are no "
         || form-data{"guess"}
         || "'s in the word."
      decrement chances
```

```
      throw game-over when chances = 0
done

; Print the word
output "<p>"
repeat scan word
   match any => the-letter
      do when right-guesses matches any** the-letter
         output the-letter
      else
         output "-"
      done
again

; Print the alphabet
output "<p>"
repeat scan "ABCDEFGHIJKLMNOPQRSTUVWXYZ"
match any => the-letter
   do unless guesses matches any** ul the-letter
      output the-letter
   else
      output "*"
   done
again

output '<P>You have '
   || 'd' % chances
   || ' wrong guesses before you die.'
   || '<P>Guess a letter'
   || '<FORM METHOD="POST" ACTION="'
   || cgi-data {"SCRIPT_NAME"}
   || '/guess">'
   || '<B>Your guess:</B>'
   || '<INPUT TYPE="hidden" NAME="word" VALUE="'
   || word || '">'
   || '<INPUT TYPE="hidden" NAME="wrong" VALUE="'
   || wrong-guesses || '">'
   || '<INPUT TYPE="hidden" NAME="right" VALUE="'
   || right-guesses || '">'
   || '<INPUT TYPE="text" NAME="guess" SIZE="1">'
   || '<INPUT TYPE="submit" VALUE="Submit guess">'
   || '</FORM>'

catch game-over
```

```
output '<P>Game over. You die.%n'
    || '<P>The word was "'
    || word || '".'

catch you-win
    output '<p>You win. <P>The word was "'
        || word || '".'
```

Chapter 10

Login page template

The login page where you start a new game:

```
<HTML><BODY>
<H1>Hangman</H1>
<P>In order to play you must provide a new word
to add to the dictionary. Please keep it clean.
<FORM METHOD="POST" ACTION="<<<Action>>>">
<B>Your word:</B>
<INPUT TYPE="TEXT" NAME="new_word" SIZE=16>
<INPUT TYPE="SUBMIT" VALUE="Submit Word">
</FORM>
</BODY></HTML>
```

Error page template

The error page if the user enters a word already in the dictionary:

```
<HTML><BODY>
<H1>Hangman</H1>
<P>Sorry, I already know <<<Word>>>.
<P>In order to play you must provide a new word
to add to the dictionary. Please keep it clean.
<FORM METHOD="POST" ACTION="<<<Action>>>">
<B>Your word:</B>
<INPUT TYPE="TEXT" NAME="new_word" SIZE=16>
<INPUT TYPE="SUBMIT" VALUE="Submit Word">
</FORM>
</BODY></HTML>
```

Winning page template

The page displayed if the user wins the game:

```
<HTML><BODY>
<H1>Hangman</H1>
<P>You win. The word was <<<Word>>>.
</BODY></HTML>
```

Losing page template

The page displayed if the user loses the game:

```
<HTML><BODY>
<H1>Hangman</H1>
<P>You lose. The word was <<<Word>>>.
</BODY></HTML>
```

hangman2.xom

```
#!omnimark.exe -sb
;hangman2.xom
;hangman with templates
include "omutil.xin"
include "omcgi.xin"

declare #main-input has unbuffered
declare catch unoriginal-new-word
declare catch game-over
declare catch you-win

;parameterizable globals
global stream num-chances initial {"7"}
global stream new-template initial {"hang\new.txt"}
global stream guess-template initial {"hang\guess.txt"}
global stream unoriginal-new-word-template
 initial {"hang\unoriginal.txt"}
global stream lose-template initial {"hang\lose.txt"}
global stream win-template initial {"hang\win.txt"}
global stream words-file-name initial {"hang\words.txt"}
global stream numwords-file-name
 initial {"hang\numwords.txt"}

global stream cgi-data variable
```

```
global stream form-data variable

define function new-page elsewhere
define function guess-page elsewhere
define function login-page elsewhere

process

    CGIGetEnv into cgi-data
    CGIGetQuery into form-data

    output "Content-type: text/html"
        || crlf
        || crlf

    ;get the extra path information
    ;used to tell us which mode to run in
    do scan cgi-data{"PATH_INFO"}
     drop ~cgi-data{"SCRIPT_NAME"}
       match "/login"
           login-page
       match "/guess"
           guess-page
       match ""
           new-page
    done

;===============================
; new-page function
;
define function new-page as
    repeat scan file new-template
       match any++ => stuff lookahead ("<<<" | =|)
           output stuff
       match "<<<Action>>>"
           output cgi-data{"SCRIPT_NAME"}
               || "/login"
    again


;===============================
; login-page function
;
define function login-page as
```

```
local integer num-words
local integer words-seen initial {0}
local integer chosen-word-offset
local stream chosen-word
local stream words-file
local integer rnd
local stream substitutes variable

; choose a word by offset into the existing list
set num-words to file numwords-file-name
UTIL_Srand(UTIL_GetMilliSecondTimer)
set rnd to UTIL_Rand
set chosen-word-offset to (rnd modulo num-words) + 1

; Make sure the new word is original
; while we're looking at the word list,
; grab the chosen word
; Avoid extra copying of pattern variable
; with test on word finding "match"
repeat scan file words-file-name
   match any-text+ => current-word
      throw unoriginal-new-word
       when form-data{"new_word"}
       matches ul current-word =|
      set chosen-word to current-word
       when words-seen = chosen-word-offset
      increment words-seen
   match "%n"
again


;update the words file
reopen words-file as file words-file-name
using output as words-file
   ;force the word to lowercase
   output "lg" format form-data{"new_word"} || "%n"
close words-file
set file numwords-file-name to "d" % (1 + num-words)


;output the guess page
repeat scan file guess-template
   match any++ => stuff lookahead ("<<<" | =|)
      output stuff
```

```
      match "<<<Result>>>"
         output ""
      match "<<<WordMask>>>"
         output "-" ||* length of chosen-word
      match "<<<AlphabetMask>>>"
         output "ABCDEFGHIJKLMNOPQRSTUVWXYZ"
      match "<<<Chances>>>"
         output num-chances
      match "<<<Action>>>"
         output cgi-data{"SCRIPT_NAME"} || "/guess"
      match "<<<Word>>>"
         output chosen-word
      match "<<<Right>>>"
         output ""
      match "<<<Wrong>>>"
         output ""
   again

   ;if word is not original, ask for a new one
   catch unoriginal-new-word

   repeat scan file new-template
      match any++ => stuff lookahead ("<<<" | =|)
         output stuff
      match "<<<Word>>>"
         output form-data {"new_word"}
      match "<<<Action>>>"
         output cgi-data{"SCRIPT_NAME"} || "/login"
   again


;=============================
; guess-page function
;
define function guess-page as
   local stream right-guesses
   local stream wrong-guesses
   local stream guess
   local stream word
   local stream word-letters initial {""}
   local stream word-mask
   local stream alphabet-mask
   local integer chances
   local stream substitutes variable
```

```
local stream result-message

set right-guesses to form-data{"right"}
set wrong-guesses to form-data{"wrong"}
set guess to "lg" % form-data{"guess"}
set word to form-data{"word"}
set chances to num-chances - length of wrong-guesses

;list the letters in the word
repeat scan word
   match any => the-letter
      do unless word-letters matches any** the-letter
         set word-letters to word-letters || the-letter
      done
again

do when word matches any** ul guess
   ;good guess
   set right-guesses to right-guesses || guess
   throw you-win
    when length of right-guesses = length of word-letters

   set result-message
    to "Right! There are one or more "
    || form-data{"guess"}
    || "'s in the word."
else
   ;bad guess
   decrement chances
   throw game-over when chances = 0
   set wrong-guesses to wrong-guesses || guess
   set result-message
    to "Wrong! There are no "
    || form-data{"guess"}
    || "'s in the word."
done

;Print the word
open word-mask as buffer
using output as word-mask
 repeat scan word
    match any => the-letter
       do when right-guesses matches any** the-letter
          output the-letter
```

```
        else
            output "-"
        done
 again
close word-mask

;Print the alphabet
open alphabet-mask as buffer
using output as alphabet-mask
 repeat scan "ABCDEFGHIJKLMNOPQRSTUVWXYZ"
    match any => the-letter
        do unless (right-guesses || wrong-guesses)
         matches any** ul the-letter
            output the-letter
        else
            output "*"
        done
 again
close alphabet-mask

;output the guess page
repeat scan file guess-template
    match any++ => stuff lookahead ("<<<" | =|)
        output stuff
    match "<<<Result>>>"
        output result-message
    match "<<<WordMask>>>"
        output word-mask
    match "<<<AlphabetMask>>>"
        output alphabet-mask
    match "<<<Chances>>>"
        output "d" format chances
    match "<<<Action>>>"
        output cgi-data{"SCRIPT_NAME"} || "/guess"
    match "<<<Word>>>"
        output word
    match "<<<Right>>>"
        output right-guesses
    match "<<<Wrong>>>"
        output wrong-guesses
again


catch game-over
```

```
    repeat scan file lose-template
    match any++ => stuff lookahead ("<<<" | =|)
       output stuff
          output stuff
       match "<<<Word>>>"
          output word
    again

  catch you-win
    repeat scan file win-template
    match any++ => stuff lookahead ("<<<" | =|)
       output stuff
       match "<<<Word>>>"
          output word
    again
```

hangman3.xom

```
#!omnimark.exe -sb
;hangman3.xom
;hangman with templates
;and centralized template handling
include "omutil.xin"
include "omcgi.xin"

declare #main-input has unbuffered
declare catch unoriginal-new-word
declare catch game-over
declare catch you-win
declare catch invalid-template

;parameterizable globals
global stream num-chances initial {"7"}
global stream new-template initial {"hang\new.txt"}
global stream guess-template initial {"hang\guess.txt"}
global stream unoriginal-new-word-template
 initial {"hang\unoriginal.txt"}
global stream lose-template initial {"hang\lose.txt"}
global stream win-template initial {"hang\win.txt"}
global stream words-file-name initial {"hang\words.txt"}
global stream numwords-file-name
 initial {"hang\numwords.txt"}

global stream cgi-data variable
```

```
global stream form-data variable

define function new-page elsewhere
define function guess-page elsewhere
define function login-page elsewhere
define function process-template
   value stream template-file
   using read-only stream substitutes
   elsewhere

process

   CGIGetEnv into cgi-data
   CGIGetQuery into form-data

   output "Content-type: text/html"
       || crlf
       || crlf

   ;get the extra path information
   ;used to tell us which mode to run in
   do scan cgi-data{"PATH_INFO"}
    drop ~cgi-data{"SCRIPT_NAME"}
      match "/login"
         login-page
      match "/guess"
         guess-page
      match ""
         new-page
   done

   catch invalid-template
      output "We're sorry, an error occurred."

;=======================
; new-page function
;
define function new-page as
   local stream substitutes variable
   set new substitutes {"Action"}
    to cgi-data{"SCRIPT_NAME"} || "/login"
   process-template new-template using substitutes
```

```
;========================
; login-page function
;
define function login-page as
    local integer num-words
    local integer words-seen initial {0}
    local integer chosen-word-offset
    local stream chosen-word
    local stream words-file
    local integer rnd
    local stream substitutes variable

    ; choose a word by offset into the existing list
    set num-words to file numwords-file-name
    UTIL_Srand(UTIL_GetMilliSecondTimer)
    set rnd to UTIL_Rand
    set chosen-word-offset to (rnd modulo num-words) + 1

    ; Make sure the new word is original
    ; While we're looking at the word list,
    ; grab the chosen word
    ; Avoid extra copying of pattern variable
    ; with test on word finding "match"
    repeat scan file words-file-name
      match any-text+ => current-word
        throw unoriginal-new-word
          when form-data{"new_word"}
          matches ul current-word =|
        set chosen-word to current-word
          when words-seen = chosen-word-offset
        increment words-seen
      match "%n"
    again

    ;update the words file
    reopen words-file as file words-file-name
    using output as words-file
      ;force the word to lowercase
      output "lg" % form-data{"new_word"} || "%n"
    close words-file
    set file numwords-file-name to "d" % (1 + num-words)


    ;output the guess page
```

```
    set new substitutes {"Result"}
     to ""

    set new substitutes {"WordMask"}
     to "-" ||* length of chosen-word

    set new substitutes {"AlphabetMask"}
     to "ABCDEFGHIJKLMNOPQRSTUVWXYZ"

    set new substitutes {"Chances"}
     to num-chances

    set new substitutes {"Action"}
     to cgi-data{"SCRIPT_NAME"} || "/guess"

    set new substitutes{"Word"}
     to chosen-word

    set new substitutes{"Right"}
     to ""

    set new substitutes{"Wrong"}
     to ""

    process-template guess-template using substitutes

    ;if word is not original, ask for a new one
    catch unoriginal-new-word
       set new substitutes {"Word"}
        to form-data{"new_word"}

       set new substitutes{"Action"}
        to cgi-data{"SCRIPT_NAME"} || "/login"

       process-template unoriginal-new-word-template
        using substitutes


;=======================
; guess-page function
;
define function guess-page as
   local stream right-guesses
   local stream wrong-guesses
```

```
local stream guess
local stream word
local stream word-letters initial {""}
local stream word-mask
local stream alphabet-mask
local integer chances
local stream substitutes variable

set right-guesses to form-data{"right"}
set wrong-guesses to form-data{"wrong"}
set guess to "lg" % form-data{"guess"}
set word to form-data{"word"}
set chances to num-chances - length of wrong-guesses

;list the letters in the word
repeat scan word
   match any => the-letter
      do unless word-letters matches any** the-letter
         set word-letters to word-letters || the-letter
      done
again

do when word matches any** ul guess
   ;good guess
   set right-guesses to right-guesses || guess
   throw you-win
    when length of right-guesses = length of word-letters

   set new substitutes{"Result"}
    to "Right! There are one or more "
    || form-data{"guess"}
    || "'s in the word."
else
   ;bad guess
   set wrong-guesses to wrong-guesses || guess
   set new substitutes{"Result"}
    to "Wrong! There are no "
    || form-data{"guess"}
    || "'s in the word."
   decrement chances
   throw game-over when chances = 0
done

;Print the word
```

```
open word-mask as buffer
using output as word-mask
 repeat scan word
    match any => the-letter
       do when right-guesses matches any** the-letter
          output the-letter
       else
          output "-"
       done
 again
close word-mask

;Print the alphabet
open alphabet-mask as buffer
using output as alphabet-mask
 repeat scan "ABCDEFGHIJKLMNOPQRSTUVWXYZ"
    match any => the-letter
       do unless (right-guesses || wrong-guesses)
        matches any** ul the-letter
          output the-letter
       else
          output "*"
       done
 again
close alphabet-mask

;output the guess page
set new substitutes{"WordMask"}
 to word-mask

set new substitutes{"AlphabetMask"}
 to alphabet-mask

set new substitutes{"Chances"}
 to "d" % chances

set new substitutes{"Action"}
 to cgi-data{"SCRIPT_NAME"} || "/guess"

set new substitutes{"Word"}
 to word

set new substitutes{"Right"}
 to right-guesses
```

```
    set new substitutes{"wrong"}
     to wrong-guesses

    process-template guess-template using substitutes

    catch game-over
        set new substitutes{"Word"}
         to word
        process-template lose-template using substitutes

    catch you-win
        set new substitutes {"Word"}
         to word
        process-template win-template using substitutes

;template processing function
define function process-template
    value stream template-file
    using read-only stream substitutes
    as

    repeat scan file template-file
        match any++ => stuff lookahead ("<<<" | =|)
            output stuff
        match "<<<" letter+ => placeholder ">>>"
            do when substitutes has key placeholder
                output substitutes{placeholder}
            else
                throw invalid-template
            done
        match any ;this should never fire
            throw invalid-template
    again
```

Chapter 16

Customer.xom

```
#!omnimark.exe -sb
;customer update
include "omcgi.xin"
include "omdb.xin"
```

```
include "omdate.xin"

declare #main-input has unbuffered
declare #main-output has binary-mode

global stream dsn initial {"customer"}

global stream cgi-data variable
global stream form-data variable
global stream now-as-http-date

declare catch customer-not-found

define function list-page elsewhere
define function detail-page elsewhere
define function edit-page elsewhere
define function new-page elsewhere
define function update-record elsewhere
define function create-record elsewhere
define function delete-record elsewhere
define function error-page
 value stream error-message
 elsewhere

process

   CGIGetEnv into cgi-data
   CGIGetQuery into form-data

   ;establish the current date
   set now-as-http-date
    to ymdhms-to-arpadate now-as-ymdhms

   ;get the extra path information
   ;used to tell us which mode to run in
   ;by dropping the script name from the full path
   do scan cgi-data{"PATH_INFO"}
    drop ~cgi-data{"SCRIPT_NAME"}
      match "/detail"
         detail-page
      match "/edit"
         edit-page
      match "/new"
         new-page
```

```
        match "/update"
           update-record
        match "/create"
           create-record
        match "/delete"
           delete-record
        else
           list-page
     done

define function list-page as
     local dbDatabase db
     local dbField current-record variable
     local stream query

     output "Content-type: text/html" || crlf
         || "Date: " || now-as-http-date || crlf
         || "Expires: " || now-as-http-date || crlf
         || crlf
         || "<HTML><BODY>%n"
         || "<H1>Customer Database</H1>%n"

     set db to dbOpenODBC dsn
     set query to "SELECT CustomerID, Title, "
               || "FirstName, LastName "
               || "FROM Customer"
     dbQuery db sql query record current-record

     output "<H2>Customer list</H2>%n"
         || "<p>Click on a customer to see details."

     throw customer-not-found
      unless dbRecordExists current-record

     output "<TABLE>"
         || "<TR><TH>Customer ID</TH>"
         || "<TH>Customer Name</TH></TR>"

     using group html-escaping
      repeat exit unless dbrecordExists current-record
        output "<TR>%n<TD>"
            || '<A HREF="'
            || cgi-data {"SCRIPT_NAME"}
            || "/detail?"
```

```
        || dbFieldValue current-record{"CustomerID"}
        || '">'
        || dbFieldValue current-record{"CustomerID"}
        || "</A></TD>%n<TD>"

    submit dbFieldValue current-record{"Title"}
        || " "
        || dbFieldValue current-record{"FirstName"}
        || " "
        || dbFieldValue current-record{"LastName"}
    output "</TD>%n</TR>%n"
    dbRecordMove current-record
  again

output "</TABLE>%n"
    ;create NEW button
    || '[<A HREF="'
    || cgi-data{"SCRIPT_NAME"}
    || '/new'
    || '">NEW</A>]'
catch customer-not-found
    output '<P>No customers found.'

catch #external-exception
  identity id
  message msg
  location loc
    output   "Error:%n"
        || "ID: %g(id)%n"
        || "Msg: %g(msg)%n"
        || "Loc: %g(loc)%n"

catch #program-error
  code c
  message m
  location l
    output "<P>We're sorry, an error occurred.%n"
        || "%d(c)%n%g(m)%n%g(l)"
always
    output "</BODY></HTML>"


define function detail-page as
```

```
local dbDatabase db
local dbField current-record variable
local stream query

output "Content-type: text/html" || crlf
    || "Date: " || now-as-http-date || crlf
    || "Expires: " || now-as-http-date || crlf
    || crlf
    || "<HTML><BODY>%n"
    || "<H1>Customer Database</H1>%n"
set db to dbOpenODBC dsn
set query to "SELECT * FROM Customer "
        || "WHERE CustomerID='"
        || cgi-data{"QUERY_STRING"}
        || "'"
dbQuery db sql query record current-record

throw customer-not-found
 unless dbRecordExists current-record

using group html-escaping
 do
    output "<H2>Customer detail</H2>%n"
       || "<TABLE>%n<TR>%n<TD>CustomerID:</TD>%n<TD>"
    submit dbFieldValue current-record {"CustomerID"}
    output "</TD></TR>%n<TR>%n<TD>Name:</TD>%n<TD>"
    submit dbFieldValue current-record{"Title"}
       || " "
       || dbFieldValue current-record{"FirstName"}
       || " "
       || dbFieldValue current-record {"LastName"}
    output "</TD></TR>%n<TR>%n<TD>Address:</TD>%n<TD>"
    submit dbFieldValue current-record{"Address"}
    output "<BR>%n"
    submit dbFieldValue current-record{"City"}
    output "<BR>%n"
    submit dbFieldValue current-record{"State"}
    output "<BR>%n"
    submit dbFieldValue current-record{"Country"}
    output "<BR>%n"
    submit dbFieldValue current-record{"Code"}
    output "</TD></TR>%n<TR>%n<TD>Phone:</TD>%n<TD>"
    submit dbFieldValue current-record {"Phone"}
    output "</TD></TR>%n<TR>%n<TD>Fax:</TD>%n<TD>"
```

```
    submit dbFieldValue current-record{"Fax"}
    output "</TD></TR>%n<TR>%n<TD>Pager:</TD>%n<TD>"
    submit dbFieldValue current-record {"Pager"}
    output "</TD></TR>%n</TABLE>"
        ; create DELETE button
        || '[<A HREF="'
        || cgi-data{"SCRIPT_NAME"}
        || '/delete?'
        || dbFieldValue current-record{"CustomerID"}
        || '">DELETE</A>]'
        ;create EDIT button
        || '[<A HREF="'
        || cgi-data{"SCRIPT_NAME"}
        || '/edit?'
        || dbFieldValue current-record{"CustomerID"}
        || '">EDIT</A>]'
        ;create NEW button
        || '[<A HREF="'
        || cgi-data{"SCRIPT_NAME"}
        || '/new'
        || '">NEW</A>]'
        ;create LIST button
        || '[<A HREF="'
        || cgi-data{"SCRIPT_NAME"}
        || '">LIST</A>]'
done

catch customer-not-found
    output "<P>That customer was not found."

catch #external-exception
 identity id
 message msg
 location loc
    output "Error:%n"
        || "ID: %g(id)%n"
        || "Msg: %g(msg)%n"
        || "Loc: %g(loc)%n"

catch #program-error
 code c
 message m
 location l
    output "<P>We're sorry, an error occurred.%n"
```

```
              || "%d(c)%n%g(m)%n%g(l)"

  always
     output "</BODY></HTML>"


define function edit-page as
    local dbDatabase db
    local dbField current-record variable
    local stream query

    throw customer-not-found
     unless cgi-data has key "QUERY_STRING"

    output "Content-type: text/html" || crlf
        || "Date: " || now-as-http-date || crlf
        || "Expires: " || now-as-http-date || crlf
        || crlf
        || "<HTML><BODY>%n"
        || "<H1>Customer Database</H1>%n"

    set db to dbOpenODBC dsn
    set query to "SELECT * FROM Customer "
            || "WHERE CustomerID='"
            || cgi-data{"QUERY_STRING"}
            || "'"
    dbQuery db sql query record current-record

    throw customer-not-found
     unless dbRecordExists current-record

    using group html-escaping
     do
       output "<H2>Edit customer</H2>%n"
           || '<FORM METHOD="POST" ACTION="'
           || cgi-data{"SCRIPT_NAME"}
           || '/update">%n'
           || '<INPUT TYPE="hidden" '
           || 'NAME="OriginalCustomerID" VALUE="'
       submit dbFieldValue current-record{"CustomerID"}
       output '">%n'
           || "<TABLE>%n<TR>%n<TD>CustomerID:</TD>%n<TD>"
           || '<INPUT TYPE="text" NAME="CustomerID" VALUE="'
       submit dbFieldValue current-record {"CustomerID"}
```

```
output '"></TD></TR>%n<TR>%n<TD>Title:</TD>%n<TD>'
    || '<INPUT TYPE="text" NAME="Title" VALUE="'
submit dbFieldValue current-record{"Title"}
output '"></TD></TR>%n<TR>%n'
    || '<TD>First name:</TD>%n<TD>'
    || '<INPUT TYPE="text" NAME="FirstName" VALUE="'
submit dbFieldValue current-record{"FirstName"}
output '"></TD></TR>%n<TR>%n<TD>Last name:</TD>%n<TD>'
    || '<INPUT TYPE="text" NAME="LastName" VALUE="'
submit dbFieldValue current-record{"LastName"}
output '"></TD></TR>%n<TR>%n<TD>Address:</TD>%n<TD>'
    || '<INPUT TYPE="text" NAME="Address" VALUE="'
submit dbFieldValue current-record{"Address"}
output '"></TD></TR>%n<TR>%n<TD>City:</TD>%n<TD>'
    || '<INPUT TYPE="text" NAME="City" VALUE="'
submit dbFieldValue current-record{"City"}
output '"></TD></TR>%n<TR>%n<TD>State:</TD>%n<TD>'
    || '<INPUT TYPE="text" NAME="State" VALUE="'
submit dbFieldValue current-record{"State"}
output '"></TD></TR>%n<TR>%n<TD>Country:</TD>%n<TD>'
    || '<INPUT TYPE="text" NAME="Country" VALUE="'
submit dbFieldValue current-record{"Country"}
output '"></TD></TR>%n<TR>%n<TD>Code:</TD>%n<TD>'
    || '<INPUT TYPE="text" NAME="Code" VALUE="'
submit dbFieldValue current-record{"Code"}
output '"></TD></TR>%n<TR>%n<TD>Phone:</TD>%n<TD>'
    || '<INPUT TYPE="text" NAME="Phone" VALUE="'
submit dbFieldValue current-record{"Phone"}
output '"></TD></TR>%n<TR>%n<TD>Fax:</TD>%n<TD>'
    || '<INPUT TYPE="text" NAME="Fax" VALUE="'
submit dbFieldValue current-record{"Fax"}
output '"</TD></TR>%n<TR>%n<TD>Pager:</TD>%n<TD>'
    || '<INPUT TYPE="text" NAME="Pager" VALUE="'
submit dbFieldValue current-record{"Pager"}
output '"></TD></TR>%n</TABLE>%n'
    || '<INPUT TYPE="submit"'
    || 'NAME="Submit" VALUE="Submit">%n'
    || '<INPUT TYPE="submit" '
    || 'NAME="Submit" VALUE="Cancel">%n'
    || '<INPUT TYPE="reset" VALUE="Reset">%n'
    || "</FORM>%n"
done

catch customer-not-found
```

```
        output "<P>That customer was not found."

    catch #external-exception
     identity id
     message msg location loc
        output "Error:%n"
             || "ID: %g(id)%n"
             || "Msg: %g(msg)%n"
             || "Loc: %g(loc)%n"

    catch #program-error
     code c
     message m
     location l
        output "<P>We're sorry, an error occurred.%n"
             || "%d(c)%n%g(m)%n%g(l)"

    always
        output "</BODY></HTML>"

define function new-page as

    output "Content-type: text/html" || crlf
         || "Date: " || now-as-http-date || crlf
         || "Expires: " || now-as-http-date || crlf
         || crlf
         || "<HTML><BODY>%n"
         || "<H1>Customer Database</H1>%n"
         || "<H2>New customer</H2>%n"
         || '<FORM METHOD="POST" ACTION="'
         || cgi-data {"SCRIPT_NAME"}
         || '/create">%n'
         || "<TABLE>%n<TR>%n<TD>CustomerID</TD>%n<TD>"
         || '<INPUT TYPE="text" NAME="CustomerID"'
         || '"></TD></TR>%n<TR>%n<TD>Title</TD>%n<TD>'
         || '<INPUT TYPE="text" NAME="Title"'
         || '"></TD></TR>%n<TR>%n<TD>First name</TD>%n<TD>'
         || '<INPUT TYPE="text" NAME="FirstName"'
         || '"></TD></TR>%n<TR>%n<TD>Last name</TD>%n<TD>'
         || '<INPUT TYPE="text" NAME="LastName"'
         || '"></TD></TR>%n<TR>%n<TD>Address</TD>%n<TD>'
         || '<INPUT TYPE="text" NAME="Address"'
         || '"></TD></TR>%n<TR>%n<TD>City</TD>%n<TD>'
         || '<INPUT TYPE="text" NAME="City"'
```

```
    || '"></TD></TR>%n<TR>%n<TD>State</TD>%n<TD>'
    || '<INPUT TYPE="text" NAME="State"'
    || '"></TD></TR>%n<TR>%n<TD>Country</TD>%n<TD>'
    || '<INPUT TYPE="text" NAME="Country"'
    || '"></TD></TR>%n<TR>%n<TD>Code</TD>%n<TD>'
    || '<INPUT TYPE="text" NAME="Code"'
    || '"></TD></TR>%n<TR>%n<TD>Phone:</TD>%n<TD>'
    || '<INPUT TYPE="text" NAME="Phone"'
    || '"></TD></TR>%n<TR>%n<TD>Fax</TD>%n<TD>'
    || '<INPUT TYPE="text" NAME="Fax"'
    || '"</TD></TR>%n<TR>%n<TD>Pager</TD>%n<TD>'
    || '<INPUT TYPE="text" NAME="Pager"'
    || '"></TD></TR>%n</TABLE>%n'
    || '<INPUT TYPE="submit" '
    || 'NAME="Submit" VALUE="Submit">%n'
    || '<INPUT TYPE="submit" '
    || 'NAME="Submit" VALUE="Cancel">%n'
    || '<INPUT TYPE="reset" VALUE="Reset">%n'
    || "</FORM>%n"

  catch #external-exception identity id
    message msg location loc
    output "Error:%n"
        || "ID: %g(id)%n"
        || "Msg: %g(msg)%n"
        || "Loc: %g(loc)%n"

  catch #program-error
   code c
   message m
   location l
    output "<P>We're sorry, an error occurred.%n"
        || "%d(c)%n%g(m)%n%g(l)"

  always
    output "</BODY></HTML>"


define function create-record as
   local dbDatabase db
   local stream query

   do unless form-data key "Submit" = "Cancel"
     open query as buffer
```

```
using output as query
using group sql-escaping
do
    output "INSERT INTO Customer ("
        || "CustomerID, "
        || "Title, "
        || "FirstName, "
        || "LastName, "
        || "Address, "
        || "City, "
        || "State, "
        || "Country, "
        || "Code, "
        || "Phone, "
        || "Fax, "
        || "Pager) VALUES ('"
    submit form-data{"CustomerID"}
    output "', '"
    submit form-data {"Title"}
    output "', '"
    submit form-data {"FirstName"}
    output "', '"
    submit form-data {"LastName"}
    output "', '"
    submit form-data {"Address"}
    output "', '"
    submit form-data {"City"}
    output "', '"
    submit form-data {"State"}
    output "', '"
    submit form-data {"Country"}
    output "', '"
    submit form-data {"Code"}
    output "', '"
    submit form-data {"Phone"}
    output "', '"
    submit form-data {"Fax"}
    output "', '"
    submit form-data {"Pager"}
    output "')"
done
close query
set db to dbOpenODBC dsn
dbExecute db sql query
```

```
    done

    ;redirect to the detail page to see result
    do when cgi-data {"SERVER_PROTOCOL"} matches "HTTP/1.1"
       output "HTTP 1.1 303 See Other" || crlf
    else
       ;technically illegal but works on most old browsers
       output "HTTP 1.0 302 Found" || crlf
    done
    output 'Location: HTTP://'
        || cgi-data{"SERVER_NAME"}
        || "/"
        || cgi-data{"SCRIPT_NAME"}
        || "/detail?"
    using group url-escaping
     submit form-data{"CustomerID"}
    output crlf
        || crlf

    catch #external-exception
     identity id
     message msg
     location loc
       error-page ("<P>ID: %g(id)%n"
                || "<P>Message: %g(msg)%n"
                || "<P>Location: %g(loc)%n")

    catch #program-error
     code code
     message msg
     location loc
       error-page ("<P>ID: %d(code)%n"
                || "<P>Message: %g(msg)%n"
                || "<P>Location: %g(loc)%n")
define function update-record as
    local dbDatabase db
    local stream query

    do unless form-data key "Submit" = "Cancel"
       open query as buffer
       using output as query
        using group sql-escaping
        do
```

```
        output "UPDATE Customer SET "
            || "CustomerID='"
        submit form-data{"CustomerID"}
        output "', Title='"
        submit form-data{"Title"}
        output "', FirstName='"
        submit form-data{"FirstName"}
        output "', LastName='"
        submit form-data{"LastName"}
        output "', Address='"
        submit form-data{"Address"}
        output "', City='"
        submit form-data{"City"}
        output "', State='"
        submit form-data{"State"}
        output "', Country='"
        submit form-data{"Country"}
        output "', Code='"
        submit form-data{"Code"}
        output "', Phone='"
        submit form-data{"Phone"}
        output "', Fax='"
        submit form-data{"Fax"}
        output "', Pager='"
        submit form-data{"Pager"}
        output "' WHERE CustomerID='"
        submit form-data{"OriginalCustomerID"}
        output "'"
    done
    close query
    set db to dbOpenODBC dsn
    dbExecute db sql query
done
;redirect to the detail page to see result
do when cgi-data{"SERVER_PROTOCOL"} matches "HTTP/1.1"
    output "HTTP 1.1 303 See Other" || crlf
else
    ;technically illegal but works on most old browsers
    output "HTTP 1.0 302 Found" || crlf
done
output 'Location: HTTP://'
    || cgi-data{"SERVER_NAME"}
    || "/"
    || cgi-data{"SCRIPT_NAME"}
```

```
          || "/detail?"
    using group url-escaping
     submit form-data {"CustomerID"}
    output crlf
         || crlf

    catch #external-exception
     identity id
     message msg
     location loc
        error-page ("<P>ID: %g(id)%n"
                 || "<P>Message: %g(msg)%n"
                 || "<P>Location: %g(loc)%n"
                 || "<P>Query: %g(query)%n")

    catch #program-error
     code code
     message msg
     location loc
        error-page ("<P>ID: %d(code)%n"
                 || "<P>Message: %g(msg)%n"
                 || "<P>Location: %g(loc)%n")

define function delete-record as
    local dbDatabase db
    local stream query

    open query as buffer
    using output as query
     using group sql-escaping
     do
        output "DELETE * FROM Customer WHERE CustomerID='"
        submit cgi-data{"QUERY_STRING"}
        output "'"
     done
    close query
    set db to dbOpenODBC dsn
    dbExecute db sql query

    ;redirect to the detail page to see result
    do when cgi-data{"SERVER_PROTOCOL"} matches "HTTP/1.1"
        output "HTTP 1.1 303 See Other" || crlf
    else
        ;technically illegal but works on most old browsers
```

```
      output "HTTP 1.0 302 Found" || crlf
   done
   output 'Location: HTTP://'
       || cgi-data{"SERVER_NAME"}
       || "/"
       || cgi-data{"SCRIPT_NAME"}
       || crlf
       || crlf

   catch #external-exception
    identity id
    message msg
    location loc
      error-page ("<P>ID: %g(id)%n"
               || "<P>Message: %g(msg)%n"
               || "<P>Location: %g(loc)%n")

   catch #program-error
    code code
    message msg
    location loc
      error-page ("<P>ID: %d(code)%n"
               || "<P>Message: %g(msg)%n"
               || "<P>Location: %g(loc)%n")

define function error-page
   value stream error-message
   as

   output "Content-type: text/html" || crlf
       || "Date: " || now-as-http-date || crlf
       || "Expires: " || now-as-http-date || crlf
       || crlf
       || "<HTML><BODY>%n"
       || "<H1>Customer Database</H1>%n"
       || "<H2>Error</H2>"
       || error-message
       ;create LIST button
       || '<P>[<A HREF="'
       || cgi-data{"SCRIPT_NAME"}
       || '">LIST</A>]'
       || "</BODY></HTML>"

 ; find rules for escaping values
```

```
; output in HTML documents
group html-escaping

find "<"
   output "&lt;"

find ">"
   output "&lt;"

find "&"
   output "&amp;"

find '"'
   output "&quot;"

; find rules for escaping values
; output in SQL statements
group sql-escaping

find "'"
   output "''"

; find rules for escaping values
; output in URL query strings
group url-escaping

find [\letter or digit or "$-_.!*'(),"] => char
   output "%%" || "16ru2fzd" % binary char
```

Chapter 17

mailbot.xom

```
;mailbot.xom
include "omdb.xin"
include "omutil.xin"
include "omtcp.xin"

declare catch pop-communication-error
declare catch no-messages

global stream mail-server initial {"mail"}
```

```
global stream mail-username initial {"user-name"}
global stream mail-password initial {"password"}
global stream dsn initial {"customer"}
global counter sleep-time initial {600} ;ten minutes
global integer pop-port initial {110}
global integer message-count

macro crlf is "%13#%10#" macro-end

define function get-mail-message
 value tcpconnection connection
 as
    do scan tcpConnectionGetSource connection
     protocol ioprotocolEndDelimited (crlf || '.' || crlf)
       match any** lookahead ul "<?xml "
          submit #current-input
    done

process
   local dbdatabase db
   local dbField record variable
   ;deamon loop
   repeat
      local integer message-count
      local stream query
      local stream commands
      local stream response initial {""}
      local tcpconnection connection

      set db to dbOpenODBC dsn
      set connection
       to tcpConnectionOpen
       on mail-server
       at pop-port

      TCPConnectionSetBuffering connection enabled false
      open commands as tcpConnectionGetOutput connection
      using output as commands & #error
       do
          repeat
             set response
              to response
              || tcpConnectionGetCharacters connection
             put #error response
```

```
      exit unless
       TCPConnectionHasCharactersToRead connection
       timeout 500
again
throw pop-communication-error
 unless response matches "+OK"
output "USER " || mail-username || crlf
set response to tcpConnectionGetLine connection
put #error response
throw pop-communication-error
 unless response matches "+OK"

output "PASS " || mail-password || crlf
set response to tcpConnectionGetLine connection
put #error response
throw pop-communication-error
 unless response matches "+OK"

output "STAT" || crlf
set response to tcpConnectionGetLine connection
put #error response
throw pop-communication-error
 unless response matches "+OK"
set message-count
 to response drop ul "+OK " take digit+

throw no-messages when message-count = 0

repeat for integer message-number
 from 1 to message-count
   output "RETR " || "d" % message-number || crlf
   using nested-referents
   do
     set query
      with referents-allowed
      defaulting {""}
      to "INSERT INTO Customer ("
     || "CustomerID, "
     || "Title, "
     || "FirstName, "
     || "LastName, "
     || "Address, "
     || "City, "
     || "State, "
```

```
                    || "Country, "
                    || "Code, "
                    || "Phone, "
                    || "Fax, "
                    || "Pager) VALUES ('"
                    || referent "CustomerID" || "', '"
                    || referent "Title" || "', '"
                    || referent "FirstName" || "', '"
                    || referent "LastName" || "', '"
                    || referent "Address" || "', '"
                    || referent "City" || "', '"
                    || referent "State" || "', '"
                    || referent "Country" || "', '"
                    || referent "Code" || "', '"
                    || referent "Phone" || "', '"
                    || referent "Fax" || "', '"
                    || referent "Pager" || "')"

            do xml-parse
             scan input get-mail-message connection
               suppress
            done
           done
          dbExecute db sql query

          output "DELE " || "d" % message-number  || crlf
          set response to tcpConnectionGetLine connection
          put #error response
        again

        output "QUIT"  || crlf
        set response to tcpConnectionGetLine connection
        put #error response

        catch pop-communication-error
           output "QUIT" || crlf

        catch no-messages
           output "QUIT" || crlf
       done

   catch #program-error
    code error-code
    message error-message
```

```
      location error-location
        put #error "This is what went wrong:%n"
          || "The error code is: "
          || "d" % error-code
          || ". %n"
          || "The OmniMark error message is: %n"
          || error-message || "%n"
          || "The location of the error is: "
          || error-location || "%n"

    always
        dbClose db
        clear record
        ;wait a while before we try again
        UTIL_Sleep(sleep-time)
  again


element field
   set referent attribute "name" to "%c"

element form
   suppress

find line-start ".."
   output "."
```

Chapter 19

linkchk.xom

```
;linkchk.xom
; html link checker

include "omhttp.xin"

declare catch page-not-found
 reason value stream message
declare catch abort-scan
declare catch page-is-redirected
 location value stream location
declare catch ignore-this-url
 url value stream url
```

```
declare catch check-existence-only
 url value stream url
declare catch check-and-scan
 url value stream url
declare catch page-exists
declare catch page-found
 contents value stream contents

macro quotes is ["%"'"] macro-end
macro identifier
 is
    (letter [letter or digit or ".-"]*)
macro-end
macro parameter-name is identifier macro-end
macro parameter-value is
 (
    ('"'  [\'"']* '"')
    or
    ("'"  [\"'"]* "'")
    or
    [\white-space or ">" ]+
 )
macro-end
macro parameter is
 (
  parameter-name
  white-space* "=" white-space*
  parameter-value
  white-space*
 )
macro-end

define  function check-page
 value stream url
 check-exists-only value switch existence-only
 optional initial {false}
 timeout value integer timeout optional initial {60000}
 elsewhere


define function normalize-url
 value stream url
 elsewhere
```

```
define stream function remove-backrefs
 value integer number-of-backrefs
 from value stream path
 elsewhere

define stream function HTTPObjectGetHeader
 read-only stream HttpObject
 for value stream HeaderName
 elsewhere

global stream pages variable
global stream external-pages variable
global stream ignored-pages variable
global stream broken-links variable
global stream current-path
global stream current-resource
global stream domain
global integer current-page initial {0}

;main process rule
process
    set new pages{#args[1] drop ul "http://"?}
     to ""
    set current-page to 1
    set domain to key of pages take [\ "/"]*

    using output as #error
     do
        repeat exit when current-page > number of pages
           using pages[current-page]
             do
               ;set the current-path and current-resource
               ;global variables used by the url normalizer
               do scan key of pages
                  match
                   [\ "/"]*
                   ([\ "/"]* "/")* => path-part
                  any* => resource-part
                     set current-path to path-part
                     set current-path to "/"
                      when current-path = ""
                     set current-resource to resource-part
               done
```

```
        output "d" % current-page
            || " Checking and scanning "
            || key of pages
        check-page key of pages

        catch page-found contents contents
            using output as #suppress
                submit contents
            output " OK%n"
            ;since its ok, we don't care
            ;where it is referenced
            set pages[current-page] to ""

        catch page-not-found reason message
            output " BROKEN (" || message || ")%n"
            set new broken-links{key of pages}
              to message

        catch page-is-redirected location location
            output " REDIRECTED TO "
                || location || "%n"
            do when pages hasnt key location
                set new pages{location}
                  after item current-page
                  to ""
            done

    always
        increment current-page
    done
again

;now check the external pages
set current-page to 1
repeat
    exit when current-page > number of external-pages
    using external-pages item current-page
    do
        output "Checking existence of "
            || key of external-pages
        check-page (key of external-pages )
          check-exists-only true
        output " OK%n"
```

```
        catch page-not-found reason message
           output " BROKEN (" || message || ")%n"
           set new broken-links{key of external-pages}
            to message

        catch page-exists
           output " OK%n"
           ;since its ok, we don't care
           ;where it is referenced
           set external-pages[current-page] to ""

        catch page-is-redirected location location
           output " REDIRECTED TO "
               || location || "%n"
           do when external-pages hasnt key location
              set new external-pages{location}
               after item current-page
               to ""
           done
        always
           increment current-page
     done
  again

  ;list ignored pages
  repeat over ignored-pages
     output "Ignored "
         || key of ignored-pages
         || "%n"
  again
done

;report
do when number of broken-links > 0
   output "%nBROKEN LINKS%n"
   repeat over broken-links
      output key of broken-links
          || "(" || broken-links || ")%n"
   again
else
   output "NO BROKEN LINKS FOUND%n"
done

repeat over broken-links
```

```
      output "%nA link to "
          || key of broken-links
          || "%nreturning the response: "
          || broken-links
          || "%noccurs on the following pages:%n"
      do when pages has key key of broken-links
          output pages{key of broken-links}
      else
          output external-pages{key of broken-links}
      done
  again

;Find rules
find ([\ "<"]+ or "<" lookahead not (ul "a" white-space))+

find ul "<a" white-space+
   repeat scan #current-input
      match
       ul "href"  white-space*
       "=" white-space*
       (
        ('"'  [\ '"']* => url-a '"')
       or
        ("'"  [\ "'"]* => url-b "'")
       or
        [\ white-space or ">" ]+ => url-c
       )
         do when url-a is specified
            normalize-url url-a
         else when url-b is specified
            normalize-url url-b
         else
            normalize-url url-c
         done

      match parameter white-space+
   again

   catch ignore-this-url url url
      do when ignored-pages hasnt key url
         new ignored-pages{url}
      done
   catch check-existence-only url url
      do when external-pages hasnt key url
```

```
        set new external-pages{url}
          to key of pages[current-page] || "%n"
      done
   catch check-and-scan url url
      do when pages hasnt key url
         set new pages{url}
           to key of pages[current-page] || "%n"
      else
         set pages{url}
           to pages{url}
           || key of pages[current-page] || "%n"
      done

;Function normalize-url
define function normalize-url
 value stream url
 as
    local stream normalized-url
    local stream page-to-check
    local switch check-only initial {false}
    local switch ignore-this initial {false}

    open normalized-url as buffer
    using output as normalized-url
    using input as url
    do
       ;is it an absolute URL?
       do scan #current-input
          match
          ul "http://" [\ "/"]+ => dom
          [\ "#?"]* => resource
          any* => stub
             set check-only to true
              unless dom = domain
             output dom || resource
             do when stub matches "?"
                output stub
                set ignore-this to true
             done
             throw abort-scan
             ;not http
          match (letter+ ":") => method
             output method
             output #current-input
```

```
            set ignore-this to true
            throw abort-scan
      done

      ;output the domain name
      output domain

   ;what kind of path is it?
   do scan #current-input
      ;absolute path on domain (drop any "." ref to root)
      match "."? ("/" ([\ "/?#."]* "/")*) => pth
            output pth
            set current-path to pth
             when current-path isnt attached
      ;path is a backward reference
      match
       "../"+ => backrefs
       ([\ "/?#"]+ "/")* => pth
            output remove-backrefs (length of backrefs / 3)
             from current-path
             || pth
      ;path relative to page
       match ([\ "/?#"]* "/")+ => pth
            output current-path || pth
      ;is it an internal page reference
      match "#"
            output current-path || current-resource
            throw abort-scan
      ;no path in url
   else
      output current-path
   done

   ;get the resource name
   do scan #current-input
      match ([\ ".?#"]+ ".")+ => resource-name
            output resource-name
      ;otherwise, output the whole thing
      match any+ => not-a-resource-name
            output not-a-resource-name
   done


   do scan #current-input
```

```
         match ul ("html" or "htm") => extension
             output extension
         match [\ "?#/"]+ => extension
             output extension
             set check-only to true
     done

     do scan #current-input
         match "?" or "/" ;query or extra path signal cgi
             set ignore-this to true
     done
   catch abort-scan
   done
   close normalized-url
   throw ignore-this-url url normalized-url
    when ignore-this
   throw check-existence-only url normalized-url
    when check-only
   throw check-and-scan url normalized-url

;function check-page
define function check-page
 value stream url
 check-exists-only value switch existence-only
 optional initial {false}
 timeout value integer timeout optional initial {60000}
 as
    local stream request variable
    local stream response variable
    local stream request-report variable
    local stream response-report variable
    local stream error-message initial {""}
    HttpRequestSetFromUrl request from url
    set request{"method"} to "HEAD" when existence-only
    HttpRequestSend request into response timeout timeout
    do when HTTPObjectIsInError request
       HttpObjectGetStatusReport request into request-report
       set error-message to " HTTP ERROR%n"
       repeat over request-report
          set error-message to error-message
                            || request-report
       again
       throw page-not-found reason error-message
    done
```

```
do scan response{"status-code"}
   match "2"
      do when existence-only
         throw page-exists
      else
         throw page-found
          contents response{"entity-body"}
      done
   match "3"
      do scan HTTPObjectGetHeader response for "location"
         match ul "http://" ? any+ => url
            throw page-is-redirected url
      done
else
   throw page-not-found
    reason (response{"status-code"}
    || " " || response{"reason-phrase"} )
done


;function remove backrefs
define stream function remove-backrefs
 value integer number-of-backrefs
 from value stream path
as
   local stream path-parts variable
   local integer i initial {0}
   local stream fixed-path initial {""}
   local switch has-trailing-slash initial {false}

   repeat scan path
      match ("/" [\ "/"]+) => part
         set new path-parts to part
      match "/"
         set has-trailing-slash to true
   again

   repeat exit when i = number-of-backrefs
      remove path-parts
      increment i
   again

   repeat over path-parts
```

```
        set fixed-path to fixed-path || path-parts
    again

    ;restore final "/" if there was one
    set fixed-path to fixed-path || "/"
     when has-trailing-slash
    return fixed-path

;this should be in the HTTP library
define stream function HTTPObjectGetHeader
 read-only stream HttpObject
 for value stream HeaderName
 as
    return HttpObject{"header-%lg(HeaderName)"}
```

Chapter 20

prodserv.xom

```
;prodsrv.xom
;a middleware application to access
;the gold product database and return
;results in XML

include "omdb.xin"
include "omtcp.xin"
global counter port-number initial {5436}
global stream dsn initial {"gold"}
global stream poison-pill initial {"_die_"}
global dbDatabase db


declare catch shut-down
declare catch record-not-found
declare catch bad-request

process
    local tcpService service


    ;start up
    ;establish db connection and TCP/IP service
    set service to tcpServiceOpen at port-number
```

```
throw shut-down when tcpServiceIsInError service
set db to dbOpenODBC dsn

;request service loop
repeat
   local tcpConnection connection
   local stream reply

   ;wait for a connection
   set connection to TCPServiceAcceptConnection service

   open reply as TCPConnectionGetOutput connection
    protocol IOProtocolMultiPacket
   using output as reply
      do xml-parse
        scan tcpConnectionGetSource connection
        protocol IOProtocolMultiPacket
          output "%c"
          catch bad-request
            output '<response status="badrequest">'
          catch record-not-found
            output '<response status="notfound"/>'
          catch #program-error
            output '<response status="error"/>'
          catch #external-exception
            output '<response status="error"/>'
      done
   catch #program-error
      put #error "A program error occurred"
   catch #external-exception
    identity id
    message msg
    location loc
      output "%n%nAn error occurred.%n"
          || "ID: %g(id)%n"
          || "Msg: %g(msg)%n"
          || "Loc: %g(loc)%n"
again

;shutdown
catch shut-down
   output "Shutting down because ..."
catch #external-exception
 identity id
```

```
    message msg
    location loc
    output "%n%nAn error occurred.%n"
        || "ID: %g(id)%n"
        || "Msg: %g(msg)%n"
        || "Loc: %g(loc)%n"

;element rules for handling request

element "request"
    output "%c"

element "product"
    local dbField record variable
    local stream query

    set query to "SELECT Product.ProductID, "
                || "Product.ProductName, "
                || "Product.ProductLineID, "
                || "ProductLine.ProductLineName, "
                || "Product.ProductTypeID, "
                || "ProductType.ProductTypeName, "
                || "Product.ProductDescription, "
                || "Product.ProductPrice "
                || "FROM (Product LEFT JOIN ProductLine "
                || "ON Product.ProductLineID = "
                || "ProductLine.ProductLineID) "
                || "LEFT JOIN ProductType "
                || "ON Product.ProductTypeID = "
                || "ProductType.ProductTypeID "
                || "WHERE ProductID=%c"


    dbQuery db sql query record record

    throw record-not-found unless dbRecordExists record

    output '<response status="ok">%n'
        || '<product>%n<id>'
        || dbFieldValue record{"ProductID"}
        || '</id>%n<name>'
    submit dbFieldValue record{"ProductName"}
    output '</name>%n<line id="'
        || dbFieldValue record{"ProductLineID"}
```

```
          || '" name="'
   submit dbFieldValue record{"ProductLineName"}
   output '</line>%n<type id="'
          || dbFieldValue record{"ProductTypeID"}
          || '" name="'
   submit dbFieldValue record{"ProductTypeName"}
   output '</type>%n'
          || dbFieldValue record{"ProductDescription"}
          || '%n<price>'
          || dbFieldValue record{"ProductPrice"}
          || '</price>%n</product>%n</response>'

element "line"
   local dbField record variable
   local stream query

   set query to "SELECT ProductLineID, "
             || "ProductLineName, "
             || "ProductLineDescription "
             || "FROM ProductLine "
             || "WHERE ProductLineID=%c"

   dbQuery db sql query record record

   throw record-not-found unless dbRecordExists record

   output '<response status="ok">%n'
          || '<line>%n<id>'
          || dbFieldValue record{"ProductLineID"}
          || '</id>%n<name>'
   submit dbFieldValue record{"ProductLineName"}
   output '</name>%n'
          || dbFieldValue record{"ProductLineDescription"}
          || '%n</line>%n</response>'

element "type"
   local dbField record variable
   local stream query

   set query to "SELECT ProductTypeID, "
             || "ProductTypeName, "
             || "ProductTypeDescription "
             || "FROM ProductType "
             || "WHERE ProductTypeID=%c"
```

```
    dbQuery db sql query record record

    throw record-not-found unless dbRecordExists record

    output '<response status="ok">%n'
        || '<type>%n<id>'
        || dbFieldValue record{"ProductTypeID"}
        || '</id>%n<name>'
    submit dbFieldValue record{"ProductTypeName"}
    output '</name>%n'
        || dbFieldValue record{"ProductTypeDescription"}
        || '%n</type>%n</response>'
element "linelist"
    local dbField record variable
    local stream query

        set query to "SELECT ProductLineID, "
                || "ProductLineName, "
                || "ProductLineDescription "
                || "FROM ProductLine"

    dbQuery db sql query record record

    throw record-not-found unless dbRecordExists record

    output '<response status="ok">%n'
    repeat exit unless dbRecordExists record
        output '<line>%n<id>'
            || dbFieldValue record{"ProductLineID"}
            || '</id>%n<name>'
        submit dbFieldValue record{"ProductLineName"}
        output '</name>%n'
            || dbFieldValue record{"ProductLineDescription"}
            || '</line>%n'
        dbRecordMove record
    again
    output '</response>'
    suppress

element "typelist"
    local dbField record variable
    local stream query
```

```
   set query to "SELECT ProductTypeID, "
             || "ProductTypeName, "
             || "ProductTypeDescription "
             || "FROM ProductType"

   dbQuery db sql query record record

   throw record-not-found unless dbRecordExists record

   output '<response status="ok">%n'
   repeat exit unless dbRecordExists record
      output '<type>%n<id>'
          || dbFieldValue record{"ProductTypeID"}
          || '</id>%n<name>'
      submit dbFieldValue record{"ProductTypeName"}
      output '</name>%n'
          || dbFieldValue record{"ProductTypeDescription"}
          || '</type>%n'
      dbRecordMove record
   again
   output '</response>'
   suppress

element "productbytype"
   local dbField record variable
   local stream query

   set query to "SELECT ProductID, "
             || "ProductName "
             || "FROM Product "
             || "WHERE ProductTypeID=%c"

   dbQuery db sql query record record

   throw record-not-found unless dbRecordExists record

   output '<response status="ok">%n'
   repeat exit unless dbRecordExists record
      output '<product>%n<id>'
          || dbFieldValue record{"ProductID"}
          || '</id>%n<name>'
      submit dbFieldValue record{"ProductName"}
      output '</name>%n</product>%n'
```

```
        dbRecordMove record
    again
    output '</response>'

element "productbyline"
    local dbField record variable
    local stream query
    local stream response
    local stream id

    ;capture the ID since we will need to use it twice
    set id to "%c"

    ;buffer the response in case we encounter an error
    open response as buffer
    using output as response
     do
        output '<response status="ok">%n'

        ;first, get information on the product line:
        set query to "SELECT ProductLineID, "
                  || "ProductLineName, "
                  || "ProductLineDescription "
                  || "FROM ProductLine "
                  || "WHERE ProductLineID=%g(id)"
        dbQuery db sql query record record
        throw record-not-found unless dbRecordExists record

        output '<line><id>'
            || dbFieldValue record{"ProductLineID"}
            || '</id><name>'
        submit dbFieldValue record{"ProductLineName"}
        output '</name>'
            || dbFieldValue record{"ProductLineDescription"}
            || '</line>'


        set query to "SELECT ProductID, "
                  || "ProductName, "
                  || "ProductDescription, "
                  || "ProductPrice "
                  || "FROM Product "
                  || "WHERE ProductLineID=%g(id)"
        dbQuery db sql query record record
```

```
        throw record-not-found unless dbRecordExists record

        repeat exit unless dbRecordExists record
          output '<product>%n<id>'
              || dbFieldValue record{"ProductID"}
              || '</id>%n<name>'
          submit dbFieldValue record{"ProductName"}
          output '</name>%n'
              || dbFieldValue record{"ProductDescription"}
              || '<price>'
              || dbFieldValue record{"ProductPrice"}
              || '</price></product>%n'
          dbRecordMove record
        again
        output '</response>'
    done
    close response
    output response

element "selectedproducts"
    local dbField record variable
    local stream query

    set query to "SELECT ProductID, "
              || "ProductName, "
              || "ProductPrice "
              || "FROM Product "
              || "WHERE "
              || "ProductID IN (%c)"

    dbQuery db sql query record record

    throw record-not-found unless dbRecordExists record

    output '<response status="ok">%n'
    repeat exit unless dbRecordExists record
      output '<product>%n<id>'
          || dbFieldValue record{"ProductID"}
          || '</id>%n<name>'
      submit dbFieldValue record{"ProductName"}
      output '</name>%n<price>'
          || dbFieldValue record{"ProductPrice"}
          || '</price></product>%n'
      dbRecordMove record
```

```
   again
   output '</response>'

element "die"
   ;check that the die request has the proper poison-pill
   throw shut-down when "%c" = poison-pill
   ;otherwise just ignore the request

element #implied
   suppress
   throw bad-request

markup-error
   throw bad-request

;find rules for escaping text in XML documents
find "<"
    output "&lt;"

find ">"
    output "&gt;"

find "&"
    output "&amp;"

find '"'
    output "&quot;"
```

gold-home.xom

```
#!omnimark.exe -sb
;gold-home.xom
declare #process-input has unbuffered
declare #main-output has binary-mode
include "omutil.xin"
include "omcgi.xin"
include "omtcp.xin"
include "omdate.xin"

declare catch connection-error
declare catch XML-error

;parameterizable globals
global stream template-file-name
```

```
 initial {"gold\gold-home.txt"}
global stream product-server-host
 initial {"localhost"}
global counter product-server-port initial {"5436"}

global stream now-as-http-date initial
 {ymdhms-to-arpadate now-as-ymdhms}

process

    output "Content-type: text/html" || crlf
       || "Date: " || now-as-http-date || crlf
       || "Expires: " || now-as-http-date || crlf
       || crlf
       || crlf

    repeat scan file template-file-name
      match
      ([\ "<"]+
       or "<" lookahead not "<<"
      )+ => stuff
        output stuff
      match "<<<LineList>>>"
         local TCPConnection connection
         set connection to TCPConnectionOpen
          on product-server-host
          at product-server-port
         throw connection-error
          when TCPConnectionIsInError connection
         set TCPConnectionGetOutput connection
          protocol IOProtocolMultiPacket
          to "<request><linelist/></request>"

         do xml-parse
          scan TCPConnectionGetSource connection
          protocol IOProtocolMultiPacket
            output "%c"
         done

       match "<<<TypeList>>>"
          local TCPConnection connection

          set connection to TCPConnectionOpen
           on product-server-host
```

```
            at product-server-port
         throw connection-error
          when TCPConnectionIsInError connection

         set TCPConnectionGetOutput connection
          protocol IOProtocolMultiPacket
          to "<request><typelist/></request>"

         do xml-parse
          scan TCPConnectionGetSource connection
          protocol IOProtocolMultiPacket
             output "%c"
         done
   again

   catch connection-error
      output "Conncetion error%n"
   catch XML-error
      output "XML error%n"

element "response"
   do scan attribute "status"
      match "ok" =|
         ;do nothing.
      match "error" =|
         output "<H3>Server Error</H3>"
             || "<P>Please try again later."
      match "notfound" =|
         output "<p>The item you requested "
             || "was not found.</p>"
      match "badrequest" =|
         output "<p>The system did not "
             || "understand your request.</p>"
   else
      output "<H3>Server Error</H3>"
          || "<P>Please try again later."
   done

   output "%c"


element "line"
   output '<a href="gold-line.xom?%c<br>'
```

```
element "type"
   output '<a href="gold-type.xom?%c<br>'

element "id"
   output '%c">'

element "name"
   output '%c:</a> '

element "description"
   output "%c"

element "p"
   do when occurrence = 1
      output "%c"
   else
      output "<p>%c"
   done

markup-error
   throw XML-error
```

gold-line.xom

```
#!omnimark.exe -sb
;gold-line.xom
;prints list of product lines
declare #process-input has unbuffered
declare #main-output has binary-mode
declare #main-output has referents-allowed defaulting {""}
include "omutil.xin"
include "omcgi.xin"
include "omtcp.xin"
include "ombcd.xin"
include "omdate.xin"

declare catch connection-error
declare catch XML-error

;parameterizable globals
global stream template-file-name
  initial {"gold\gold-line.txt"}
global stream product-server-host
  initial {"localhost"}
```

```
global counter product-server-port
 initial {"5436"}

global stream ProductByLineText
global stream current-product-id

global stream cgi-data variable
global stream now-as-http-date

process
   local TCPConnection connection

   ;establish the current date
   set now-as-http-date
    to ymdhms-to-arpadate now-as-ymdhms

   CGIGetEnv into cgi-data

   output "Content-type: text/html" || crlf
       || "Date: " || now-as-http-date || crlf
       || "Expires: " || now-as-http-date || crlf
       || crlf
       || crlf


   repeat scan file template-file-name
     match
      ([\ "<"]+
       or "<" lookahead not "<<"
      )+ => stuff
         output stuff
     match "<<<" letter+ => placeholder ">>>"
         output referent placeholder
   again


   set connection to TCPConnectionOpen
    on product-server-host
    at product-server-port
   throw connection-error
    when TCPConnectionIsInError connection
   set TCPConnectionGetOutput connection
    protocol IOProtocolMultiPacket
    to '<request><productbyline>'
```

```
      || cgi-data{"QUERY_STRING"}
      || '</productbyline></request>'

   do xml-parse
    scan TCPConnectionGetSource connection
    protocol IOProtocolMultiPacket
      output "%c"
   done

   ;catch #program-error
   ;catch #external-exception

   catch connection-error
      output "Connection error%n"
   catch XML-error
      output "XML error%n"

element "response"
   do scan attribute "status"
      match "ok" =|
         open ProductByLineText as referent "ProductByLine"
         using output as ProductByLineText
         output "%c"
         close ProductByLineText
      match "error" =|
         output "<H3>Server Error</H3>"
            || "<P>Please try again later.%c"
      match "notfound" =|
         output "<p>The item you requested "
            || "was not found.</p>%c"
      match "badrequest" =|
         output "<p>The system did not "
            || "understand your request.</p>%c"
   else
      output "<H3>Server Error</H3>"
         || "<P>Please try again later.%c"
   done

element "line"
   output '%c'

element "product"
   output '%c%n<HR>%n'
```

```
element "type"
   output '<a href="gold-type.xom?%c<br>%n'

element "id" when parent is "product"
   set current-product-id to "%c"
   output '<H3><a href="gold-product.xom?'
      || "g" % current-product-id
      || '>%n'

element "id" when parent is "line"
   suppress

element "name"
   do when parent is "line"
      set referent "ProductLineName" to "%c"
   else
      output '%c</a></H3>%n'
   done

element "description"
   do when parent is "line"
      set referent "ProductLineDescription" to "%c%n"
   else
      output '%c%n'
   done

element "p"
   output "<P>%c%n"

element "prodref"
   output '<B><A HREF="gold-product.xom?%v(id)">%c</A></B>'

element "price"
   local bcd price

   set price to bcd "%c"
   output '<p>Price: '
      || "<$,NNZ.ZZ>" % price
      || '<FORM ACTION="gold-cart.xom" METHOD="POST">'
      || '<INPUT TYPE="HIDDEN" NAME="id" '
      || 'VALUE="%g(current-product-id)">'
      || '<INPUT TYPE="SUBMIT" NAME="Add" '
      || 'VALUE="Add to shopping cart">'
      || ' Qty: <INPUT TYPE="TEXT" VALUE="1" '
```

```
        || 'NAME="Quantity" SIZE="3">'
        || '</FORM>'

markup-error
    throw XML-error
```

gold-cart.xom

```
#!omnimark.exe -sb
;gold-cart.xom
;manages the shopping cart
declare #process-input has unbuffered
declare #main-output has binary-mode
declare #main-output has referents-allowed defaulting {""}
include "omutil.xin"
include "omcgi.xin"
include "omtcp.xin"
include "ombcd.xin"
include "omdate.xin"

declare catch connection-error
declare catch XML-error
declare catch bad-request
declare catch template-error


;parameterizable globals
global stream template-file-name
 initial {"gold\gold-cart.txt"}
global stream product-server-host
 initial {"localhost"}
global counter product-server-port
 initial {"5436"}

global stream CartTableText
global stream current-product-id

global bcd grand-total
global bcd tax-rate

global stream cgi-data variable
global stream form-data variable

global stream order variable
```

```
define stream function get-cookie-value
 value stream name
 as
    do scan cgi-data {"HTTP_COOKIE"}
       match any** name "=" any** => cookie (";" | value-end)
       return cookie
    else
       throw XML-error
    done

global stream now-as-http-date

process
    local TCPConnection connection
    local stream ordered-products-ids

    ;establish the current date
    set now-as-http-date to ymdhms-to-arpadate now-as-ymdhms
    set tax-rate to 0.07

    CGIGetEnv into cgi-data
    CGIGetQuery into form-data

    output "Content-type: text/html" || crlf
        || "Date: " || now-as-http-date || crlf
        || "Expires: " || now-as-http-date || crlf
        || referent "order cookie"
        || crlf
        || crlf


    repeat scan file template-file-name
       match
        ([\"<"]+
         or "<" lookahead not "<<"
        )+ => stuff
           output stuff
       match "<<<" letter+ => placeholder ">>>"
           output referent placeholder
       match any
           throw template-error
    again
```

```
;check for an existing order
do when cgi-data has key "HTTP_COOKIE"

   using group process-cookie
   do xml-parse
    scan get-cookie-value "order"
      suppress
   done
done


;is this an add, a change, or a view?
do when cgi-data key "REQUEST_METHOD" = "GET"
   ;it's a view
else
   local stream quantity

   do scan form-data key "Quantity"
     match value-start digit+ => qty value-end
        set quantity to qty
   else
     throw bad-request
   done

   do when form-data has key "Add"
     do when order hasnt key form-data key "id"
        set new order
         key form-data key "id"
         to quantity
     else
        set order
         key form-data key "id"
         to quantity
     done
   else when form-data has key "Change"
     do when quantity > 0
        set order
         key form-data key "id"
         to quantity
     else
        remove order key form-data key "id"
     done
   else
```

```
      ;we're lost
   done
done

do when number of order > 0
   open ordered-products-ids as buffer
   using output as ordered-products-ids
    repeat over order
      output key of order
      output "," unless #last
    again
   close ordered-products-ids

   set connection to TCPConnectionOpen
    on product-server-host
    at product-server-port
   throw connection-error
    when TCPConnectionIsInError connection
   set TCPConnectionGetOutput connection
    protocol IOProtocolMultiPacket
    to '<request><selectedproducts>'
    || ordered-products-ids
    || '</selectedproducts></request>'

   using group process-database-response
    do xml-parse
    scan TCPConnectionGetSource connection
    protocol IOProtocolMultiPacket
      output "%c"
    done

   do
      local stream cookie
      open cookie as referent "order cookie"
      using output as cookie
       do
         output 'Set-Cookie: order=<order>'
         repeat over order
           output "<item id=%""
                || key of order
                || '" qty="'
                || order
                || '"/>'
         again
```

```
                  output '</order>'
               done
           done

       else
          set referent "OrderTable"
           to "<P>No items ordered."
          set referent "order cookie"
           to 'Set-Cookie: order=; '
           || 'expires=sat, 01-Jan-2000 12:12:12 GMT'
       done
       catch #program-error
       catch #external-exception

       catch connection-error
          output "Connection error%n"

       catch XML-error
          output "XML error%n"

       catch bad-request
          output "Bad request%n"

group process-database-response

element "response"
   do scan attribute "status"
      match value-start "ok" =|
         open CartTableText as referent "OrderTable"
         using output as CartTableText
          output "<TABLE BORDER='1'>%n"
              || " <TR>%n"
              || "  <TD><B>Item</B></TD>%n"
              || "  <TD><B>Price</B></TD>%n"
              || "  <TD><B>Quantity</B></TD>%n"
              || "  <TD><B>Total</B></TD>%n"
              || " </TR>%n"
              || "%c"
              || " <TR>%n"
              || "  <TD></TD>%n"
              || "  <TD></TD>%n"
              || "  <TD>Total price</TD>%n"
              || "  <TD>"
              || "<$,NNZ.ZZ>" % grand-total
```

```
                 || "   </TD>"
                 || "  </TR>"
                 || "  <TR>%n"
                 || "    <TD></TD>%n"
                 || "    <TD></TD>%n"
                 || "    <TD>Taxes at "
                 || "<W%%>" % tax-rate * 100
                 || "</TD>%n   <TD>"
                 || "<$,NNZ.ZZ>" % grand-total * (tax-rate)
                 || "   </TD>%n"
                 || "  </TR>"
                 || "  <TR>%n"
                 || "    <TD></TD>%n"
                 || "    <TD></TD>%n"
                 || "    <TD>Total price</TD>%n"
                 || "    <TD>"
                 || "<$,NNZ.ZZ>" % grand-total * (tax-rate + 1)
                 || "   </TD>"
                 || "  </TR>"
                 || "</TABLE>%n"
          close CartTableText
       match value-start "error" value-end
          output "<H3>Server Error</H3>"
             || "<P>Please try again later.%c"
       match value-start "notfound" value-end
          output "<p>The item you requested "
             || "was not found.</p>%c"
       match value-start "badrequest" value-end
          output "<p>The system did not "
             || "understand your request.</p>%c"
    else
       output "<H3>Server Error</H3>"
          || "<P>Please try again later.%c"
    done

element "product"
   output '<TR>%c</TR>%n'

element "id"
   set current-product-id to "%c"
   output '<TD><a href="gold-product.xom?'
      || "g" % current-product-id
      || '>%n'
```

```
element "name"
   output '%c</a></TD>%n'

element "price"
   local bcd price initial {"%c"}
   local integer quantity
    initial {order{current-product-id}}
   set grand-total to grand-total + (price * quantity)
   output '<TD>'
       || "<$,NNZ.ZZ>" % price
       || '</TD>%n'
       || '<TD><FORM ACTION="gold-cart.xom" METHOD="POST">'
       || '<INPUT TYPE="TEXT" VALUE="%d(quantity)" '
       || 'NAME="Quantity" SIZE="3">'
       || '<INPUT TYPE="HIDDEN" NAME="id" '
       || 'VALUE="%g(current-product-id)">'
       || '<INPUT TYPE="SUBMIT" VALUE="Change" '
       || 'NAME="Change"></FORM></TD>%n'
       || '<TD>'
       || "<$,NNZ.ZZ>" % (price * quantity)
       || '</TD>%n'


group process-cookie

element "order"
   suppress

element "item"
   set new order{attribute "id"} to attribute "qty"
   suppress

group #implied

markup-error
   output "{message{%g(#message) on line %d(#line-number)"
   output "%n%g(#additional-info)"
    when #additional-info is attached
   output "}"
```

gold-home.txt

```
<HTML>
```

```
<HEAD></HEAD>
<BODY>
<H1>Goldilocks Online</H1>
<P>Goldilocks online is your complete source
for home decorating ideas for your little house in the woods.
<P>You can browse our catalog by product
line or by product type.
<TABLE>
 <TR>
  <TH>Product Lines</TH>
  <TH>Product Types</TH>
 </TR>
 <TR>
  <TD><<<LineList>>></TD>
  <TD><<<TypeList>>></TD>
 </TR>
</TABLE>
<<<CartLink>>>
<P>[<A HREF="gold-home.xom">HOME</A>]
[<A HREF="gold-cart.xom">SHOPPING CART</A>]
</BODY>
</HTML>
```

gold-line.txt

```
<HTML>
<HEAD></HEAD>
<BODY>
<H1>Goldilocks Online</H1>
<H2><<<ProductLineName>>> Line</H2>
<<<ProductLineDescription>>>
<HR>
<<<ProductByLine>>>
<<<CartLink>>>
<P>[<A HREF="gold-home.xom">HOME</A>]
[<A HREF="gold-cart.xom">SHOPPING CART</A>]
</BODY>
</HTML>
```

Chapter 21

hangsrv.xom

```
;hangman OMASF server

declare catch unoriginal-new-word
declare catch game-over
declare catch you-win
include "omutil.xin"

;parameterizable globals
global stream num-chances initial {"7"}
global stream new-template initial {"hang\new.htm"}
global stream guess-template initial {"hang\guess.htm"}
global stream unoriginal-new-word-template
 initial {"hang\unoriginal.htm"}
global stream lose-template initial {"hang\lose.htm"}
global stream win-template initial {"hang\win.htm"}
global stream words-file-name initial {"hang\words.txt"}
global stream word-list variable


define function newpage
 (read-only stream requestHeader,
  read-only stream requestBody
 )
 elsewhere
define function guesspage
 (read-only stream requestHeader,
  read-only stream requestBody
 )
 elsewhere
define function loginpage
 (read-only stream requestHeader,
  read-only stream requestBody
 )
 elsewhere

; include the OmniMark Web Services base functions
include 'omasf.xin'


;=======================
```

```
; ServiceInitialize
define function ServiceInitialize
as

    repeat scan file words-file-name
      match any-text+ => the-word "%n"
          new word-list{the-word}
    again


;==============================
; ServiceMain
define function ServiceMain
 (read-only stream requestHeader,
  read-only stream requestBody
 )
 as

    output "Content-type: text/html"
        || crlf
        || crlf

    ;get the query string information
    ;used to tell us which mode to run in
    do scan requestHeader{"QUERY_STRING"}
       match "login" =|
           loginpage (requestHeader, requestBody)
       match "guess" =|
           guesspage (requestHeader, requestBody)
    else
       newpage (requestHeader, requestBody)
    done


;==================
; ServiceTerminate
define function ServiceTerminate
 as
    local stream words-file
    ;update the words file
    reopen words-file as file words-file-name
    using output as words-file
     repeat over word-list
       output key of word-list || "%n"
```

```
      again
   close words-file


;================================
;newpage function
;
define function newpage
 (read-only stream requestHeader,
  read-only stream requestBody
 )
 as
   repeat scan file new-template
      match
       ([\ "<"]+
        or "<" lookahead not "<<"
       )+ => stuff
         output stuff
      match "<<<Action>>>"
         output requestHeader{"SCRIPT_NAME"}
               || "/hangman?login"
   again


;================================
;loginpage function
;
define function loginpage
 (read-only stream requestHeader,
  read-only stream requestBody
 )
 as
   local stream chosen-word
   local stream words-file
   local integer rnd
   local stream substitutes variable
   local integer selected-word-offset

   ; Make sure the new word is original
   throw unoriginal-new-word
    when word-list has key requestBody{"new_word"}

   ; choose a word by offset into the list
   UTIL_Srand(UTIL_GetMilliSecondTimer)
```

```
set rnd to UTIL_Rand
set selected-word-offset
 to (rnd modulo number of word-list) + 1
set chosen-word
 to key of word-list[selected-word-offset]

;now delete it from the list
remove word-list[selected-word-offset]


;add new word to the list
new word-list {("lg" % requestBody{"new_word"})}


;output the guess page
repeat scan file guess-template
   match
    ([any except "<"]+
     or "<" lookahead not "<<"
    )+ => stuff
      output stuff
   match "<<<Result>>>"
      output ""
   match "<<<WordMask>>>"
      output "-" ||* length of chosen-word
   match "<<<AlphabetMask>>>"
      output "ABCDEFGHIJKLMNOPQRSTUVWXYZ"
   match "<<<Chances>>>"
      output num-chances
   match "<<<Action>>>"
      output RequestHeader{"SCRIPT_NAME"}
          || "/hangman?guess"
   match "<<<Word>>>"
      output chosen-word
   match "<<<Right>>>"
      output ""
   match "<<<Wrong>>>"
      output ""
again

;if word is not original, ask for a new one
catch unoriginal-new-word

repeat scan file new-template
```

```
   match
    ([\ "<"]+
     or "<" lookahead not "<<"
    )+ => stuff
       output stuff
    match "<<<Word>>>"
       output RequestBody{"new_word"}
    match "<<<Action>>>"
       output RequestHeader{"SCRIPT_NAME"}
           || "/hangman?login"
  again


;============================
;guesspage function
;
define function guesspage
 (read-only stream requestHeader,
  read-only stream requestBody
 )
 as
   local stream right-guesses
   local stream wrong-guesses
   local stream guess
   local stream word
   local stream word-letters initial {""}
   local stream word-mask
   local stream alphabet-mask
   local integer chances
   local stream substitutes variable
   local stream result-message

   set right-guesses to RequestBody{"right"}
   set wrong-guesses to RequestBody{"wrong"}
   set guess to "lg" % RequestBody{"guess"}
   set word to RequestBody{"word"}
   set chances to num-chances - length of wrong-guesses

   ;list the letters in the word
   repeat scan word
      match any => the-letter
         do unless word-letters matches any** the-letter
            set word-letters to word-letters || the-letter
         done
   again
```

```
do when word matches unanchored ul guess
   ;good guess
   set right-guesses to right-guesses || guess
   throw you-win
    when length of right-guesses = length of word-letters

   set result-message
    to "Right! There are one or more "
    || RequestBody{"guess"}
    || "'s in the word."
else
   ;bad guess
   decrement chances
   throw game-over when chances = 0
   set wrong-guesses to wrong-guesses || guess
   set result-message
    to "Wrong! There are no "
    || RequestBody{"guess"}
    || "'s in the word."
done

;Print the word
open word-mask as buffer
using output as word-mask
   repeat scan word
      match any => the-letter
         do when right-guesses matches any** the-letter
            output the-letter
         else
            output "-"
         done
   again
close word-mask

;Print the alphabet
open alphabet-mask as buffer
using output as alphabet-mask
   repeat scan "ABCDEFGHIJKLMNOPQRSTUVWXYZ"
      match any => the-letter
         do unless (right-guesses || wrong-guesses)
          matches any** ul the-letter
            output the-letter
         else
```

```
                output "*"
            done
    again
close alphabet-mask

;output the guess page
repeat scan file guess-template
  match
    ([\ "<"]+
     or "<" lookahead not "<<"
    )+ => stuff
      output stuff
  match "<<<Result>>>"
      output result-message

  match "<<<WordMask>>>"
      output word-mask

  match "<<<AlphabetMask>>>"
      output alphabet-mask

  match "<<<Chances>>>"
      output "d" % chances

  match "<<<Action>>>"
      output RequestHeader{"SCRIPT_NAME"}
          || "/hangman?guess"

  match "<<<Word>>>"
      output word

  match "<<<Right>>>"
      output right-guesses

  match "<<<Wrong>>>"
      output wrong-guesses

again


catch game-over
  repeat scan file lose-template
  match
    ([\ "<"]+
```

```
   or "<" lookahead not "<<"
  )+ => stuff
  output stuff
  match "<<<word>>>"
    output word
  again

catch you-win
  repeat scan file win-template
    match
    ([\ "<"]+
     or "<" lookahead not "<<"
    )+ => stuff
      output stuff
    match "<<<word>>>"
      output word
  again
```

Index

D

G